Learn Data Structures and Algorithms with Golang

Level up your Go programming skills to develop faster and more efficient code

Bhagvan Kommadi

BIRMINGHAM - MUMBAI

Learn Data Structures and Algorithms with Golang

Commissioning Editor: Richa Tripathi
Acquisition Editor: Shahnish Khan
Content Development Editor: Zeeyan Pinheiro
Technical Editor: Ketan Kamble
Copy Editor: Safis Editing
Project Coordinator: Vaidehi Sawant
Proofreader: Safis Editing
Indexer: Tejal Daruwale Soni
Graphics: Alishon Mendonsa
Production Coordinator: Deepika Naik

First published: March 2019

Production reference: 1290319

Published by Packt Publishing Ltd.
Livery Place
35 Livery Street
Birmingham
B3 2PB, UK.

ISBN 978-1-78961-850-1

`www.packtpub.com`

Mapt

Contributors

About the author

Bhagvan Kommadi, the founder of Quantica Computacao and Architect Corner, has around 18 years' experience in the industry, ranging from large-scale enterprise development to incubating software product startups. He has a master's degree in Industrial Systems Engineering from the Georgia Institute of Technology (1997) and a bachelor's degree in Aerospace Engineering from the IIT Madras (1993). He is a member of the IFX forum and an individual member of Oracle JCP.

He has developed Go-based blockchain solutions in the retail, education, banking, and financial service sectors. He has experience of building high-transactional applications using Java, Python, Go, Ruby, and JavaScript frameworks.

About the reviewer

Eduard Bondarenko is a software developer living in Kiev, Ukraine. He started programming using Basic on a ZX Spectrum many, many years ago. Later, he worked in the web development domain. He has used Ruby on Rails for over 8 years. Having used Ruby for a long time, he discovered Clojure in early 2009, and liked the simplicity of the language. Besides Ruby and Clojure, he is interested in Go and ReasonML development.

I want to thank my wonderful wife, my children, and my parents for all the love, support, and help they have given me.

Packt is searching for authors like you

If you're interested in becoming an author for Packt, please visit `authors.packtpub.com` and apply today. We have worked with thousands of developers and tech professionals, just like you, to help them share their insight with the global tech community. You can make a general application, apply for a specific hot topic that we are recruiting an author for, or submit your own idea.

Table of Contents

Section 2: Basic Data Structures and Algorithms using Go

Section 3: Advanced Data Structures and Algorithms using Go

Preface

Learn Data Structures and Algorithms with Go covers topics related to simple and advanced concepts in computer programming. The primary objective is to choose the correct algorithm and data structures for a problem. This book explains the concepts for comparing algorithm complexity and data structures in terms of code performance and efficiency.

Golang has been the buzzword for the last two years, with tremendous improvements being seen in this area. Many developers and organizations are slowly migrating to Golang, adopting its fast, lightweight, and inbuilt concurrency features. This means we need to have a solid foundation in data structures and algorithms with this growing language.

Who this book is for

This comprehensive book is for developers who want to understand how to select the best data structures and algorithms that will help to solve specific problems. Some basic knowledge of Go programming would be an added advantage.

This book is for anyone who wants to learn how to write efficient programs and use the proper data structures and algorithms.

What this book covers

`Chapter 1`, *Data Structures and Algorithms*, focuses on the definition of abstract data types, classifying data structures into linear, non-linear, homogeneous, heterogeneous, and dynamic types. Abstract data types, such as container, list, set, map, graph, stack, and queue, are presented in this chapter. This chapter also covers the performance analysis of data structures, as well as the correct choice of data structures and structural design patterns.

`Chapter 2`, *Getting Started with Go for Data Structures and Algorithms*, covers Go-specific data structures, such as arrays, slices, two-dimensional slices, maps, structs, and channels. Variadic functions, deferred function calls, and panic and recover operations are introduced. Slicing operations, such as enlarging using append and copy, assigning parts, appending a slice, and appending part of a slice, are also presented in this chapter.

`Chapter 3`, *Linear Data Structures*, covers linear data structures such as lists, sets, tuples, stacks, and heaps. The operations related to these types, including insertion, deletion, updating, reversing, and merging are shown with various code samples. In this chapter, we present the complexity analysis of various data structure operations that display accessing, search, insertion, and deletion times.

`Chapter 4`, *Non-Linear Data Structures*, covers non-linear data structures, such as trees, tables, containers, and hash functions. Tree types, including binary tree, binary search tree, T-tree, treap, symbol table, B- tree, and B+ tree, are explained with code examples and complexity analysis. Hash function data structures are presented, along with examples in cryptography for a variety of scenarios, such as open addressing, linear probing, universal hashing, and double hashing.

`Chapter 5`, *Homogeneous Data Structures*, covers homogeneous data structures such as two-dimensional and multi-dimensional arrays. Array shapes, types, literals, printing, construction, indexing, modification, transformation, and views are presented together with code examples and performance analysis. Matrix representation, multiplication, addition, subtraction, inversion, and transpose scenarios are shown to demonstrate the usage of multi-dimensional arrays.

`Chapter 6`, *Heterogeneous Data Structures*, covers heterogeneous data structures, such as linked lists, ordered, and unordered lists. We present the singly linked list, doubly linked list, and circular linked list, along with code samples and efficiency analysis. Ordered and unordered lists from HTML 3.0 are shown to demonstrate the usage of lists and storage management.

`Chapter 7`, *Dynamic Data Structures*, covers dynamic data structures, such as dictionaries, TreeSets, and sequences. Synchronized TreeSets and mutable TreeSets are covered in this chapter along with Go code exhibits. Sequence types including Farey, Fibonacci, look-and-say, and Thue-Morse, are discussed with Go programs. This chapter also explains the usage anti-patterns of dictionaries, TreeSets, and sequences.

`Chapter 8`, *Classic Algorithms*, covers pre-order, post-order, in-order, level-order tree traversals and linked list traversals. Sorting algorithms, such as bubble, selection, insertion, shell, merge, and quick are explained with code exhibits. Search algorithms, as well as linear, sequential, binary, and interpolation methods, are also covered in this chapter. Recursion and hashing are shown by means of code samples.

`Chapter 9`, *Network and Sparse Matrix Representation*, covers data structures such as graphs and lists of lists. Different use cases from real-life applications, such as social network representation, map layouts, and knowledge catalogs, are shown with code examples and efficiency analysis.

`Chapter 10`, *Memory Management*, covers dynamic data structures, such as AVL trees and stack frames. Garbage collection, cache management, and space allocation algorithms are presented with code samples and efficiency analysis. Garbage collection algorithms, such as simple/deferred/one-bit/weighted reference counting, mark and sweep, and generational collection, are explained with an analysis of their advantages and disadvantages.

`Appendix`, *Next Steps*, shares the learning outcomes for the reader arising from the book. The code repository links and key takeaways are presented. References are included for the latest data structures and algorithms. Tips and techniques are provided to keep yourself updated with the latest on data structures and algorithms.

To get the most out of this book

The knowledge we assume is basic programming in a language and mathematical skills related to topics including matrices, set operations, and statistical concepts. The reader should have the ability to write pseudo code based on a flowchart or a specified algorithm. Writing functional code, testing, following guidelines, and building a complex project in the Go language are the prerequisites that we assume in terms of reader skills.

Download the example code files

You can download the example code files for this book from your account at `www.packt.com`. If you purchased this book elsewhere, you can visit `www.packt.com/support` and register to have the files emailed directly to you.

You can download the code files by following these steps:

1. Log in or register at `www.packt.com`.
2. Select the **SUPPORT** tab.
3. Click on **Code Downloads & Errata**.
4. Enter the name of the book in the **Search** box and follow the onscreen instructions.

Once the file is downloaded, please make sure that you unzip or extract the folder using the latest version of:

- WinRAR/7-Zip for Windows
- Zipeg/iZip/UnRarX for Mac
- 7-Zip/PeaZip for Linux

The code bundle for the book is also hosted on GitHub at `https://github.com/PacktPublishing/Learn-Data-Structures-and-Algorithms-with-Golang`. In case there's an update to the code, it will be updated on the existing GitHub repository.

We also have other code bundles from our rich catalog of books and videos available at `https://github.com/PacktPublishing/`. Check them out!

Download the color images

We also provide a PDF file that has color images of the screenshots/diagrams used in this book. You can download it here:
`http://www.packtpub.com/sites/default/files/downloads/9781789618501_ColorImages.pdf`.

Conventions used

There are a number of text conventions used throughout this book.

`CodeInText`: Indicates code words in text, database table names, folder names, filenames, file extensions, pathnames, dummy URLs, user input, and Twitter handles. Here is an example: "Let's take a look at the `len` function in the next section."

A block of code is set as follows:

```
//main package has examples shown
// in Hands-On Data Structures and algorithms with Go book
package main

// importing fmt package
import (
  "fmt"
)
// main method
func main() {
  fmt.Println("Hello World")
}
```

Any command-line input or output is written as follows:

```
go build
./hello_world
```

Bold: Indicates a new term, an important word, or words that you see on screen.

Warnings or important notes appear like this.

Tips and tricks appear like this.

Get in touch

Feedback from our readers is always welcome.

General feedback: If you have questions about any aspect of this book, mention the book title in the subject of your message and email us at `customercare@packtpub.com`.

Errata: Although we have taken every care to ensure the accuracy of our content, mistakes do happen. If you have found a mistake in this book, we would be grateful if you would report this to us. Please visit `www.packt.com/submit-errata`, selecting your book, clicking on the Errata Submission Form link, and entering the details.

Piracy: If you come across any illegal copies of our works in any form on the internet, we would be grateful if you would provide us with the location address or website name. Please contact us at `copyright@packt.com` with a link to the material.

If you are interested in becoming an author: If there is a topic that you have expertise in, and you are interested in either writing or contributing to a book, please visit `authors.packtpub.com`.

Reviews

Please leave a review. Once you have read and used this book, why not leave a review on the site that you purchased it from? Potential readers can then see and use your unbiased opinion to make purchase decisions, we at Packt can understand what you think about our products, and our authors can see your feedback on their book. Thank you!

For more information about Packt, please visit `packt.com`.

1

Section 1: Introduction to Data Structures and Algorithms and the Go Language

We will be introducing the abstract data types, definition, and classification of data structures. Readers will be well-versed with performance analysis of algorithms and choosing appropriate data structures for structural design patterns after reading this part.

This section contains the following chapters:

- `Chapter 1`, *Data Structures and Algorithms*
- `Chapter 2`, *Getting Started with Go for Data Structures and Algorithms*

1
Data Structures and Algorithms

A data structure is the organization of data to reduce the storage space used and to reduce the difficulty while performing different tasks. Data structures are used to handle and work with large amounts of data in various fields, such as database management and internet indexing services.

In this chapter, we will focus on the definition of abstract datatypes, classifying data structures into linear, nonlinear, homogeneous, heterogeneous, and dynamic types. Abstract datatypes, such as Container, List, Set, Map, Graph, Stack, and Queue, are presented in this chapter. We will also cover the performance analysis of data structures, choosing the right data structures, and structural design patterns.

The reader can start writing basic algorithms using the right data structures in Go. Given a problem, choosing the data structure and different algorithms will be the first step. After this, doing performance analysis is the next step. Time and space analysis for different algorithms helps compare them and helps you choose the optimal one. It is essential to have basic knowledge of Go to get started.

In this chapter, we will cover the following topics:

- Classification of data structures and structural design patterns
- Representation of algorithms
- Complexity and performance analysis
- Brute force algorithms
- Divide and conquer algorithms
- Backtracking algorithms

Technical requirements

Install Go version 1.10 from `https://golang.org/doc/install` for your operating system.

The code files for this chapter can be found at the following GitHub URL: `https://github.com/PacktPublishing/Learn-Data-Structures-and-Algorithms-with-Golang/tree/master/Chapter01`.

Check the installation of Go by running the hello world program at `https://github.com/PacktPublishing/Learn-Data-Structures-and-Algorithms-with-Golang/tree/master/hello_world`:

```
//main package has examples shown
// in Hands-On Data Structures and algorithms with Go book
package main

// importing fmt package
import (
  "fmt"
)
// main method
func main() {
  fmt.Println("Hello World")
}
```

Run the following commands:

```
go build
./hello_world
```

The following screenshot displays the output:

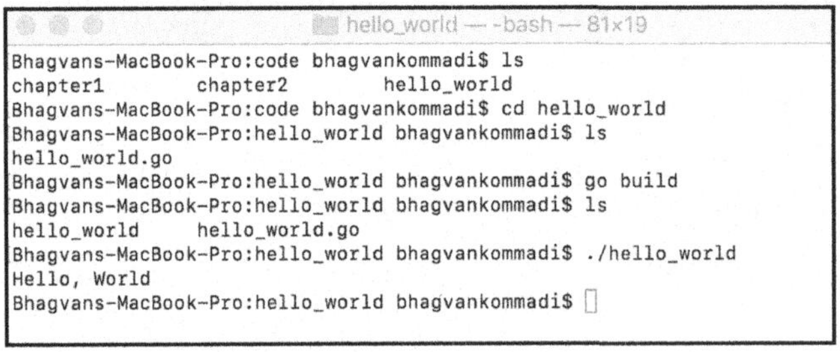

```
hello_world — -bash — 81x19
Bhagvans-MacBook-Pro:code bhagvankommadi$ ls
chapter1        chapter2        hello_world
Bhagvans-MacBook-Pro:code bhagvankommadi$ cd hello_world
Bhagvans-MacBook-Pro:hello_world bhagvankommadi$ ls
hello_world.go
Bhagvans-MacBook-Pro:hello_world bhagvankommadi$ go build
Bhagvans-MacBook-Pro:hello_world bhagvankommadi$ ls
hello_world     hello_world.go
Bhagvans-MacBook-Pro:hello_world bhagvankommadi$ ./hello_world
Hello, World
Bhagvans-MacBook-Pro:hello_world bhagvankommadi$
```

Let's take a look at the classification of data structures and structural design patterns in the next section.

Classification of data structures and structural design patterns

You can choose a data structure by using classification. In this section, we discuss data structure classification in detail. The design patterns related to the data structure are covered after the classification.

In the next section, we'll take a look at classification of data structures.

Classification of data structures

The term **data structure** refers to the organization of data in a computer's memory, in order to retrieve it quickly for processing. It is a scheme for data organization to decouple the functional definition of a data structure from its implementation. A data structure is chosen based on the problem type and the operations performed on the data.

If the situation requires various datatypes within a data structure, we can choose heterogeneous data structures. Linked, ordered, and unordered lists are grouped as heterogeneous data structures. Linear data structures are lists, sets, tuples, queues, stacks, and heaps. Trees, tables, and containers are categorized as nonlinear data structures. Two-dimensional and multidimensional arrays are grouped as homogeneous data structures. Dynamic data structures are dictionaries, tree sets, and sequences.

The classification of **Data Structures** is show in the following diagram:

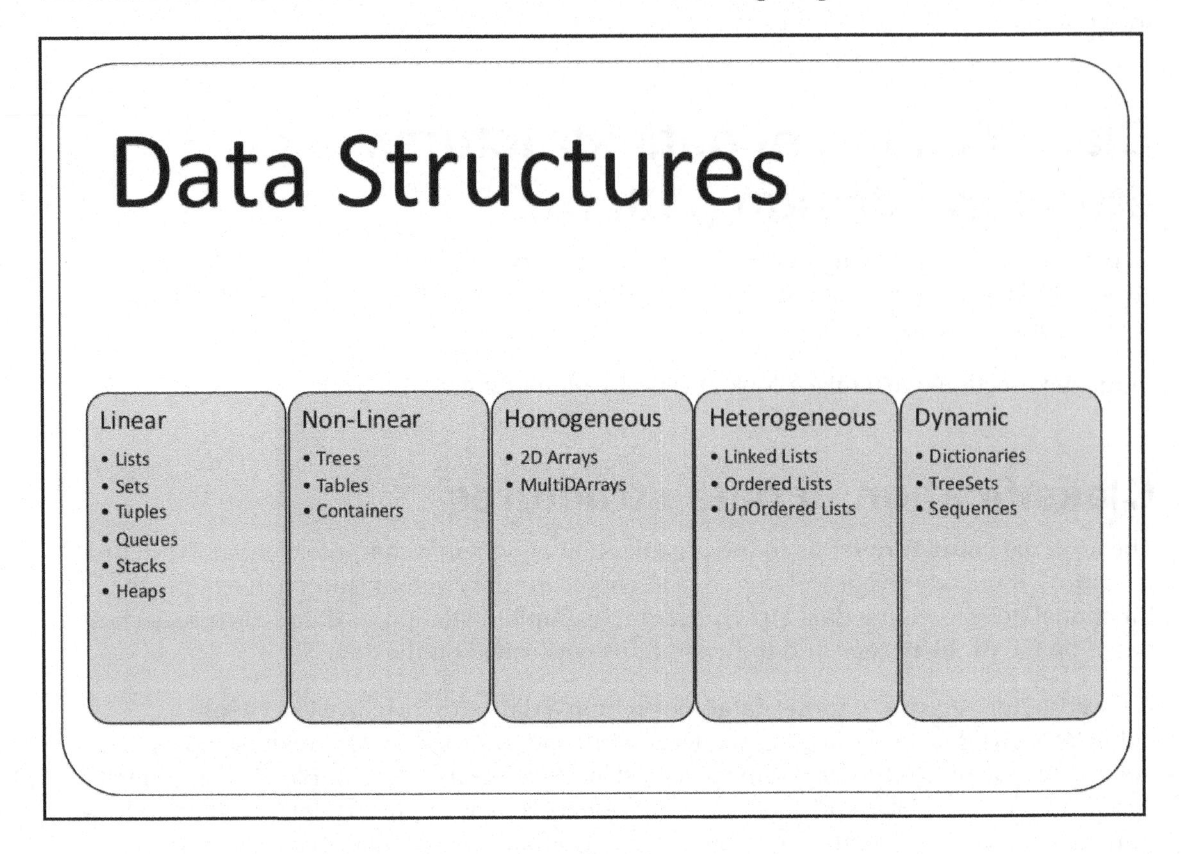

Let's take a look at lists, tuples and heaps in the next sections.

Lists

A list is a sequence of elements. Each element can be connected to another with a link in a forward or backward direction. The element can have other payload properties. This data structure is a basic type of container. Lists have a variable length and developer can remove or add elements more easily than an array. Data items within a list need not be contiguous in memory or on disk. Linked lists were proposed by Allen Newell, Cliff Shaw, and Herbert A. Simon at RAND Corporation.

To get started, a list can be used in Go, as shown in the following example; elements are added through the `PushBack` method on the list, which is in the `container/list` package:

```
//main package has examples shown
// in Hands-On Data Structures and algorithms with Go book
package main

// importing fmt and container list packages
import (
   "fmt"
   "container/list")

// main method
func main() {
    var intList list.List
    intList.PushBack(11)
    intList.PushBack(23)
    intList.PushBack(34)

    for element := intList.Front(); element != nil; element=element.Next()
{
        fmt.Println(element.Value.(int))
    }
}
```

The list is iterated through the `for` loop, and the element's value is accessed through the `Value` method.

Run the following commands:

```
go run list.go
```

The following screenshot displays the output:

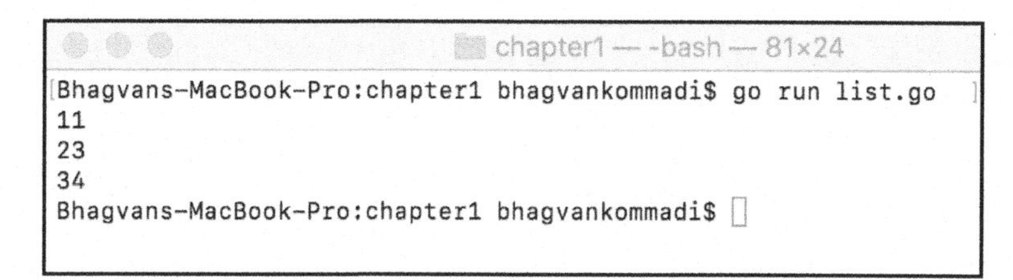

Let's take a look at Tuples in the next section.

Tuples

A tuple is a finite sorted list of elements. It is a data structure that groups data. Tuples are typically immutable sequential collections. The element has related fields of different datatypes. The only way to modify a tuple is to change the fields. Operators such as + and * can be applied to tuples. A database record is referred to as a tuple. In the following example, power series of integers are calculated and the square and cube of the integer is returned as a tuple:

```
//main package has examples shown
// in Hands-On Data Structures and algorithms with Go book
package main

// importing fmt package
import (
  "fmt"

)
//gets the power series of integer a and returns tuple of square of a
// and cube of a
func powerSeries(a int) (int,int) {

  return a*a, a*a*a

}
```

The `main` method calls the `powerSeries` method with `3` as a parameter. The `square` and `cube` values are returned from the method:

```
// main method
func main() {

  var square int
  var cube int
  square, cube = powerSeries(3)

  fmt.Println("Square ", square, "Cube", cube)

}
```

Run the following commands:

```
go run tuples.go
```

The following screenshot displays the output:

```
chapter1 — -bash — 81×24
Bhagvans-MacBook-Pro:chapter1 bhagvankommadi$ go run tuples.go
Square  9 Cube 27
16 64
25 125 <nil>
Bhagvans-MacBook-Pro:chapter1 bhagvankommadi$
```

The tuples can be named in the `powerSeries` function, as shown in the following code:

```
func powerSeries(a int) (square int, cube int) {

  square = a*a

  cube = square*a
  return

}
```

If there is an error, it can be passed with tuples, as shown in the following code:

```
func powerSeries(a int) (int, int, error) {

  square = a*a

  cube = square*a
  return square,cube,nil

}
```

Heaps

A heap is a data structure that is based on the `heap` property. The heap data structure is used in selection, graph, and k-way merge algorithms. Operations such as finding, merging, insertion, key changes, and deleting are performed on heaps. Heaps are part of the `container/heap` package in Go. According to the heap order (maximum heap) property, the value stored at each node is greater than or equal to its children.

If the order is descending, it is referred to as a maximum heap; otherwise, it's a minimum heap. The heap data structure was proposed by J.W.J. Williams in 1964 for a heap sorting algorithm. It is not a sorted data structure, but partially ordered. The following example shows how to use the `container/heap` package to create a heap data structure:

```
//main package has examples shown
//in Hands-On Data Structures and algorithms with Go book
package main

// importing fmt package and container/heap
import (
  "container/heap"
  "fmt"
)
// integerHeap a type
type IntegerHeap []int

// IntegerHeap method - gets the length of integerHeap
func (iheap IntegerHeap) Len() int { return len(iheap) }

// IntegerHeap method - checks if element of i index is less than j index
func (iheap IntegerHeap) Less(i, j int) bool { return iheap[i] < iheap[j] }
// IntegerHeap method -swaps the element of i to j index
func (iheap IntegerHeap) Swap(i, j int) { iheap[i], iheap[j] = iheap[j],
iheap[i] }
```

`IntegerHeap` has a `Push` method that pushes the item with the interface:

```
//IntegerHeap method -pushes the item
func (iheap *IntegerHeap) Push(heapintf interface{}) {

 *iheap = append(*iheap, heapintf.(int))
}
//IntegerHeap method -pops the item from the heap
func (iheap *IntegerHeap) Pop() interface{} {
 var n int
 var x1 int
 var previous IntegerHeap = *iheap
 n = len(previous)
 x1 = previous[n-1]
 *iheap = previous[0 : n-1]
 return x1
}

// main method
func main() {
 var intHeap *IntegerHeap = &IntegerHeap{1,4,5}
```

```
    heap.Init(intHeap)
    heap.Push(intHeap, 2)
    fmt.Printf("minimum: %d\n", (*intHeap)[0])
    for intHeap.Len() > 0 {
    fmt.Printf("%d \n", heap.Pop(intHeap))
    }
  }
```

Run the following commands:

```
go run heap.go
```

The following screenshot displays the output:

```
chapter1 — -bash — 81×24
Bhagvans-MacBook-Pro:chapter1 bhagvankommadi$ go run heap.go
minimum: 1
1
2
4
5
Bhagvans-MacBook-Pro:chapter1 bhagvankommadi$
```

Let's take a look at structural design patterns in the next section

Structural design patterns

Structural design patterns describe the relationships between the entities. They are used to form large structures using classes and objects. These patterns are used to create a system with different system blocks in a flexible manner. Adapter, bridge, composite, decorator, facade, flyweight, private class data, and proxy are the **Gang of Four** (**GoF**) structural design patterns. The private class data design pattern is the other design pattern covered in this section.

We will take a look at adapter and bridge design patterns in the next sections.

Adapter

The adapter pattern provides a wrapper with an interface required by the API client to link incompatible types and act as a translator between the two types. The adapter uses the interface of a class to be a class with another compatible interface. When requirements change, there are scenarios where class functionality needs to be changed because of incompatible interfaces.

The dependency inversion principle can be adhered to by using the adapter pattern, when a class defines its own interface to the next level module interface implemented by an `adapter` class. Delegation is the other principle used by the adapter pattern. Multiple formats handling source-to-destination transformations are the scenarios where the adapter pattern is applied.

The adapter pattern comprises the target, adaptee, adapter, and client:

- Target is the interface that the client calls and invokes methods on the adapter and adaptee.
- The client wants the incompatible interface implemented by the adapter.
- The adapter translates the incompatible interface of the adaptee into an interface that the client wants.

Let's say you have an `IProcessor` interface with a `process` method, the `Adapter` class implements the `process` method and has an `Adaptee` instance as an attribute. The `Adaptee` class has a `convert` method and an `adapterType` instance variable. The developer while using the API client calls the `process` interface method to invoke `convert` on `Adaptee`. The code is as follows:

```
//main package has examples shown
// in Hands-On Data Structures and algorithms with Go book
package main
// importing fmt package
import (
 "fmt"
)
//IProcess interface
type IProcess interface {
 process()
}
//Adapter struct
type Adapter struct {
 adaptee Adaptee
}
```

The `Adapter` class has a `process` method that invokes the `convert` method on `adaptee`:

```
//Adapter class method process
func (adapter Adapter) process() {
 fmt.Println("Adapter process")
 adapter.adaptee.convert()
}
//Adaptee Struct
type Adaptee struct {
 adapterType int
}
// Adaptee class method convert
func (adaptee Adaptee) convert() {
 fmt.Println("Adaptee convert method")
}
// main method
func main() {
var processor IProcess = Adapter{}
processor.process()
}
```

Run the following commands:

```
go run adapter.go
```

The following screenshot displays the output:

```
chapter1 — -bash — 81×24
Bhagvans-MacBook-Pro:chapter1 bhagvankommadi$ go run adapter.go
Adapter process
Adaptee convert method
Bhagvans-MacBook-Pro:chapter1 bhagvankommadi$
```

Let's take a look at Bridge pattern in the next section.

Bridge

Bridge decouples the implementation from the abstraction. The abstract base class can be subclassed to provide different implementations and allow implementation details to be modified easily. The interface, which is a bridge, helps in making the functionality of concrete classes independent from the interface implementer classes. The bridge patterns allow the implementation details to change at runtime.

The bridge pattern demonstrates the principle, preferring composition over inheritance. It helps in situations where one should subclass multiple times orthogonal to each other. Runtime binding of the application, mapping of orthogonal class hierarchies, and platform independence implementation are the scenarios where the bridge pattern can be applied.

The bridge pattern components are abstraction, refined abstraction, implementer, and concrete implementer. Abstraction is the interface implemented as an abstract class that clients invoke with the method on the concrete implementer. Abstraction maintains a *has-a* relationship with the implementation, instead of an *is-a* relationship. The *has-a* relationship is maintained by composition. Abstraction has a reference of the implementation. Refined abstraction provides more variations than abstraction.

Let's say `IDrawShape` is an interface with the `drawShape` method. `DrawShape` implements the `IDrawShape` interface. We create an `IContour` bridge interface with the `drawContour` method. The contour class implements the `IContour` interface. The `ellipse` class will have *a, b , r* properties and `drawShape` (an instance of `DrawShape`). The `ellipse` class implements the `contour` bridge interface to implement the `drawContour` method. The `drawContour` method calls the `drawShape` method on the `drawShape` instance.

The following code demonstrates the bridge implementation:

```
//main package has examples shown
// in Hands-On Data Structures and algorithms with Go book
package main
// importing fmt package
import (
 "fmt"
)
//IDrawShape interface
type IDrawShape interface {
 drawShape(x[5] float32,y[5] float32)
}
//DrawShape struct
type DrawShape struct{}
```

drawShape method

The `drawShape` method draws the shape given the coordinates, as shown in the following code:

```
// DrawShape struct has method draw Shape with float x and y coordinates
func (drawShape DrawShape) drawShape(x[5] float32, y[5] float32) {
 fmt.Println("Drawing Shape")
}
```

```
//IContour interace
type IContour interface {
 drawContour(x[5] float32 ,y[5] float32)
 resizeByFactor(factor int)
}
//DrawContour struct
type DrawContour struct {
 x[5] float32
 y[5] float32
 shape DrawShape
 factor int
}
```

drawContour method

The `drawContour` method of the `DrawContour` class calls the `drawShape` method on the `shape` instance, this is shown in the following code:

```
//DrawContour method drawContour given the coordinates
func (contour DrawContour) drawContour(x[5] float32,y[5] float32) {
 fmt.Println("Drawing Contour")
 contour.shape.drawShape(contour.x,contour.y)
}
//DrawContour method resizeByFactor given factor
func (contour DrawContour) resizeByFactor(factor int) {
 contour.factor = factor
}
// main method
func main() {
var x = [5]float32{1,2,3,4,5}
var y = [5]float32{1,2,3,4,5}
var contour IContour = DrawContour{x,y,DrawShape{},2}
contour.drawContour(x,y)
 contour.resizeByFactor(2)
}
```

Run the following commands:

```
go run bridge.go
```

The following screenshot displays the output:

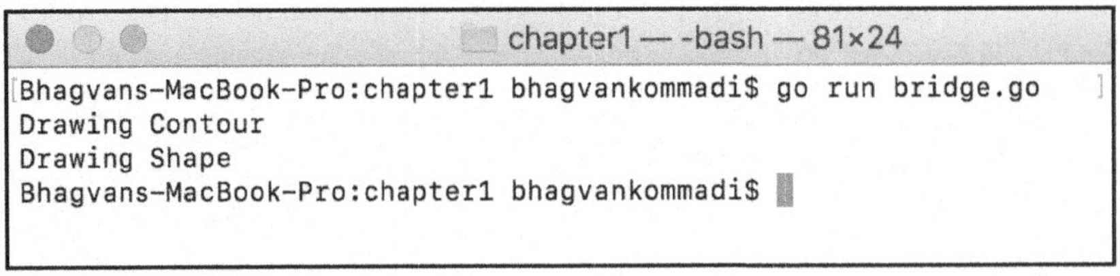

```
chapter1 — -bash — 81×24
Bhagvans-MacBook-Pro:chapter1 bhagvankommadi$ go run bridge.go
Drawing Contour
Drawing Shape
Bhagvans-MacBook-Pro:chapter1 bhagvankommadi$
```

We will take a look at Composite, Decorator, Facade and Flyweight design patterns in the next sections.

Composite

A composite is a group of similar objects in a single object. Objects are stored in a tree form to persist the whole hierarchy. The composite pattern is used to change a hierarchical collection of objects. The composite pattern is modeled on a heterogeneous collection. New types of objects can be added without changing the interface and the client code. You can use the composite pattern, for example, for UI layouts on the web, for directory trees, and for managing employees across departments. The pattern provides a mechanism to access the individual objects and groups in a similar manner.

The composite pattern comprises the `component` interface, `component` class, composite, and client:

- The `component` interface defines the default behavior of all objects and behaviors for accessing the components of the composite.
- The `composite` and `component` classes implement the `component` interface.
- The client interacts with the component interface to invoke methods in the composite.

Let's say there is an `IComposite` interface with the `perform` method and `BranchClass` that implements `IComposite` and has the `addLeaf`, `addBranch`, and `perform` methods. The `Leaflet` class implements `IComposite` with the `perform` method. `BranchClass` has a one-to-many relationship with `leafs` and `branches`. Iterating over the branch recursively, one can traverse the composite tree, as shown in the following code:

```
//main package has examples shown
// in Hands-On Data Structures and algorithms with Go book
package main
// importing fmt package
```

```
import (
 "fmt"
)
// IComposite interface
type IComposite interface {
 perform()
}
// Leaflet struct
type Leaflet struct {
 name string
}
// Leaflet class method perform
func (leaf *Leaflet) perform() {
fmt.Println("Leaflet " + leaf.name)
}
// Branch struct
type Branch struct {
 leafs []Leaflet
 name string
 branches[]Branch
}
```

The `perform` method of the `Branch` class calls the `perform` method on `branch` and `leafs`, as seen in the code:

```
// Branch class method perform
func (branch *Branch) perform() {
fmt.Println("Branch: " + branch.name)
 for _, leaf := range branch.leafs {
 leaf.perform()
 }
for _, branch := range branch.branches {
 branch.perform()
 }
}
// Branch class method add leaflet
func (branch *Branch) add(leaf Leaflet) {
 branch.leafs = append(branch.leafs, leaf)
}
```

As shown in the following code, the `addBranch` method of the `Branch` class adds a new `branch`:

```
//Branch class method addBranch branch
func (branch *Branch) addBranch(newBranch Branch) {
branch.branches = append(branch.branches,newBranch)
}
//Branch class method getLeaflets
```

```
func (branch *Branch) getLeaflets() []Leaflet {
 return branch.leafs
}
// main method
func main() {
var branch = &Branch{name:"branch 1"}
var leaf1 = Leaflet{name:"leaf 1"}
var leaf2 = Leaflet{name:"leaf 2"}
var branch2 = Branch{name:"branch 2"}
branch.add(leaf1)
branch.add(leaf2)
branch.addBranch(branch2)
branch.perform()
}
```

Run the following commands:

```
go run composite.go
```

The following screenshot displays the output:

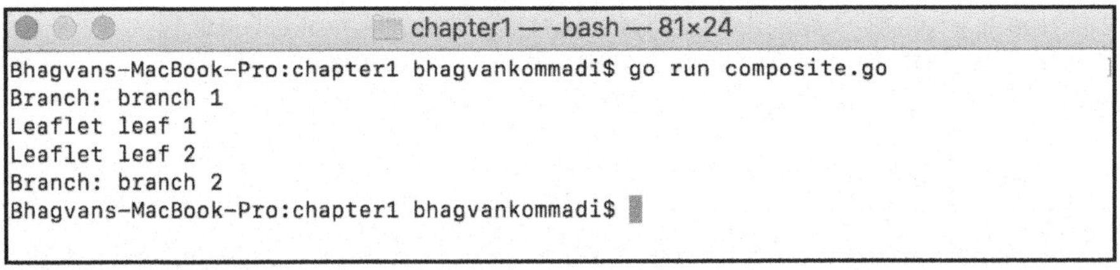

```
chapter1 — -bash — 81×24
Bhagvans-MacBook-Pro:chapter1 bhagvankommadi$ go run composite.go
Branch: branch 1
Leaflet leaf 1
Leaflet leaf 2
Branch: branch 2
Bhagvans-MacBook-Pro:chapter1 bhagvankommadi$
```

Let's take a look at Decorator pattern in the next section.

Decorator

In a scenario where class responsibilities are removed or added, the decorator pattern is applied. The decorator pattern helps with subclassing when modifying functionality, instead of static inheritance. An object can have multiple decorators and run-time decorators. The single responsibility principle can be achieved using a decorator. The decorator can be applied to window components and graphical object modeling. The decorator pattern helps with modifying existing instance attributes and adding new methods at run-time.

The decorator pattern participants are the component interface, the concrete component class, and the `decorator` class:

- The concrete component implements the component interface.
- The `decorator` class implements the component interface and provides additional functionality in the same method or additional methods. The decorator base can be a participant representing the base class for all decorators.

Let 's say `IProcess` is an interface with the `process` method. `ProcessClass` implements an interface with the `process` method. `ProcessDecorator` implements the process interface and has an instance of `ProcessClass`. `ProcessDecorator` can add more functionality than `ProcessClass`, as shown in the following code:

```
//main package has examples shown
 // in Hands-On Data Structures and algorithms with Go book
 package main
// importing fmt package
 import (
 "fmt"
 )
// IProcess Interface
 type IProcess interface {
 process()
 }
//ProcessClass struct
 type ProcessClass struct{}
//ProcessClass method process
 func (process *ProcessClass) process() {
 fmt.Println("ProcessClass process")
 }
//ProcessDecorator struct
 type ProcessDecorator struct {
 processInstance *ProcessClass
 }
```

In the following code, the `ProcessDecorator` class `process` method invokes the `process` method on the decorator instance of `ProcessClass`:

```
//ProcessDecorator class method process
func (decorator *ProcessDecorator) process() {
if decorator.processInstance == nil {
fmt.Println("ProcessDecorator process")
} else {
fmt.Printf("ProcessDecorator process and ")
decorator.processInstance.process()
}
```

```
  }
//main method
 func main() {
var process = &ProcessClass{}
var decorator = &ProcessDecorator{}
decorator.process()
decorator.processInstance = process
decorator.process()
}
```

Run the following commands:

```
go run decorator.go
```

The following screenshot displays the output:

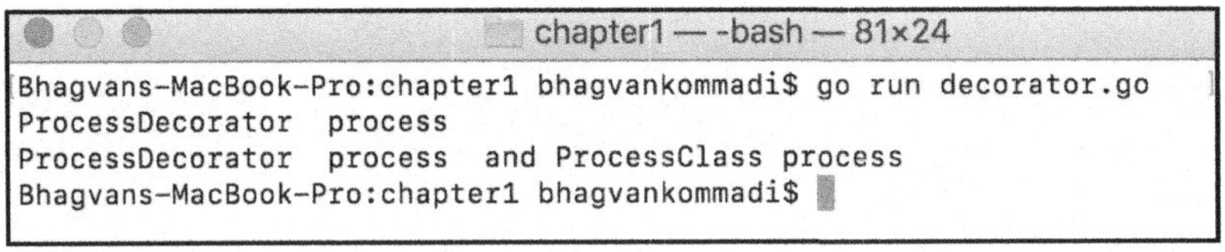

```
chapter1 — -bash — 81×24
Bhagvans-MacBook-Pro:chapter1 bhagvankommadi$ go run decorator.go
ProcessDecorator  process
ProcessDecorator  process  and ProcessClass process
Bhagvans-MacBook-Pro:chapter1 bhagvankommadi$
```

Let's take a look at Facade pattern in the next section.

Facade

Facade is used to abstract subsystem interfaces with a helper. The facade design pattern is used in scenarios when the number of interfaces increases and the system gets complicated. Facade is an entry point to different subsystems, and it simplifies the dependencies between the systems. The facade pattern provides an interface that hides the implementation details of the hidden code.

A loosely coupled principle can be realized with a facade pattern. You can use a facade to improve poorly designed APIs. In SOA, a service facade can be used to incorporate changes to the contract and implementation.

The facade pattern is made up of the `facade` class, module classes, and a client:

- The facade delegates the requests from the client to the module classes. The `facade` class hides the complexities of the subsystem logic and rules.
- Module classes implement the behaviors and functionalities of the module subsystem.
- The client invokes the `facade` method. The `facade` class functionality can be spread across multiple packages and assemblies.

For example, account, customer, and transaction are the classes that have account, customer, and transaction creation methods. `BranchManagerFacade` can be used by the client to create an account, customer, and transaction:

```
//main package has examples shown
// in Hands-On Data Structures and algorithms with Go book
package main
// importing fmt package
import (
 "fmt"
 )
 //Account struct
 type Account struct{
id string
accountType string
}
//Account class method create - creates account given AccountType
func (account *Account) create(accountType string) *Account{
 fmt.Println("account creation with type")
 account.accountType = accountType
return account
}
//Account class method getById given id string
func (account *Account) getById(id string) *Account {
 fmt.Println("getting account by Id")
 return account
 }
```

The `account` class has the `deleteById` method, which is used to delete an account with a given ID, as shown in the following code:

```
 //Account class method deleteById given id string
 func (account *Account) deleteById(id string)() {
 fmt.Println("delete account by id")
 }
//Customer struct
 type Customer struct{
```

```
name string
id int
}
```

In the following code, the `customer` class has a method that creates a new customer with `name`:

```
//Customer class method create - create Customer given name
 func (customer *Customer) create(name string) *Customer {
 fmt.Println("creating customer")
 customer.name = name
 return customer
 }
//Transaction struct
 type Transaction struct{
 id string
 amount float32
 srcAccountId string
 destAccountId string
 }
```

As shown in the following code, the `transaction` class has the `create` method for creating a transaction:

```
//Transaction class method create Transaction
 func (transaction *Transaction) create(srcAccountId string, destAccountId
string,amount float32) *Transaction {
 fmt.Println("creating transaction")
 transaction.srcAccountId = srcAccountId
 transaction.destAccountId = destAccountId
 transaction.amount = amount
 return transaction
 }
 //BranchManagerFacade struct
 type BranchManagerFacade struct {
 account *Account
 customer *Customer
 transaction *Transaction
 }
//method NewBranchManagerFacade
 func NewBranchManagerFacade() *BranchManagerFacade {
 return &BranchManagerFacade{ &Account{}, &Customer{}, &Transaction{}}
 }
```

`BranchManagerFacade` has the `createCustomerAccount` method, which calls the `create` method on the `customer` class instance, as shown in the following code:

```
//BranchManagerFacade class method createCustomerAccount
 func (facade *BranchManagerFacade) createCustomerAccount(customerName
string, accountType string) (*Customer,*Account) {
 var customer = facade.customer.create(customerName)
 var account = facade.account.create(accountType)
 return customer, account
 }
 //BranchManagerFacade class method createTransaction
 func (facade *BranchManagerFacade) createTransaction(srcAccountId string,
destAccountId string, amount float32) *Transaction {
var transaction =
facade.transaction.create(srcAccountId,destAccountId,amount)
 return transaction
}
```

The `main` method calls the `NewBranchManagerFacade` method to create a facade. The methods on `facade` are invoked to create `customer` and `account`:

```
//main method
func main() {
    var facade = NewBranchManagerFacade()
    var customer *Customer
    var account *Account
    customer, account = facade.createCustomerAccount("Thomas Smith",
    "Savings")
    fmt.Println(customer.name)
    fmt.Println(account.accountType)
    var transaction = facade.createTransaction("21456","87345",1000)
    fmt.Println(transaction.amount)
}
```

Run the following commands:

```
go run facade.go
```

The following screenshot displays the output:

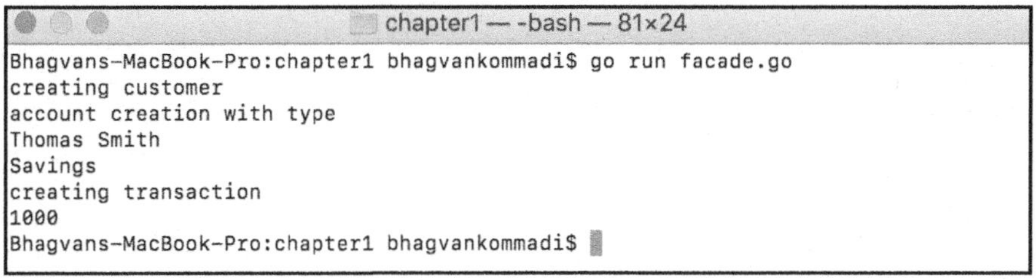

```
chapter1 — -bash — 81×24
Bhagvans-MacBook-Pro:chapter1 bhagvankommadi$ go run facade.go
creating customer
account creation with type
Thomas Smith
Savings
creating transaction
1000
Bhagvans-MacBook-Pro:chapter1 bhagvankommadi$
```

Let's take a look at Flyweight pattern in the next section.

Flyweight

Flyweight is used to manage the state of an object with high variation. The pattern allows us to share common parts of the object state among multiple objects, instead of each object storing it. Variable object data is referred to as extrinsic state, and the rest of the object state is intrinsic. Extrinsic data is passed to flyweight methods and will never be stored within it. Flyweight pattern helps reduce the overall memory usage and the object initializing overhead. The pattern helps create interclass relationships and lower memory to a manageable level.

Flyweight objects are immutable. Value objects are a good example of the flyweight pattern. Flyweight objects can be created in a single thread mode, ensuring one instance per value. In a concurrent thread scenario, multiple instances are created. This is based on the equality criterion of flyweight objects.

The participants of the flyweight pattern are the `FlyWeight` interface, `ConcreteFlyWeight`, `FlyWeightFactory`, and the `Client` classes:

- The `FlyWeight` interface has a method through which flyweights can get and act on the extrinsic state.
- `ConcreteFlyWeight` implements the `FlyWeight` interface to represent flyweight objects.
- `FlyweightFactory` is used to create and manage flyweight objects. The client invokes `FlyweightFactory` to get a flyweight object. `UnsharedFlyWeight` can have a functionality that is not shared.
- `Client` classes

Let's say `DataTransferObject` is an interface with the `getId` method. `DataTransferObjectFactory` creates a data transfer object through `getDataTransferObject` by the `DTO` type. The `DTO` types are customer, employee, manager, and address, as shown in the following code:

```
//main package has examples shown
// in Hands-On Data Structures and algorithms with Go book
 package main
// importing fmt package
 import (
 "fmt"
 )
 //DataTransferObjectFactory struct
```

```
 type DataTransferObjectFactory struct {
 pool map[string] DataTransferObject
 }
//DataTransferObjectFactory class method getDataTransferObject
 func (factory DataTransferObjectFactory) getDataTransferObject(dtoType
string) DataTransferObject {
var dto = factory.pool[dtoType]
if dto == nil {
fmt.Println("new DTO of dtoType: " + dtoType)
 switch dtoType{
 case "customer":
 factory.pool[dtoType] = Customer{id:"1"}
 case "employee":
 factory.pool[dtoType] = Employee{id:"2"}
 case "manager":
 factory.pool[dtoType] = Manager{id:"3"}
 case "address":
 factory.pool[dtoType] = Address{id:"4"}
 }
dto = factory.pool[dtoType]
}

 return dto
 }
```

In the following code, the `DataTransferObject` interface is implemented by the `Customer` class:

```
// DataTransferObject interface
 type DataTransferObject interface {
 getId() string
 }
 //Customer struct
 type Customer struct {
 id string //sequence generator
 name string
 ssn string
 }
 // Customer class method getId
 func (customer Customer) getId() string {
 //fmt.Println("getting customer Id")
 return customer.id
}
 //Employee struct
 type Employee struct {
 id string
 name string
 }
```

```
//Employee class method getId
func (employee Employee) getId() string {
return employee.id
}
//Manager struct
type Manager struct {
id string
name string
dept string
}
```

The `DataTransferObject` interface is implemented by the `Manager` class, as shown in the following code:

```
//Manager class method getId
 func (manager Manager) getId() string {
 return manager.id
 }
 //Address struct
 type Address struct {
 id string
 streetLine1 string
 streetLine2 string
 state string
 city string
}
//Address class method getId
 func (address Address) getId() string{
 return address.id
 }
 //main method
 func main() {
 var factory =
DataTransferObjectFactory{make(map[string]DataTransferObject)}
 var customer DataTransferObject =
factory.getDataTransferObject("customer")
 fmt.Println("Customer ",customer.getId())
 var employee DataTransferObject =
factory.getDataTransferObject("employee")
 fmt.Println("Employee ",employee.getId())
 var manager DataTransferObject = factory.getDataTransferObject("manager")
 fmt.Println("Manager",manager.getId())
 var address DataTransferObject = factory.getDataTransferObject("address")
 fmt.Println("Address",address.getId())
 }
```

Run the following commands:

```
go run flyweight.go
```

The following screenshot displays the output:

```
chapter1 — -bash — 81×24
Bhagvans-MacBook-Pro:chapter1 bhagvankommadi$ go run flyweight.go
new DTO of dtoType: customer
Customer  1
new DTO of dtoType: employee
Employee  2
new DTO of dtoType: manager
Manager 3
new DTO of dtoType: address
Address 4
Bhagvans-MacBook-Pro:chapter1 bhagvankommadi$
```

We will take a look at Private class and Proxy data patterns in the next sections.

Private class data

The private class data pattern secures the data within a class. This pattern encapsulates the initialization of the class data. The write privileges of properties within the private class are protected, and properties are set during construction. The private class pattern prints the exposure of information by securing it in a class that retains the state. The encapsulation of class data initialization is a scenario where this pattern is applicable.

`Account` is a class with account details and a customer name. `AccountDetails` is the private attribute of `Account` , and `CustomerName` is the public attribute. JSON marshaling of `Account` has `CustomerName` as a public property. `AccountDetails` is the package property in Go (modeled as private class data):

```
//main package has examples shown
 // in Hands-On Data Structures and algorithms with Go book
 package main
// importing fmt and encoding/json packages
import (
 "encoding/json"
 "fmt"
 )
 //AccountDetails struct
 type AccountDetails struct {
 id string
 accountType string
 }
 //Account struct
```

```
type Account struct {
details *AccountDetails
CustomerName string
}
// Account class method setDetails
func (account *Account) setDetails(id string, accountType string) {
account.details = &AccountDetails{id, accountType}
}
```

As shown in the following code, the `Account` class has the `getId` method, which returns the `id` private class attribute:

```
//Account class method getId
func (account *Account) getId() string{
return account.details.id
}
//Account class method getAccountType
func (account *Account) getAccountType() string{
return account.details.accountType
}
```

The `main` method calls the `Account` initializer with `CustomerName`. The details of the account are set details with the `setDetails` method:

```
// main method
func main() {
var account *Account = &Account{CustomerName: "John Smith"}
account.setDetails("4532","current")
jsonAccount, _ := json.Marshal(account)
fmt.Println("Private Class hidden",string(jsonAccount))
fmt.Println("Account Id",account.getId())
fmt.Println("Account Type",account.getAccountType())
}
```

Run the following commands:

```
go run privateclass.go
```

The following screenshot displays the output:

```
chapter1 — -bash — 81×24
Bhagvans-MacBook-Pro:chapter1 bhagvankommadi$ go run privateclass.go
Private Class hidden {"CustomerName":"John Smith"}
Account Id 4532
Account Type current
Bhagvans-MacBook-Pro:chapter1 bhagvankommadi$
```

Let's take a look at Proxy pattern in the next section.

Proxy

The proxy pattern forwards to a real object and acts as an interface to others. The proxy pattern controls access to an object and provides additional functionality. The additional functionality can be related to authentication, authorization, and providing rights of access to the resource-sensitive object. The real object need not be modified while providing additional logic. Remote, smart, virtual, and protection proxies are the scenarios where this pattern is applied. It is also used to provide an alternative to extend functionality with inheritance and object composition. A proxy object is also referred to as a surrogate, handle, or wrapper.

The proxy pattern comprises the subject interface, the `RealSubject` class, and the `Proxy` class:

- Subject is an interface for the `RealObject` and `Proxy` class.
- The `RealSubject` object is created and maintained as a reference in the `Proxy` class. `RealSubject` is resource sensitive, required to be protected, and expensive to create. `RealObject` is a class that implements the `IRealObject` interface. It has a `performAction` method.
- `VirtualProxy` is used to access `RealObject` and invoke the `performAction` method.

The following code shows an implementation of proxy pattern:

```
//main package has examples shown
// in Hands-On Data Structures and algorithms with Go book
package main
// importing fmt package
import (
"fmt"
)
//IRealObject interface
type IRealObject interface {
performAction()
}
//RealObject struct
type RealObject struct{}
RealObject class implements IRealObject interface. The class has method
performAction.
//RealObject class method performAction
func (realObject *RealObject) performAction() {
fmt.Println("RealObject performAction()")
```

```
}
//VirtualProxy struct
type VirtualProxy struct {
realObject *RealObject
}
//VirtualProxy class method performAction
func (virtualProxy *VirtualProxy) performAction() {
if virtualProxy.realObject == nil {
virtualProxy.realObject = &RealObject{}
}
fmt.Println("Virtual Proxy performAction()")
virtualProxy.realObject.performAction()
}
// main method
func main() {
var object VirtualProxy = VirtualProxy{}
object.performAction()
}
```

Run the following commands:

```
go run virtualproxy.go
```

The following screenshot displays the output:

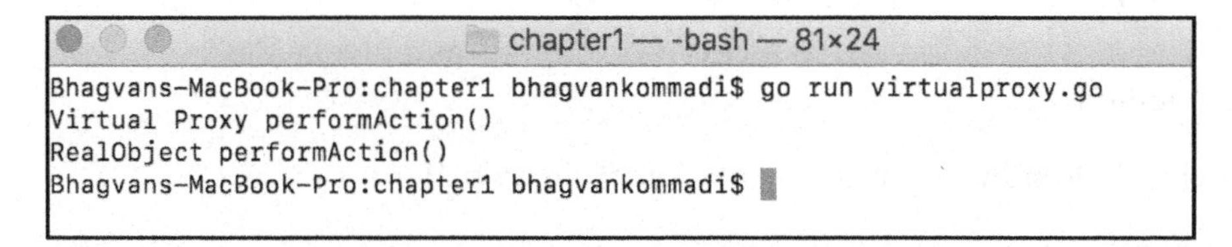

Now that we know the classification of data structures and the design patterns used, let's go ahead and take a look at the representation of algorithms.

Representation of algorithms

A flow chart and pseudo code are methods of representing algorithms. An algorithm shows the logic of how a problem is solved. A flow chart has different representation symbols such as Entry, Exit, Task, Input/Output, Decision Point, and Inter Block. A structured program consists of a series of these symbols to perform a specific task. Pseudo code has documentation, action, and flow control keywords to visualize an algorithm. The documentation keywords are **TASK** and **REM**. **SET**, **PUT**, and **GET** are the action keywords.

Let's take a look at the different representations of algorithms, that is, flow charts and Pseudo code in the next sections.

Flow chart

The flow control keywords are **SET**, **LOOP**, **(WHILE**, **UNTIL)**, **REP**, and **POST**. The following flow chart shows a formula or an algorithm to calculate the dividend given a number of shares, the face value, and the dividend percentage. The start and end are the Entry and Exit symbols. The input number of shares, share face value, and dividend percentage use the Input symbol. The compute dividend and output dividend use the Task symbol and Output symbol respectively:

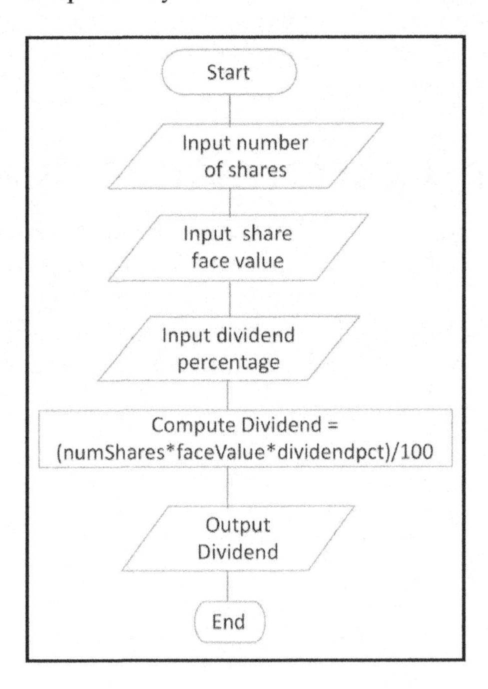

In the next section, we'll take a look at pseudo code, representation of algorithms.

Pseudo code

Pseudo code is a high-level design of a program or algorithm. Sequence and selection are two constructs used in pseudo code. Pseudo code is easier than a flow chart visualizes the algorithm while pseudo code can be easily modified and updated. Errors in design can be caught very early in pseudo code. This saves the cost of fixing defects later.

To give an example, we want to find the `max` value in an array of length *n*. The pseudo code will be written as follows:

```
maximum(arr) {
    n <- len(arr)
    max <- arr[0]
    for k <- 0,n do  {
        If  arr[k] > max {
            max <- arr[k]
        }
    }
    return max
}
```

Now that we know the different ways to represent the algorithm, let's take a look at how we can monitor its complexity and performance in the next section.

Complexity and performance analysis

The efficiency of an algorithm is measured through various parameters, such as CPU time, memory, disk, and network. The complexity is how the algorithm scales when the number of input parameters increases. Performance is a measure of time, space, memory, and other parameters. Algorithms are compared by their processing time and resource consumption. Complexity measures the parameters and is represented by the Big O notation.

Complexity analysis of algorithms

The complexity of an algorithm is measured by the speed of the algorithm. Typically, the algorithm will perform differently based on processor speed, disk speed, memory, and other hardware parameters. Hence, asymptotical complexity is used to measure the complexity of an algorithm. An algorithm is a set of steps to be processed by different operations to achieve a task. The time taken for an algorithm to complete is based on the number of steps taken.

Let's say an algorithm iterates through an array, `m`, of size `10` and update the elements to the sum of index and `200`. The computational time will be 10*t, where t is the time taken to add two integers and update them to an array. The next step will be printing them after iterating over an array. The t time parameter will vary with the hardware of the computer used. Asymptotically, the computational time grows as a factor of `10`, as shown in the following code:

```
//main package has examples shown
// in Hands-On Data Structures and algorithms with Go book
package main
// importing fmt package
import (
 "fmt"
)
// main method
func main() {
 var m [10]int
 var k int
for k = 0; k < 10; k++ {
 m[k] = k + 200
fmt.Printf("Element[%d] = %d\n", k, m[k] )
 }
}
```

Run the following commands:

```
go run complexity.go
```

The following screenshot displays the output:

```
chapter1 — -bash — 81×24
Bhagvans-MacBook-Pro:chapter1 bhagvankommadi$ go run complexity.go
Element[0] = 200
Element[1] = 201
Element[2] = 202
Element[3] = 203
Element[4] = 204
Element[5] = 205
Element[6] = 206
Element[7] = 207
Element[8] = 208
Element[9] = 209
Bhagvans-MacBook-Pro:chapter1 bhagvankommadi$
```

Let's take a look at the different complexity types in the next sections.

Big O notation

The $T(n)$ time function represents the algorithm complexity based on Big O notation. $T(n) = O(n)$ states that an algorithm has a linear time complexity. Using Big O notation, the constant time, linear time, logarithmic time, cubic time, and quadratic time complexity are different complexity types for an algorithm.

Linear time, $O(n)$, is used as a measure of complexity in scenarios such as linear search, traversing, and finding the minimum and maximum number of array elements. ArrayList and queue are data structures that have these methods. An algorithm that has logarithmic time, $O(log\ n)$, is a binary search in a tree data structure. Bubble sort, selection sort, and insertion sort algorithms have complexity of quadratic time, $O(n^2)$. Big Omega Ω and big Theta Θ are notations for the lower and upper bounds for a particular algorithm.

The worst case, best case, average case, and amortized run-time complexity is used for analysis of algorithms. Amortized run-time complexity is referred to as 2^n. Asymptotically, it will tend to $O(1)$.

Big O notation is also used to determine how much space is consumed by the algorithm. This helps us find the best and worst case scenarios, relative to space and time.

Let's take a look at linear complexity in the next section.

Linear complexity

An algorithm is of linear complexity if the processing time or storage space is directly proportional to the number of input elements to be processed. In Big O notation, linear complexity is presented as $O(n)$. String matching algorithms such as the Boyer-Moore and Ukkonen have linear complexity.

Linear complexity, $O(n)$, is demonstrated in an algorithm as follows:

```
//main package has examples shown
// in Go Data Structures and algorithms book
package main
// importing fmt package
import (
  "fmt"
)
// main method
func main() {
  var m [10]int
  var k int
for k = 0; k < 10; k++ {
  m[k] = k * 200
fmt.Printf("Element[%d] = %d\n", k, m[k] )
  }
}
```

Run the following commands:

```
go run linear_complexity.go
```

The following screenshot displays the output:

```
chapter1 — -bash — 81×24
Bhagvans-MacBook-Pro:chapter1 bhagvankommadi$ go run linear_complexity.go
Element[0] = 0
Element[1] = 200
Element[2] = 400
Element[3] = 600
Element[4] = 800
Element[5] = 1000
Element[6] = 1200
Element[7] = 1400
Element[8] = 1600
Element[9] = 1800
Bhagvans-MacBook-Pro:chapter1 bhagvankommadi$
```

Let's take a look at quadratic complexity in the next section.

Quadratic complexity

An algorithm is of quadratic complexity if the processing time is proportional to the square of the number of input elements. In the following case, the complexity of the algorithm is 10*10 = 100. The two loops have a maximum of `10`. The quadratic complexity for a multiplication table of *n* elements is $O(n^2)$.

Quadratic complexity, $O(n^2)$, is shown in the following example:

```
//main package has examples shown
// in Go Data Structures and algorithms book
package main
// importing fmt package
import (
    "fmt"
)
// main method
func main() {
    var k,l int
    for k = 1; k <= 10; k++ {
        fmt.Println(" Multiplication Table", k)
        for l=1; l <= 10; l++ {
            var x int = l *k
            fmt.Println(x)
        }
    }
}
```

Run the following commands:

```
go run quadratic_complexity.go
```

The following screenshot displays the output:

```
chapter1 — -bash — 81×30
Bhagvans-MacBook-Pro:chapter1 bhagvankommadi$ go run quadratic_complexity.go
 Multiplication Table 1
1
2
3
4
5
6
7
8
9
10
 Multiplication Table 2
2
4
6
8
10
12
14
16
18
20
 Multiplication Table 3
3
6
9
12
15
18
```

Let's take a look at cubic complexity in the next section.

Cubic complexity

In the case of cubic complexity, the processing time of an algorithm is proportional to the cube of the input elements. The complexity of the following algorithm is 10*10*10 = 1,000. The three loops have a maximum of 10. The cubic complexity for a matrix update is $O(n^3)$.

Cubic complexity $O(n^3)$ is explained in the following example:

```
//main package has examples shown
// in Hands-On Data Structures and algorithms with Go book
package main
// importing fmt package
import (
 "fmt"
)
// main method
func main() {
var k,l,m int
var arr[10][10][10] int
```

```
 for k = 0; k < 10; k++ {
for l=0; l < 10; l++ {
for m=0; m < 10; m++ {
arr[k][l][m] = 1
fmt.Println("Element value ",k,l,m," is", arr[k][l][m])
}
}
}
}
```

Run the following commands:

```
go run cubic_complexity.go
```

The following screenshot displays the output:

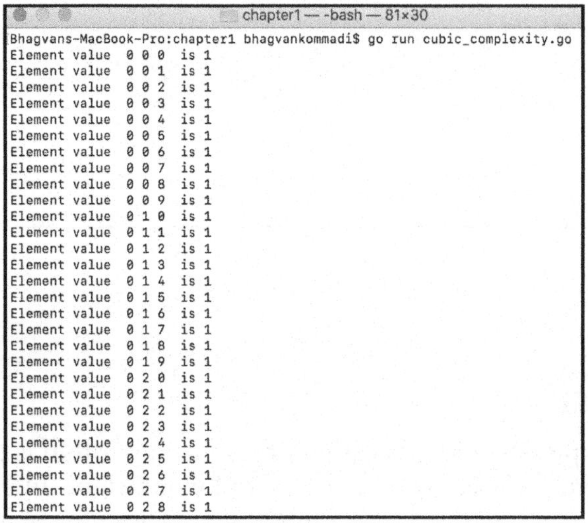

```
chapter1 — -bash — 81×30
Bhagvans-MacBook-Pro:chapter1 bhagvankommadi$ go run cubic_complexity.go
Element value  0 0 0  is 1
Element value  0 0 1  is 1
Element value  0 0 2  is 1
Element value  0 0 3  is 1
Element value  0 0 4  is 1
Element value  0 0 5  is 1
Element value  0 0 6  is 1
Element value  0 0 7  is 1
Element value  0 0 8  is 1
Element value  0 0 9  is 1
Element value  0 1 0  is 1
Element value  0 1 1  is 1
Element value  0 1 2  is 1
Element value  0 1 3  is 1
Element value  0 1 4  is 1
Element value  0 1 5  is 1
Element value  0 1 6  is 1
Element value  0 1 7  is 1
Element value  0 1 8  is 1
Element value  0 1 9  is 1
Element value  0 2 0  is 1
Element value  0 2 1  is 1
Element value  0 2 2  is 1
Element value  0 2 3  is 1
Element value  0 2 4  is 1
Element value  0 2 5  is 1
Element value  0 2 6  is 1
Element value  0 2 7  is 1
Element value  0 2 8  is 1
```

Let's take a look at logarithmic complexity in the next section.

Logarithmic complexity

An algorithm is of logarithmic complexity if the processing time is proportional to the logarithm of the input elements. The logarithm base is typically 2. The following tree is a binary tree with `LeftNode` and `RightNode`. The insert operation is of *O(log n)* complexity, where *n* is the number of nodes.

Logarithmic complexity is presented as follows:

```
//main package has examples shown
// in Hands-On Data Structures and algorithms with Go book
package main
// importing fmt package
import (
    "fmt"
)
// Tree struct
type Tree struct {
    LeftNode *Tree
    Value int
    RightNode *Tree
}
```

As shown in the following code, the `Tree` class has the `insert` method, which inserts the element given `m` is the integer element:

```
// Tree insert method for inserting at m position
func (tree *Tree) insert( m int) {
 if tree != nil {
if tree.LeftNode == nil {
tree.LeftNode = &Tree{nil,m,nil}
 } else {
 if tree.RightNode == nil {
 tree.RightNode = &Tree{nil,m,nil}
 } else {
if tree.LeftNode != nil {
tree.LeftNode.insert(m)
} else {
tree.RightNode.insert(m)
}
}
}
} else {
tree = &Tree{nil,m,nil}
 }
}
//print method for printing a Tree
func print(tree *Tree) {
 if tree != nil {
fmt.Println(" Value",tree.Value)
 fmt.Printf("Tree Node Left")
 print(tree.LeftNode)
 fmt.Printf("Tree Node Right")
 print(tree.RightNode)
 } else {
```

```
 fmt.Printf("Nil\n")
 }
}
```

The `main` method calls the `insert` method on `tree` to insert the `1`, `3`, `5`, and `7` elements, as shown in the following code:

```
// main method
func main() {
 var tree *Tree = &Tree{nil,1,nil}
 print(tree)
 tree.insert(3)
 print(tree)
 tree.insert(5)
 print(tree)
 tree.LeftNode.insert(7)
 print(tree)
}
```

Run the following commands:

```
go run tree.go
```

The following screenshot displays the output:

```
chapter1 — -bash — 81×30
Bhagvans-MacBook-Pro:chapter1 bhagvankommadi$ go run tree.go
 Value 1
Tree Node LeftNil
Tree Node RightNil
 Value 1
Tree Node Left Value 3
Tree Node LeftNil
Tree Node RightNil
Tree Node RightNil
 Value 1
Tree Node Left Value 3
Tree Node LeftNil
Tree Node RightNil
Tree Node Right Value 5
Tree Node LeftNil
Tree Node RightNil
 Value 1
Tree Node Left Value 3
Tree Node Left Value 7
Tree Node LeftNil
Tree Node RightNil
Tree Node RightNil
Tree Node Right Value 5
Tree Node LeftNil
Tree Node RightNil
Bhagvans-MacBook-Pro:chapter1 bhagvankommadi$
```

Now that we know about the complexities in algorithms and analyzing their performance, let's take a look at brute force algorithms in the next section.

Brute force algorithms

A brute force algorithm solves a problem based on the statement and the problem definition. Brute force algorithms for search and sort are sequential search and selection sort. Exhaustive search is another brute force algorithm where the solution is in a set of candidate solutions with definitive properties. The space in which the search happens is a state and combinatorial space, which consists of permutations, combinations, or subsets.

Brute Force algorithms are known for wide applicability and simplicity in solving complex problems. Searching, string matching, and matrix multiplication are some scenarios where they are used. Single computational tasks can be solved using brute force algorithms. They do not provide efficient algorithms. The algorithms are slow and non-performant. Representation of a brute force algorithm is shown in the following code:

```
//main package has examples shown
//in Hands-On Data Structures and algorithms with Go book
package main
// importing fmt package
import (
    "fmt"
)
//findElement method given array and k element
func findElement(arr[10] int, k int) bool {
    var i int
    for i=0; i< 10; i++ {
        if arr[i]==k {
            return true
        }
    }
    return false
}
// main method
func main() {
    var arr = [10]int{1,4,7,8,3,9,2,4,1,8}
    var check bool = findElement(arr,10)
    fmt.Println(check)
    var check2 bool = findElement(arr,9)
    fmt.Println(check2)
}
```

Run the following commands:

```
go run bruteforce.go
```

The following screenshot displays the output:

```
chapter1 — -bash — 81×30
Bhagvans-MacBook-Pro:chapter1 bhagvankommadi$ go run bruteforce.go
false
true
Bhagvans-MacBook-Pro:chapter1 bhagvankommadi$
```

After brute force algorithms, let's cover divide and conquer algorithms in the next section.

Divide and conquer algorithms

A divide and conquer algorithm breaks a complex problem into smaller problems and solves these smaller problems. The smaller problem will be further broken down till it is a known problem. The approach is to recursively solve the sub-problems and merge the solutions of the sub-problems.

Recursion, quick sort, binary search, fast Fourier transform, and merge sort are good examples of divide and conquer algorithms. Memory is efficiently used with these algorithms. Performance is sometimes an issue in the case of recursion. On multiprocessor machines, these algorithms can be executed on different processors after breaking them down into sub-problems. A divide and conquer algorithm is shown in the following code:

```
//main package has examples shown
// in Hands-On Data Structures and algorithms with Go book
package main
// importing fmt package
import (
    "fmt"
)
```

As shown in the following code, the Fibonacci method takes the *k* integer parameter and returns the Fibonacci number for *k*. The method uses recursion to calculate the Fibonacci numbers. The recursion algorithm is applied by dividing the problem into the `k-1` integer and the `k-2` integer:

```
// fibonacci method given k integer
func fibonacci(k int) int {
if k<=1{
```

```
    return 1
    }
    return fibonacci(k-1)+fibonacci(k-2)
}
// main method
func main() {
var m int = 5
for m=0; m < 8; m++ {
var fib = fibonacci(m)
fmt.Println(fib)
 }
}
```

Run the following commands:

```
go run divide.go
```

The following screenshot displays the output:

```
chapter1 — -bash — 81×30
Bhagvans-MacBook-Pro:chapter1 bhagvankommadi$ go run divide.go
1
1
2
3
5
8
13
21
Bhagvans-MacBook-Pro:chapter1 bhagvankommadi$
```

Let's take a look at what backtracking algorithms are in the next section.

Backtracking algorithms

A backtracking algorithm solves a problem by constructing the solution incrementally. Multiple options are evaluated, and the algorithm chooses to go to the next component of the solution through recursion. Backtracking can be a chronological type or can traverse the paths, depending on the problem that you are solving.

Backtracking is an algorithm that finds candidate solutions and rejects a candidate on the basis of its feasibility and validity. Backtracking is useful in scenarios such as finding a value in an unordered table. It is faster than a brute force algorithm, which rejects a large number of solutions in an iteration. Constraint satisfaction problems such as parsing, rules engine, knapsack problems, and combinatorial optimization are solved using backtracking.

The following is an example of a backtracking algorithm. The problem is to identify the combinations of elements in an array of 10 elements whose sum is equal to `18`. The `findElementsWithSum` method recursively tries to find the combination. Whenever the sum goes beyond the `k` target, it backtracks:

```
//main package has examples shown
// in Hands-On Data Structures and algorithms with Go book
package main
// importing fmt package
import (
 "fmt"
)
//findElementsWithSum of k from arr of size
func findElementsWithSum(arr[10] int,combinations[19] int,size int, k int,
addValue int, l int, m int) int {
var num int = 0
if addValue > k {
 return -1
 }
if addValue == k {
 num = num +1
 var p int =0
 for p=0; p < m; p++ {
  fmt.Printf("%d,",arr[combinations[p]])
  }
 fmt.Println(" ")
 }
var i int
for i=l; i< size; i++ {
//fmt.Println(" m", m)
combinations[m] = l
findElementsWithSum(arr,combinations,size,k,addValue+arr[i],l,m+1)
l = l+1
 }
 return num
}
// main method
func main() {
var arr = [10]int{1,4,7,8,3,9,2,4,1,8}
var addedSum int = 18
var combinations [19]int
```

```
findElementsWithSum(arr,combinations,10,addedSum,0,0,0)
//fmt.Println(check)//var check2 bool = findElement(arr,9)
//fmt.Println(check2)
}
```

Run the following commands:

```
go run backtracking.go
```

The following screenshot displays the output:

```
chapter1 — -bash — 81×30
Bhagvans-MacBook-Pro:chapter1 bhagvankommadi$ go run backtracking.go
1,1,1,1,1,1,1,1,1,1,1,1,1,1,1,1,1,1,
1,1,1,1,1,1,1,1,1,1,1,1,1,1,1,1,1,1,
1,1,1,1,1,1,1,1,1,1,1,1,1,1,1,1,2,
1,1,1,1,1,1,1,1,1,1,1,1,1,1,1,1,1,1,
1,1,1,1,1,1,1,1,1,1,1,1,1,1,1,3,
1,1,1,1,1,1,1,1,1,1,1,1,1,1,1,2,1,
1,1,1,1,1,1,1,1,1,1,1,1,1,1,1,1,1,1,
1,1,1,1,1,1,1,1,1,1,1,1,1,1,4,
1,1,1,1,1,1,1,1,1,1,1,1,1,1,3,1,
1,1,1,1,1,1,1,1,1,1,1,1,1,1,2,2,
1,1,1,1,1,1,1,1,1,1,1,1,1,1,2,1,1,
1,1,1,1,1,1,1,1,1,1,1,1,1,1,4,
1,1,1,1,1,1,1,1,1,1,1,1,1,1,1,1,1,1,
1,1,1,1,1,1,1,1,1,1,1,1,1,4,1,
1,1,1,1,1,1,1,1,1,1,1,1,1,3,2,
1,1,1,1,1,1,1,1,1,1,1,1,1,3,1,1,
1,1,1,1,1,1,1,1,1,1,1,1,1,2,2,1,
1,1,1,1,1,1,1,1,1,1,1,1,1,2,1,1,1,
1,1,1,1,1,1,1,1,1,1,1,1,1,4,1,
1,1,1,1,1,1,1,1,1,1,1,1,1,1,1,1,1,1,
1,1,1,1,1,1,1,1,1,1,1,1,4,2,
1,1,1,1,1,1,1,1,1,1,1,1,4,1,1,
1,1,1,1,1,1,1,1,1,1,1,1,3,3,
1,1,1,1,1,1,1,1,1,1,1,1,3,2,1,
1,1,1,1,1,1,1,1,1,1,1,1,3,1,1,1,
1,1,1,1,1,1,1,1,1,1,1,1,2,2,2,
1,1,1,1,1,1,1,1,1,1,1,1,2,2,1,1,
1,1,1,1,1,1,1,1,1,1,1,1,2,4,
1,1,1,1,1,1,1,1,1,1,1,1,2,1,1,1,1,
```

Summary

This chapter covered the definition of abstract datatypes, classifying data structures into linear, nonlinear, homogeneous, heterogeneous, and dynamic types. Abstract datatypes such as container, list, set, map, graph, stack, and queue were presented in this chapter. The chapter covered the performance analysis of data structures and structural design patterns.

We looked at the classification of data structures and structural design patterns. You can use algorithms such as brute force, divide and conquer, and backtracking by calculating the complexity and performance analysis. The choice of algorithm and the use of design patterns and data structures are the key takeaways.

In the next chapter, we will discuss data structures in Go. The following data structures will be covered:

- Arrays
- Slices
- Two-dimensional slices
- Maps

Questions and exercises

1. Give an example where you can use a composite pattern.
2. For an array of 10 elements with a random set of integers, identify the maximum and minimum. Calculate the complexity of the algorithm.
3. To manage the state of an object, which structural pattern is relevant?
4. A window is sub-classed to add a scroll bar to make it a scrollable window. Which pattern is applied in this scenario?
5. Find the complexity of a binary tree search algorithm.
6. Identify the submatrices of 2x2 in a 3x3 matrix. What is the complexity of the algorithm that you have used?
7. Explain with a scenario the difference between brute force and backtracking algorithms.

8. A rules engine uses backtracking to identify the rules affected by the change. Show an example where backtracking identifies the affected rules.
9. Draw a flow chart for the algorithm of the calculation of profit-loss given the cost price, selling price, and quantity.
10. Write the pseudo code for an algorithm that compares the strings and identifies the substring within a string.

Further reading

The following books are recommended if you want to find out more about Gang of Four design patterns, algorithms, and data structures:

- *Design Patterns*, by Erich Gamma, Richard Helm, Ralph Johnson, and John Vlissides
- *Introduction to Algorithms – Third Edition*, by Thomas H. Cormen, Charles E. Leiserson, Ronald L. Rivest, and Clifford Stein
- *Data structures and Algorithms: An Easy Introduction*, by Rudolph Russell

2
Getting Started with Go for Data Structures and Algorithms

The Go programming language has been rapidly adopted by developers for building web applications. With its impressive performance and ease of development, Go enjoys the support of a wide variety of open source frameworks for building scalable and highly performant web services and apps. The migration to Golang has taken place mainly because of its fast, lightweight, and inbuilt concurrency features. This brings with it the need to learn data structures and algorithms with this growing language.

In data structures, a collection of elements of a single type is called an **array**. **Slices** are similar to arrays except that they have unusual properties. Slice operations such as enlarging a slice using `append` and `copy` methods, assigning parts of a slice, appending a slice, and appending a part of a slice are presented with code samples. Database operations and CRUD web forms are the scenarios in which Go data structures and algorithms are demonstrated.

In this chapter, we will discuss the following Go language-specific data structures:

- Arrays
- Slices
- Two-dimensional slices
- Maps
- Database operations
- Variadic functions
- CRUD web forms

Technical requirements

Install Go Version 1.10 at `https://golang.org/doc/install`, depending on your operating system.

The code files for this chapter can be found at the following GitHub URL: `https://github.com/PacktPublishing/Learn-Data-Structures-and-Algorithms-with-Golang/tree/master/Chapter02`.

In this chapter, database operations require the `github.com/go-sql-driver/mysql` package. In addition to this, MySQL (4.1+) needs to be installed from `https://dev.mysql.com/downloads/mysql/`.

Run the following command:

```
go get -u github.com/go-sql-driver/mysql
```

Arrays

Arrays are the most famous data structures in different programming languages. Different data types can be handled as elements in arrays such as `int`, `float32`, `double`, and others. The following code snippet shows the initialization of an array (`arrays.go`):

```
var arr = [5]int {1,2,4,5,6}
```

An array's size can be found with the `len()` function. A `for` loop is used for accessing all the elements in an array, as follows:

```
var i int
for i=0; i< len(arr); i++ {
    fmt.Println("printing elements ",arr[i]
}
```

In the following code snippet, the `range` keyword is explained in detail. The `range` keyword can be used to access the index and `value` for each element:

```
var value int
for i, value = range arr{
    fmt.Println(" range ",value)
}
```

The _ blank identifier is used if the index is ignored. The following code shows how a _ blank identifier can be used:

```
for _, value = range arr{
    fmt.Println("blank range",value)
}
```

Run the following command:

```
go run arrays.go
```

The following screenshot displays the output:

```
chapter2 — -bash — 80×30
Bhagvans-MacBook-Pro:chapter2 bhagvankommadi$ go run arrays.go
printing elements  1
printing elements  2
printing elements  4
printing elements  5
printing elements  6
 range  1
 range  2
 range  4
 range  5
 range  6
blank range 1
blank range 2
blank range 4
blank range 5
blank range 6
Bhagvans-MacBook-Pro:chapter2 bhagvankommadi$
```

Go arrays are not dynamic but have a fixed size. To add more elements than the size, a bigger array needs to be created and all the elements of the old one need to be copied. An array is passed as a value through functions by copying the array. Passing a big array to a function might be a performance issue.

Now that we have covered what arrays are, let's take a look at slices in the next section.

Slices

Go Slice is an abstraction over **Go Array**. Multiple data elements of the same type are allowed by Go arrays. The definition of variables that can hold several data elements of the same type are allowed by Go Array, but it does not have any provision of inbuilt methods to increase its size in Go. This shortcoming is taken care of by Slices. A Go slice can be appended to elements after the capacity has reached its size. Slices are dynamic and can double the current capacity in order to add more elements.

Let's take a look at the `len` function in the next section.

The len function

The `len()` function gives the current length of `slice`, and the capacity of `slice` can be obtained using the `cap()` function. The following code sample shows the basic slice creation and appending a slice (`basic_slice.go`):

```
var slice = []int{1,3,5,6}
slice = append(slice, 8)
fmt.Println("Capacity", cap(slice))
fmt.Println("Length", len(slice))
```

Run the following command to execute the preceding code:

```
go run basic_slice.go
```

The following screenshot displays the output:

```
chapter2 — -bash — 80×30
Bhagvans-MacBook-Pro:chapter2 bhagvankommadi$ go run basic_slice.go
Capacity 8
Length 5
Bhagvans-MacBook-Pro:chapter2 bhagvankommadi$
```

Let's take a look at the `slice` function in the next section.

Slice function

Slices are passed by referring to functions. Big slices can be passed to functions without impacting performance. Passing a slice as a reference to a function is demonstrated in the code as follows (`slices.go`):

```
//twiceValue method given slice of int type
func twiceValue(slice []int) {
      var i int
      var value int
for i, value = range  slice {
      slice[i] = 2*value
   }
    }
// main method
func main() {
```

```
        var slice = []int{1,3,5,6}
        twiceValue(slice)
        var i int
        for i=0; i< len(slice); i++ {
            fmt.Println("new slice value", slice[i])
    }
    }
```

Run the following command:

```
go run slices.go
```

The following screenshot displays the output:

```
Bhagvans-MacBook-Pro:chapter2 bhagvankommadi$ go run slices.go
new slice value 2
new slice value 6
new slice value 10
new slice value 12
Bhagvans-MacBook-Pro:chapter2 bhagvankommadi$
```

Now that we know what slices are, let's move on to two-dimensional slices in the next section.

Two-dimensional slices

Two-dimensional slices are descriptors of a two-dimensional array. A two-dimensional slice is a contiguous section of an array that is stored away from the slice itself. It holds references to an underlying array. A two-dimensional slice will be an array of arrays, while the capacity of a slice can be increased by creating a new slice and copying the contents of the initial slice into the new one. This is also referred to as a **slice of slices**. The following is an example of a two-dimensional array. A 2D array is created and the array elements are initialized with values.

`twodarray.go` is the code exhibit that's presented in the following code:

```
//main package has examples shown
// in Go Data Structures and algorithms book
package main
// importing fmt package
import (
 "fmt"
)
// main method
```

```
func main() {
  var TwoDArray [8][8]int
   TwoDArray[3][6] = 18
  TwoDArray[7][4] = 3
   fmt.Println(TwoDArray)
}
```

Run the following command:

```
go run twodarray.go
```

The following screenshot displays the output:

```
chapter2 — -bash — 80×30
Bhagvans-MacBook-Pro:chapter2 bhagvankommadi$ go run twodarray.go
[[0 0 0 0 0 0 0 0] [0 0 0 0 0 0 0 0] [0 0 0 0 0 0 0 0] [0 0 0 0 0 0 18 0] [0 0 0
 0 0 0 0 0] [0 0 0 0 0 0 0 0] [0 0 0 0 0 0 0 0] [0 0 0 0 3 0 0 0]]
Bhagvans-MacBook-Pro:chapter2 bhagvankommadi$
```

For dynamic allocation, we use slice of slices. In the following code, slice of slices is explained as two-dimensional slices—`twodslices.go`:

```
// in Go Data Structures and algorithms book
package main
// importing fmt package
import (
 "fmt"
)
// main method
func main() {
   var rows int
   var cols int
   rows = 7
   cols = 9
   var twodslices = make([][]int, rows)
   var i int
   for i = range twodslices {
      twodslices[i] = make([]int,cols)
   }
    fmt.Println(twodslices)
}
```

Run the following commands:

```
go run twodslices.go
```

The following screenshot displays the output:

```
chapter2 — -bash — 80×24
Bhagvans-MacBook-Pro:chapter2 bhagvankommadi$ go run twodslices.go
[[0 0 0 0 0 0 0 0 0] [0 0 0 0 0 0 0 0 0] [0 0 0 0 0 0 0 0 0] [0 0 0 0 0 0 0 0 0]
 [0 0 0 0 0 0 0 0 0] [0 0 0 0 0 0 0 0 0] [0 0 0 0 0 0 0 0 0]]
Bhagvans-MacBook-Pro:chapter2 bhagvankommadi$
```

The `append` method on the slice is used to append new elements to the slice. If the slice capacity has reached the size of the underlying array, then append increases the size by creating a new underlying array and adding the new element. `slic1` is a sub slice of `arr` starting from zero to 3 (excluded), while `slic2` is a sub slice of `arr` starting from 1 (inclusive) to 5 (excluded). In the following snippet, the `append` method calls on `slic2` to add a new `12` element (`append_slice.go`):

```
var arr = [] int{5,6,7,8,9}
var slic1 = arr[: 3]
fmt.Println("slice1",slic1)
var slic2 = arr[1:5]
fmt.Println("slice2",slic2)
var slic3 = append(slic2, 12)
fmt.Println("slice3",slic3)
```

Run the following commands:

```
go run append_slice.go
```

The following screenshot displays the output:

```
chapter2 — -bash — 80×30
Bhagvans-MacBook-Pro:chapter2 bhagvankommadi$ go run append_slice.go
slice1 [5 6 7]
slice2 [6 7 8 9]
slice3 [6 7 8 9 12]
Bhagvans-MacBook-Pro:chapter2 bhagvankommadi$
```

Now that we have covered what two-dimensional slices are, let's take a look at maps in the next section.

Maps

Maps are used to keep track of keys that are types, such as integers, strings, float, double, pointers, interfaces, structs, and arrays. The values can be of different types. In the following example, the language of the map type with a key integer and a value string is created (`maps.go`):

```
var languages = map[int]string {
      3: "English",
       4: "French",
        5: "Spanish"
}
```

Maps can be created using the `make` method, specifying the key type and the value type. Products of a map type with a key integer and value string are shown in the following code snippet:

```
var products = make(map[int]string)
products[1] = "chair"
products[2] = "table"
```

A `for` loop is used for iterating through the map. The languages map is iterated as follows:

```
var i int
var value string
for i, value = range languages {
   fmt.Println("language",i, ":",value)
}
fmt.Println("product with key 2",products[2])
```

Retrieving value and deleting slice operations using the products map is shown in the following code:

```
fmt.Println(products[2])
delete(products,"chair")
fmt.Println("products",products)
```

Run the following commands:

```
go run maps.go
```

The following screenshot displays the output:

```
chapter2 — -bash — 80×30
Bhagvans-MacBook-Pro:chapter2 bhagvankommadi$ go run maps.go
language 3 : English
language 4 : French
language 5 : Spanish
product with key 2 table
products map[2:table]
Bhagvans-MacBook-Pro:chapter2 bhagvankommadi$
```

Now that we've covered maps, let's move on to database operations.

Database operations

In this section, we will take a look at some of database operations using appropriate examples.

Let's start with the `GetCustomer` method in the next section.

The GetCustomer method

The `GetCustomer` method retrieves the `Customer` data from the database. To start with, the `create` database operation is shown in the following example. `Customer` is the table with the `Customerid`, `CustomerName`, and `SSN` attributes. The `GetConnection` method returns the database connection, which is used to query the database. The query then returns the rows from the database table. In the following code, database operations are explained in detail (`database_operations.go`):

```
//main package has examples shown
// in Hands-On Data Structures and algorithms with Go book
package main

// importing fmt,database/sql, net/http, text/template package
import (
    "fmt"
    "database/sql"
    _ "github.com/go-sql-driver/mysql"
)

// Customer Class
type Customer struct {
    CustomerId int
```

```
        CustomerName string
        SSN string
    }
    // GetConnection method which returns sql.DB
    func GetConnection() (database *sql.DB) {
        databaseDriver := "mysql"
        databaseUser := "newuser"
        databasePass := "newuser"
        databaseName := "crm"
        database, error := sql.Open(databaseDriver,
    databaseUser+":"+databasePass+"@/"+databaseName)
        if error != nil {
            panic(error.Error())
        }
        return database
    }
    // GetCustomers method returns Customer Array
    func GetCustomers() []Customer {
        var database *sql.DB
        database = GetConnection()

        var error error
        var rows *sql.Rows
        rows, error = database.Query("SELECT * FROM Customer ORDER BY
    Customerid DESC")
        if error != nil {
            panic(error.Error())
        }
        var customer Customer
        customer = Customer{}

        var customers []Customer
        customers= []Customer{}
        for rows.Next() {
            var customerId int
            var customerName string
            var ssn string
            error = rows.Scan(&customerId, &customerName, &ssn)
            if error != nil {
                panic(error.Error())
            }
            customer.CustomerId = customerId
            customer.CustomerName = customerName
            customer.SSN = ssn
            customers = append(customers, customer)
        }

        defer database.Close()
```

```
        return customers
}

//main method
func main() {

     var customers []Customer
    customers = GetCustomers()
    fmt.Println("Customers",customers)

}
```

Run the following commands:

```
go run database_operations.go
```

The following screenshot displays the output:

```
chapter2 — -bash — 80×24
Bhagvans-MacBook-Pro:chapter2 bhagvankommadi$ go run database_operations.go
Customers [{9 Arnie Smith 2386343} {8 Martin Rod 2376343} {6 Steve Rod 237343} {
4 Jacob Martinez 23423232423} {1 John Smith 453454934}]
Bhagvans-MacBook-Pro:chapter2 bhagvankommadi$
```

Let's take a look at the `InsertCustomer` method in the next section.

The InsertCustomer method

The `INSERT` operation is as follows. The `InsertCustomer` method takes the `Customer` parameter and creates a prepared statement for the `INSERT` statement. The statement is used to execute the insertion of customer rows into the table, as shown in the following snippet:

```
// InsertCustomer method with parameter customer
func InsertCustomer(customer Customer) {
     var database *sql.DB
     database= GetConnection()

      var error error
      var insert *sql.Stmt
      insert,error = database.Prepare("INSERT INTO
CUSTOMER(CustomerName,SSN) VALUES(?,?)")
          if error != nil {
              panic(error.Error())
          }
          insert.Exec(customer.CustomerName,customer.SSN)
```

```
        defer database.Close()


    }
```

Let's take a look at the variadic functions in the next section.

Variadic functions

A function in which we pass an infinite number of arguments, instead of passing them one at a time, is called a variadic function. The type of the final parameter is preceded by an ellipsis (...), while declaring a variadic function; this shows us that the function might be called with any number of arguments of this type.

Variadic functions can be invoked with a variable number of parameters. `fmt.Println` is a common variadic function, as follows:

```
//main method
func main() {
     var customers []Customer
    customers = GetCustomers()
    fmt.Println("Before Insert",customers)
    var customer Customer
    customer.CustomerName = "Arnie Smith"
    customer.SSN = "2386343"
    InsertCustomer(customer)
    customers = GetCustomers()
    fmt.Println("After Insert",customers)
    }
```

Run the following commands:

```
go run database_operations.go
```

The following screenshot displays the output:

```
chapter2 — -bash — 80×30
[Bhagvans-MacBook-Pro:chapter2 bhagvankommadi$ go run database_operations.go     ]
Before Insert [{8 Martin Rod 2376343} {6 Steve Rod 237343} {5 Michael  Thompson
8834344} {4 Jacob Martinez 23423232423} {1 John Smith 453454934}]
After Insert [{9 Arnie Smith 2386343} {8 Martin Rod 2376343} {6 Steve Rod 237343
} {5 Michael  Thompson 8834344} {4 Jacob Martinez 23423232423} {1 John Smith 453
454934}]
Bhagvans-MacBook-Pro:chapter2 bhagvankommadi$ 
```

Let's start the `update` operation in the next section.

The update operation

The `update` operation is as follows. The `UpdateCustomer` method takes the `Customer` parameter and creates a prepared statement for the `UPDATE` statement. The statement is used to update a customer row in the table:

```
// Update Customer method with parameter customer
func UpdateCustomer(customer Customer){
     var database *sql.DB
     database= GetConnection()
     var error error
      var update *sql.Stmt
      update,error = database.Prepare("UPDATE CUSTOMER SET CustomerName=?,
SSN=? WHERE CustomerId=?")
          if error != nil {
           panic(error.Error())
          }
      update.Exec(customer.CustomerName,customer.SSN,customer.CustomerId)
defer database.Close()
}
// main method
func main() {
    var customers []Customer
    customers = GetCustomers()
   fmt.Println("Before Update",customers)
   var customer Customer
    customer.CustomerName = "George Thompson"
    customer.SSN = "23233432"
    customer.CustomerId = 5
    UpdateCustomer(customer)
    customers = GetCustomers()
    fmt.Println("After Update",customers)
}
```

Run the following commands:

```
go run database_operations.go
```

The following screenshot displays the output:

```
chapter2 — -bash — 80×30
Bhagvans-MacBook-Pro:chapter2 bhagvankommadi$ go run database_operations.go
Before Update [{9 Arnie Smith 2386343} {8 Martin Rod 2376343} {6 Steve Rod 23734
3} {5 Michael  Thompson 8834344} {4 Jacob Martinez 23423232423} {1 John Smith 45
3454934}]
After Update [{9 Arnie Smith 2386343} {8 Martin Rod 2376343} {6 Steve Rod 237343
} {5 George Thompson 23233432} {4 Jacob Martinez 23423232423} {1 John Smith 4534
54934}]
Bhagvans-MacBook-Pro:chapter2 bhagvankommadi$
```

Let's take a look at the `delete` operation in the next section.

The delete operation

The `delete` operation is as follows. The `DeleteCustomer` method takes the `Customer` parameter and creates a prepared statement for the `DELETE` statement. The statement is used to execute the deletion of a customer row in the table:

```
// Delete Customer method with parameter customer
func deleteCustomer(customer Customer){
     var database *sql.DB
     database= GetConnection()
     var error error
      var delete *sql.Stmt
      delete,error = database.Prepare("DELETE FROM Customer WHERE
Customerid=?")
          if error != nil {
             panic(error.Error())
         }
          delete.Exec(customer.CustomerId)
      defer database.Close()
}
// main method
func main() {
     var customers []Customer
    customers = GetCustomers()
    fmt.Println("Before Delete",customers)
  var customer Customer
  customer.CustomerName = "George Thompson"
  customer.SSN = "23233432"
  customer.CustomerId = 5
    deleteCustomer(customer)
    customers = GetCustomers()
    fmt.Println("After Delete",customers)
```

```
}
```

Run the following commands:

```
go run database_operations.go
```

The following screenshot displays the output:

```
chapter2 — -bash — 80×30
Bhagvans-MacBook-Pro:chapter2 bhagvankommadi$ go run database_operations.go
Before Delete [{9 Arnie Smith 2386343} {8 Martin Rod 2376343} {6 Steve Rod 23734
3} {5 George Thompson 23233432} {4 Jacob Martinez 23423232423} {1 John Smith 453
454934}]
After Delete [{9 Arnie Smith 2386343} {8 Martin Rod 2376343} {6 Steve Rod 237343
} {4 Jacob Martinez 23423232423} {1 John Smith 453454934}]
Bhagvans-MacBook-Pro:chapter2 bhagvankommadi$
```

Now that we are done with variadic functions, let's go ahead and look at CRUD web forms in the next section.

CRUD web forms

In this section, we will explain web forms using basic examples, showing you how to perform various actions.

To start a basic HTML page with the Go `net/http` package, the web forms example is as follows (`webforms.go`). This has a welcome greeting in `main.html`:

```
//main package has examples shown
// in Hands-On Data Structures and algorithms with Go book
package main
// importing fmt, database/sql, net/http, text/template package
import (
    "net/http"
    "text/template"
    "log")
// Home method renders the main.html
func Home(writer http.ResponseWriter, reader *http.Request) {
    var template_html *template.Template
    template_html = template.Must(template.ParseFiles("main.html"))
    template_html.Execute(writer,nil)
}
// main method
func main() {
    log.Println("Server started on: http://localhost:8000")
    http.HandleFunc("/", Home)
```

```
    http.ListenAndServe(":8000", nil)
}
```

The code for `main.html` is as follows:

```
<html>
    <body>
        <p> Welcome to Web Forms</p>
    </body>
</html>
```

Run the following commands:

```
go run webforms.go
```

The following screenshot displays the output:

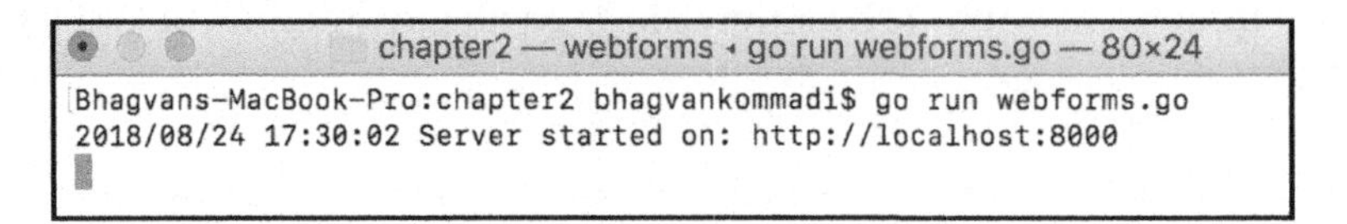

The web browser output is shown in the following screenshot:

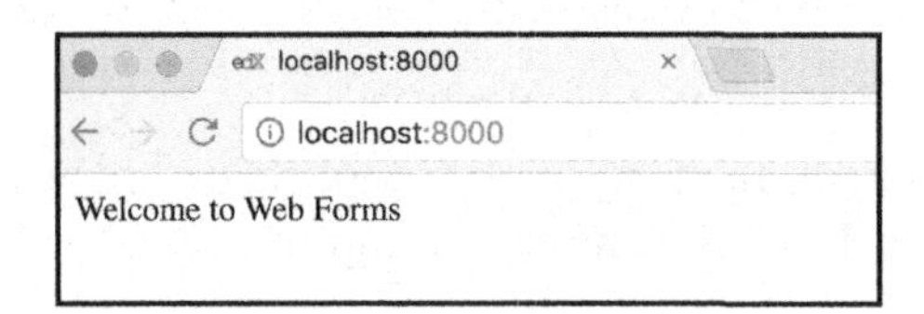

The CRM application is built with web forms as an example to demonstrate CRUD operations. We can use the database operations we built in the previous section. In the following code, the `crm` database operations are presented. The `crm` database operations consist of CRUD methods such as `CREATE`, `READ`, `UPDATE`, and `DELETE` customer operations. The `GetConnection` method retrieves the database connection for performing the database operations (`crm_database_operations.go`):

```
//main package has examples shown
// in Hands-On Data Structures and algorithms with Go book
package main
// importing fmt,database/sql, net/http, text/template package
import (
   "database/sql"
    _ "github.com/go-sql-driver/mysql"
)
// Customer Class
```

```
type Customer struct {
    CustomerId    int
    CustomerName  string
    SSN string
}
//  GetConnection method  which returns sql.DB
func GetConnection() (database *sql.DB) {
    databaseDriver := "mysql"
    databaseUser := "newuser"
    databasePass := "newuser"
    databaseName := "crm"
    database, error := sql.Open(databaseDriver,
databaseUser+":"+databasePass+"@/"+databaseName)
    if error != nil {
        panic(error.Error())
    }
    return database
}
```

As shown in the following code, the `GetCustomerById` method takes the `customerId` parameter to look up in the customer database. The `GetCustomerById` method returns the customer object:

```
//GetCustomerById with parameter customerId returns Customer
func GetCustomerById(customerId int) Customer {
  var database *sql.DB
  database = GetConnection()
  var error error
  var rows *sql.Rows
  rows, error = database.Query("SELECT * FROM Customer WHERE
CustomerId=?",customerId)
  if error != nil {
      panic(error.Error())
  }
  var customer Customer
  customer = Customer{}
    for rows.Next() {
        var customerId int
        var customerName string
        var SSN  string
        error = rows.Scan(&customerId, &customerName, &SSN)
        if error != nil {
           panic(error.Error())
        }
        customer.CustomerId = customerId
        customer.CustomerName = customerName
       customer.SSN = SSN
```

```
    }
```

Now that we have covered CRUD web forms, let's move on to `defer` and `panic` in the next section.

The defer and panic statements

The `defer` statement defers the execution of the function until the surrounding function returns. The `panic` function stops the current flow and control. Deferred functions are executed normally after the `panic` call. In the following code example, the `defer` call gets executed even when the `panic` call is invoked:

```
    defer database.Close()
    return customer
}
// GetCustomers method returns Customer Array
func GetCustomers() []Customer {
    var database *sql.DB
    database = GetConnection()
    var error error
    var rows *sql.Rows
    rows, error = database.Query("SELECT * FROM Customer ORDER BY
Customerid DESC")
    if error != nil {
       panic(error.Error())
    }
   var customer Customer
    customer = Customer{}
    var customers []Customer
    customers= []Customer{}
   for rows.Next() {
       var customerId int
        var customerName string
       var ssn string
        error = rows.Scan(&customerId, &customerName, &ssn)
        if error != nil {
            panic(error.Error())
        }
        customer.CustomerId = customerId
        customer.CustomerName = customerName
        customer.SSN = ssn
        customers = append(customers, customer)
    }
   defer database.Close()
    return customers
```

```
}
```

Let's take a look at the `InsertCustomer`, `UpdateCustomer`, and `DeleteCustomer` methods in the following sections.

The InsertCustomer method

In the following code, the `InsertCustomer` method takes `customer` as a parameter to execute the SQL statement for inserting into the `CUSTOMER` table:

```
// InsertCustomer method with parameter customer
func InsertCustomer(customer Customer) {
      var database *sql.DB
      database= GetConnection()
      var error error
       var insert *sql.Stmt
      insert,error = database.Prepare("INSERT INTO
CUSTOMER(CustomerName,SSN) VALUES(?,?)")
            if error != nil {
                panic(error.Error())
            }
      insert.Exec(customer.CustomerName,customer.SSN)
       defer database.Close()
}
```

The UpdateCustomer method

The `UpdateCustomer` method prepares the `UPDATE` statement by passing the `CustomerName` and `SSN` from the `customer` object; this is shown in the following code:

```
// Update Customer method with parameter customer
func UpdateCustomer(customer Customer) {
      var database *sql.DB
      database= GetConnection()
      var error error
       var update *sql.Stmt
       update,error = database.Prepare("UPDATE CUSTOMER SET CustomerName=?,
SSN=? WHERE CustomerId=?")
            if error != nil {
                panic(error.Error())
            }
update.Exec(customer.CustomerName,customer.SSN,customer.CustomerId)
      defer database.Close()
}
```

The DeleteCustomer method

The `DeleteCustomer` method deletes the customer that's passed by executing the `DELETE` statement:

```
// Delete Customer method with parameter customer
func DeleteCustomer(customer Customer) {
     var database *sql.DB
     database= GetConnection()
      var error error
      var delete *sql.Stmt
      delete,error = database.Prepare("DELETE FROM Customer WHERE
Customerid=?")
          if error != nil {
              panic(error.Error())
          }
          delete.Exec(customer.CustomerId)
     defer database.Close()
}
```

Let's take a look at the CRM web application in the next section.

CRM web application

The CRM web application is shown as follows, with various web paths handled. The CRM application code is shown in the following code. The `Home` function executes the `Home` template with the writer parameter and the customers array (`crm_app.go`):

```
//main package has examples shown
// in Hands-On Data Structures and algorithms with Go book
package main

// importing fmt,database/sql, net/http, text/template package
import (
    "fmt"
    "net/http"
    "text/template"
    "log"
)


var template_html = template.Must(template.ParseGlob("templates/*"))

// Home - execute Template
func Home(writer http.ResponseWriter, request *http.Request) {
    var customers []Customer
```

```
        customers = GetCustomers()
        log.Println(customers)
        template_html.ExecuteTemplate(writer,"Home",customers)

    }
```

Let's take a look at the Create, Insert, Alter, Update, and Delete functions, as well as the main method in the following sections.

The Create function

As shown in the following code, the Create function takes the writer and request parameters to render the Create template:

```
    // Create - execute Template
    func Create(writer http.ResponseWriter, request *http.Request) {

        template_html.ExecuteTemplate(writer,"Create",nil)
    }
```

The Insert function

The Insert function invokes the GetCustomers method to get an array of customers and renders the Home template with the writer and customers arrays as parameters by invoking the ExecuteTemplate method. This is shown in the following code:

```
    // Insert - execute template
    func Insert(writer http.ResponseWriter, request *http.Request) {

        var customer Customer
        customer.CustomerName = request.FormValue("customername")
        customer.SSN = request.FormValue("ssn")
        InsertCustomer(customer)
        var customers []Customer
        customers = GetCustomers()
        template_html.ExecuteTemplate(writer,"Home",customers)

    }
```

The Alter function

The following code shows how the `Alter` function renders the `Home` template by invoking the `ExecuteTemplate` method with the `writer` and `customers` arrays as parameters:

```
// Alter - execute template
func Alter(writer http.ResponseWriter, request *http.Request) {

    var customer Customer
    var customerId int
    var customerIdStr string
    customerIdStr = request.FormValue("id")
    fmt.Sscanf(customerIdStr, "%d", &customerId)
    customer.CustomerId = customerId
    customer.CustomerName = request.FormValue("customername")
    customer.SSN = request.FormValue("ssn")
    UpdateCustomer(customer)
    var customers []Customer
    customers = GetCustomers()
    template_html.ExecuteTemplate(writer,"Home",customers)

}
```

The Update function

The `Update` function invokes the `ExecuteTemplate` method with `writer` and `customer` looked up by `id`. The `ExecuteTemplate` method renders the `UPDATE` template:

```
// Update - execute template
func Update(writer http.ResponseWriter, request *http.Request) {

  var customerId int
  var customerIdStr string
  customerIdStr = request.FormValue("id")
  fmt.Sscanf(customerIdStr, "%d", &customerId)
  var customer Customer
  customer = GetCustomerById(customerId)

    template_html.ExecuteTemplate(writer,"Update",customer)

}
```

The Delete function

The `Delete` method renders the `Home` template after deleting the customer that's found by the `GetCustomerById` method. The `View` method renders the `View` template after finding the customer by invoking the `GetCustomerById` method:

```
// Delete - execute Template
func Delete(writer http.ResponseWriter, request *http.Request) {
  var customerId int
  var customerIdStr string
  customerIdStr = request.FormValue("id")
  fmt.Sscanf(customerIdStr, "%d", &customerId)
  var customer Customer
  customer = GetCustomerById(customerId)
   DeleteCustomer(customer)
   var customers []Customer
   customers = GetCustomers()
  template_html.ExecuteTemplate(writer,"Home",customers)

}
// View - execute Template
func View(writer http.ResponseWriter, request *http.Request) {
    var customerId int
    var customerIdStr string
    customerIdStr = request.FormValue("id")
    fmt.Sscanf(customerIdStr, "%d", &customerId)
    var customer Customer
    customer = GetCustomerById(customerId)
    fmt.Println(customer)
    var customers []Customer
    customers= []Customer{customer}
    customers.append(customer)
    template_html.ExecuteTemplate(writer,"View",customers)

}
```

The main method

The main method handles the `Home`, `Alter`, `Create`, `Update`, `View`, `Insert`, and `Delete` functions with different aliases for lookup and renders the templates appropriately. `HttpServer` listens to port `8000` and waits for template alias invocation:

```
// main method
func main() {
    log.Println("Server started on: http://localhost:8000")
    http.HandleFunc("/", Home)
```

```
        http.HandleFunc("/alter", Alter)
        http.HandleFunc("/create", Create)
        http.HandleFunc("/update", Update)
        http.HandleFunc("/view", View)
        http.HandleFunc("/insert", Insert)
        http.HandleFunc("/delete", Delete)
        http.ListenAndServe(":8000", nil)
}
```

Let's take a look at the `Header`, `Footer`, `Menu`, `Create`, `Update`, and `View` templates in the following sections.

The Header template

The `Header` template has the HTML `head` and `body` defined in the code snippet, as follows. The TITLE tag of the web page is set to `CRM` and the web page has `Customer Management – CRM` as content (`Header.tmpl`):

```
{{ define "Header" }}
<!DOCTYPE html>
<html>
    <head>
        <title>CRM</title>
        <meta charset="UTF-8" />
    </head>
    <body>
        <h1>Customer Management - CRM</h1>
{{ end }}
```

The Footer template

The `Footer` template has the HTML and BODY close tags defined. The `Footer` template is presented in the following code snippet (`Footer.tmpl`):

```
{{ define "Footer" }}
    </body>
  </html>
{{ end }}
```

The Menu template

The `Menu` template has the links defined for `Home` and `Create Customer`, as shown in the following code (`Menu.tmpl`):

```
{{ define "Menu" }}
<a href="/">Home</a> |<a href="/create">Create Customer</a>
{{ end }}
```

The Create template

The `Create` template consists of `Header`, `Menu`, and `Footer` templates. The form to create customer fields is found in the `create` template. This form is submitted to a web path—`/insert`, as shown in the following code snippet (`Create.tmpl`):

```
{{ define "Create" }}
  {{ template "Header" }}
  {{ template "Menu"  }}
  <br>
    <h1>Create Customer</h1>
  <br>
  <br>
  <form method="post" action="/insert">
    Customer Name: <input type="text" name="customername"
placeholder="customername" autofocus/>
    <br>
    <br>
    SSN: <input type="text" name="ssn" placeholder="ssn"/>
    <br>
    <br>
    <input type="submit" value="Create Customer"/>
   </form>
{{ template "Footer" }}
{{ end }}
```

The Update template

The `Update` template consists of the `Header`, `Menu`, and `Footer` templates, as follows. The form to update customer fields is found in the `Update` template. This form is submitted to a web path, `/alter` (`Update.tmpl`):

```
{{ define "Update" }}
  {{ template "Header" }}
```

```
    {{ template "Menu" }}
<br>
<h1>Update Customer</h1>
    <br>
    <br>
  <form method="post" action="/alter">
    <input type="hidden" name="id" value="{{ .CustomerId }}" />
    Customer Name: <input type="text" name="customername"
placeholder="customername" value="{{ .CustomerName }}" autofocus>
    <br>
    <br>
    SSN: <input type="text" name="ssn" value="{{ .SSN }}"
placeholder="ssn"/>
    <br>
    <br>
    <input type="submit" value="Update Customer"/>
   </form>
{{ template "Footer" }}
{{ end }}
```

The View template

The `View` template consists of `Header`, `Menu`, and `Footer` templates. The form to view the customer fields is found in the `View` template, which is presented in code as follows (`View.tmpl`):

```
{{ define "View" }}
  {{ template "Header" }}
  {{ template "Menu"  }}
    <br>
       <h1>View Customer</h1>
      <br>
      <br>
<table border="1">
<tr>
<td>CustomerId</td>
<td>CustomerName</td>
<td>SSN</td>
<td>Update</td>
<td>Delete</td>
</tr>
{{ if . }}
       {{ range . }}
<tr>
<td>{{ .CustomerId }}</td>
<td>{{ .CustomerName }}</td>
```

```
<td>{{ .SSN }}</td>
<td><a href="/delete?id={{.CustomerId}}" onclick="return confirm('Are you
sure you want to delete?');">Delete</a> </td>
<td><a href="/update?id={{.CustomerId}}">Update</a> </td>
</tr>
{{ end }}
     {{ end }}
</table>
{{ template "Footer" }}
{{ end }}
```

Run the following commands:

```
go run crm_app.go crm_database_operations.go
```

The following screenshot displays the output:

```
chapter2 — crm_app ◂ go run crm_app.go crm_database_operations.go — 94×24
Bhagvans-MacBook-Pro:chapter2 bhagvankommadi$ go run crm_app.go crm_database_operations.go
2018/08/24 17:38:14 Server started on: http://localhost:8000
```

The web browser output is shown in the following screenshot:

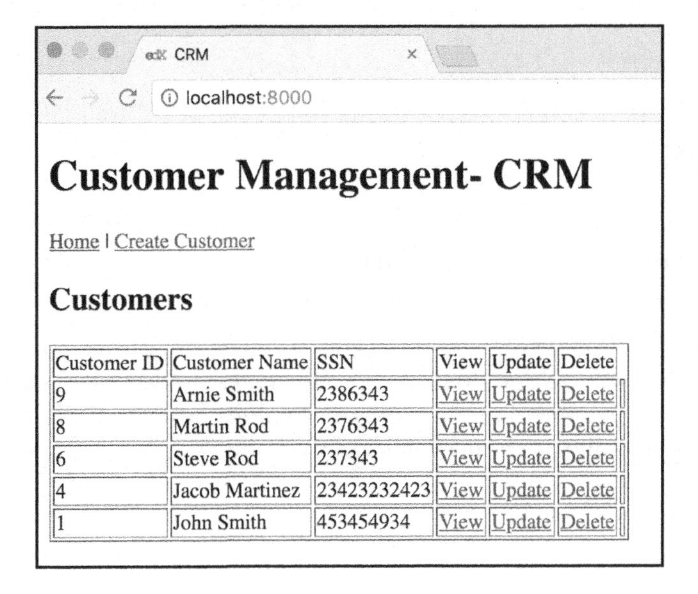

Summary

This chapter introduced database operations and web forms. Now, you will be able to build web applications that can store data in databases. Arrays, slices, two-dimensional slices, and maps were covered with code samples. Array methods such as `len`, iterating through an array using `for`, and `range` were explained in this chapter using code snippets. Two-dimensional arrays and slice of slices were discussed in the *Slices* section.

Maps were explained with various scenarios such as adding keys and values, as well as retrieving and deleting values. Maps of different types, such as strings and integers, were also discussed in this chapter. Furthermore, variadic functions, deferred function calls, and panic and recover operations were demonstrated in the *Database operations* and *CRUD web forms* sections.

The CRM application was built as a web application with data persisted in the MySQL database. Database operations for adding, deleting, updating, and retrieving data were shown in code snippets. In addition, web forms for creating, updating, deleting, and viewing customer data were presented using web forms with templates. MySQL driver and its installation details were provided in the *Technical requirements* section of this chapter. How to create a web application using Go was demonstrated with execution details.

The next chapter will have topics related to linear data structures such as lists, sets, tuples, and stacks.

Questions

1. What is the name of the method to get the size of an array?
2. How do you find the capacity of the slice?
3. How do you initialize the 2D slice of a string type?
4. How do you add an element to the slice?
5. Using code, can you demonstrate how to create a map of key strings and value strings? Initialize the map with keys and values in the code, iterate them in a loop, and print the keys and values in the code.

6. How do you delete a value in a map?
7. What parameters are required for getting a database connection?
8. Which `sql.Rows` class method makes it possible to read the attributes of the entity in a table?
9. What does `defer` do when a database connection is closed?
10. Which method allows the `sql.DB` class to create a prepared statement?

Further reading

To read more about arrays, maps and slices, the following links are recommended:

- *Learning Go Data Structures and Algorithms [Video]*, by Gustavo Chaín
- *Mastering Go*, by Mihalis Tsoukalos

2

Section 2: Basic Data Structures and Algorithms using Go

We will talk about data structures, including linear, non-linear, homogeneous, heterogeneous, and dynamic types, as well as classic algorithms. This section covers different types of lists, trees, arrays, sets, dictionaries, tuples, heaps, queues, and stacks, along with sorting, recursion, searching, and hashing algorithms.

This section contains the following chapters:

3 Linear Data Structures

Various applications, such as Facebook, Twitter, and Google, use lists and linear data structures. As we have discussed previously, data structures allow us to organize vast swathes of data in a sequential and organized manner, thereby reducing time and effort in working with such data. Lists, stacks, sets, and tuples are some of the commonly used linear data structures.

In this chapter, we will discuss these data structures by giving examples of various procedures involving them. We will discuss the various operations related to these data structures, such as insertion, deletion, updating, traversing (of lists), reversing, and merging with various code samples.

We will cover the following linear data structures in this chapter:

- Lists
- Sets
- Tuples
- Stacks

Technical requirements

Install Go version 1.10 at `https://golang.org/doc/install`, depending on your operating system.

The code files for this chapter can be found at the following GitHub URL: `https://github.com/PacktPublishing/Learn-Data-Structures-and-Algorithms-with-Golang/tree/master/Chapter03`.

Lists

A list is a collection of ordered elements that are used to store list of items. Unlike array lists, these can expand and shrink dynamically.

Lists also be used as a base for other data structures, such as stack and queue. Lists can be used to store lists of users, car parts, ingredients, to-do items, and various other such elements. Lists are the most commonly used linear data structures. These were introduced in the lisp programming language. In this chapter, linked list and doubly linked list are the lists we will cover in the Go language.

Let's discuss the operations related to add, update, remove, and lookup on linked list and doubly linked list in the following section.

LinkedList

`LinkedList` is a sequence of nodes that have properties and a reference to the next node in the sequence. It is a linear data structure that is used to store data. The data structure permits the addition and deletion of components from any node next to another node. They are not stored contiguously in memory, which makes them different arrays.

The following sections will look at the structures and methods in a linked list.

The Node class

The `Node` class has an integer typed variable with the name `property`. The class has another variable with the name `nextNode`, which is a node pointer. Linked list will have a set of nodes with integer properties, as follows:

```
//Node class
type Node struct {
    property int
    nextNode *Node
}
```

The LinkedList class

The `LinkedList` class has the `headNode` pointer as its property. By traversing to `nextNode` from `headNode`, you can iterate through the linked list, as shown in the following code:

```
// LinkedList class
type LinkedList struct {
    headNode *Node
}
```

The different methods of the `LinkedList` class, such as `AddtoHead`, `IterateList`, `LastNode`, `AddtoEnd`, `NodeWithValue`, `AddAfter`, and the `main` method, are discussed in the following sections.

The AddToHead method

The `AddToHead` method adds the node to the start of the linked list. The `AddToHead` method of the `LinkedList` class has a parameter integer property. The property is used to initialize the node. A new node is instantiated and its property is set to the `property` parameter that's passed. The `nextNode` points to the current `headNode` of `linkedList`, and `headNode` is set to the pointer of the new node that's created, as shown in the following code:

```
//AddToHead method of LinkedList class
func (linkedList *LinkedList) AddToHead(property int) {
    var node = Node{}
    node.property = property
    if node.nextNode != nil {
        node.nextNode = linkedList.headNode
    }
    linkedList.headNode = &node
}
```

When the node with the `1` property is added to the head, adding the `1` property to the head of `linkedList` sets `headNode` to `currentNode` with a value of `1`, as you can see in the following screenshot:

```
Add To Head method
headNode is set to the currentNode 1
```

Let's execute this command using the `main` method. Here, we have created an instance of a `LinkedList` class and added the `1` and `3` integer properties to the head of this instance. The linked list's `headNode` property is printed after adding the elements, as follows:

```
// main method
func main() {
    var linkedList LinkedList
    linkedList = LinkedList{}
    linkedList.AddToHead(1)
    linkedList.AddToHead(3)
    fmt.Println(linkedList.headNode.property)
}
```

Run the following commands to execute the `linked_list.go` file:

```
go run linked_list.go
```

After executing the preceding command, we get the following output:

```
chapter3 — -bash — 80×24
Bhagvans-MacBook-Pro:chapter3 bhagvankommadi$ go run linked_list.go
3
Bhagvans-MacBook-Pro:chapter3 bhagvankommadi$
```

Let's take a look at the `IterateList` method in the next section.

The IterateList method

The `IterateList` method of the `LinkedList` class iterates from the `headNode` property and prints the property of the current head node. The iteration happens with the head node moves to `nextNode` of the `headNode` property until the current node is no longer equal to `nil`. The following code shows the `IterateList` method of the `LinkedList` class:

```
//IterateList method iterates over LinkedList
func (linkedList *LinkedList) IterateList() {
    var node *Node
    for node = linkedList.headNode; node != nil; node = node.nextNode {
        fmt.Println(node.property)
    }
}
```

The LastNode method

The `LastNode` method of `LinkedList` returns the node at the end of the list. The list is traversed to check whether `nextNode` is `nil` from `nextNode` of `headNode`, as follows:

```
//LastNode method returns the last Node

func (linkedList *LinkedList) LastNode() *Node{
 var node *Node
 var lastNode *Node
 for node = linkedList.headNode; node != nil; node = node.nextNode {
 if node.nextNode ==nil {
 lastNode = node
 }
 }
 return lastNode
}
```

The AddToEnd method

The `AddToEnd` method adds the node at the end of the list. In the following code, the current `lastNode` is found and its `nextNode` property is set as the added node:

```
//AddToEnd method adds the node with property to the end

func (linkedList *LinkedList) AddToEnd(property int) {
 var node = &Node{}
 node.property = property
 node.nextNode = nil
 var lastNode *Node
 lastNode = linkedList.LastNode()
 if lastNode != nil {
 lastNode.nextNode = node
 }
}
```

In the following screenshot, the `AddToEnd` method is invoked when the node with a property value of **5** is added to the end. Adding the property through this method creates a node with a value of **5**. The last node of the list has a property value of **5**. The `nextNode` property of `lastNode` is `nil`. The `nextNode` of `lastNode` is set to the node with a value of **5**:

```
Add To End method
linked list's lastNode property value 1
current node property value 5
 lastNode's next node property value <nil>
 lastNode's next node property value after adding the current node 5
```

Let's take a look at the `NodeWithValue` method in the next section.

The NodeWithValue method

In the following code snippet, the `NodeWithValue` method of `LinkedList` returns the node with the `property` value. The list is traversed and checked to see whether the `property` value is equal to the parameter property:

```
//NodeWithValue method returns Node given parameter property

func (linkedList *LinkedList) NodeWithValue(property int) *Node{
 var node *Node
 var nodeWith *Node
 for node = linkedList.headNode; node != nil; node = node.nextNode {
 if node.property == property {
 nodeWith = node
 break;
 }
 }
 return nodeWith
}
```

The AddAfter method

The `AddAfter` method adds the node after a specific node. The `AddAfter` method of `LinkedList` has `nodeProperty` and `property` parameters. A node with the `nodeProperty` value is retrieved using the `NodeWithValue` method. A node with `property` is created and added after the `NodeWith` node, as follows:

```
//AddAfter method adds a node with nodeProperty after node with property

func (linkedList *LinkedList) AddAfter(nodeProperty int,property int) {
 var node = &Node{}
 node.property = property
 node.nextNode = nil
 var nodeWith *Node
 nodeWith = linkedList.NodeWithValue(nodeProperty)
 if nodeWith != nil {
 node.nextNode = nodeWith.nextNode
 nodeWith.nextNode = node
 }
}
```

You then get the following output when the `AddAfter` method is invoked when the node with a property value of **7** is added after the node with a value of **1**. The `nextNode` property of the node with a property value of **1** is **nil**. The `nextNode` property of the node with a property value of **1** is set to the node with a value of **5**:

```
Add After method
current node property value 7
linked list's Node with value equal to property  1
 current node's next node property value <nil>
 current node's next node property value after adding current node 5
 linked list's Node with value equal to property's next Node after adding curren
t node 5
```

Let's take a look at the `main` method in the next section.

The main method

The `main` method adds the nodes with integer properties of `1`, `3`, and `5`, as shown in the following code. A node with an integer property of `7` is added after the node with an integer property of `1`. The `IterateList` method is invoked on the `linkedList` instance, as follows:

```
// main method
func main() {
    var linkedList LinkedList
    linkedList = LinkedList{}
    linkedList.AddToHead(1)
    linkedList.AddToHead(3)
    linkedList.AddToEnd(5)
    linkedList.AddAfter(1,7)
    linkedList.IterateList()
}
```

The main method adds `1` and `3` to the head of the linked list. `5` is added to the end. `7` is added after `1`. The linked list will be `3`, `1`, `7`, and `5`.

Run the following commands to execute the `linked_list.go` file:

```
go run linked_list.go
```

After executing the preceding command, we get the following output:

```
chapter3 — -bash — 80×24
Bhagvans-MacBook-Pro:chapter3 bhagvankommadi$ go run linked_list.go
3
1
7
5
Bhagvans-MacBook-Pro:chapter3 bhagvankommadi$
```

Let's take a look at doubly linked list in the next section.

Doubly linked list

In a doubly linked list, all nodes have a pointer to the node they are connected to, on either side of them, in the list. This means that each node is connected to two nodes, and we can traverse forward through to the next node or backward through to the previous node. Doubly linked lists allow insertion, deletion and, obviously, traversing operations. The node class definition is presented in the following code example:

```
// Node class
type Node struct {
    property int
    nextNode *Node
    previousNode *Node
}
```

The following sections explain doubly linked list methods, such as the `NodeBetweenValues`, `AddToHead`, `AddAfter`, `AddToEnd`, and `main` methods.

The NodeBetweenValues method

The `NodeBetweenValues` method of the `LinkedList` class returns the node that has a property lying between the `firstProperty` and `secondProperty` values. The method traverses the list to find out whether the `firstProperty` and `secondProperty` integer properties match on consecutive nodes, as follows:

```
//NodeBetweenValues method of LinkedList
func (linkedList *LinkedList) NodeBetweenValues(firstProperty
int,secondProperty int) *Node{
    var node *Node
    var nodeWith *Node
    for node = linkedList.headNode; node != nil; node = node.nextNode {
```

```
        if node.previousNode != nil && node.nextNode != nil {
            if node.previousNode.property == firstProperty &&
node.nextNode.property ==
            secondProperty{
                nodeWith = node
                break;
            }
        }
    }
    return nodeWith
}
```

The example output after the node between the values method was invoked with **1** and **5** is shown in the following screenshot. The `nextNode` of the `lastNode` is set to the node with a value of **5**. The node with a property value of **7** is between the nodes with property values of **1** and **5**:

```
Node Between values method
Add To End method
first property 1
second property 5
node with property between values of firstProperty and secondProperty 7
```

Let's take a look at the `AddToHead` method in the next section.

The AddToHead method

The `AddToHead` method of the doubly `LinkedList` class sets the `previousNode` property of the current `headNode` of the linked list to the node that's added with property. The node with property will be set as the `headNode` of the `LinkedList` method in the following code:

```
//AddToHead method of LinkedList
func (linkedList *LinkedList) AddToHead(property int) {
 var node = &Node{}
 node.property = property
 node.nextNode = nil
 if linkedList.headNode != nil {
 node.nextNode = linkedList.headNode
 linkedList.headNode.previousNode = node
 }
 linkedList.headNode = node
}
```

The example output after the `AddToHead` method was invoked with property **3** is as follows. A node with property **3** is created. The `headNode` property of the list has a property value of **1**. The current node with property **3** has a `nextNode` property of **nil**. The `nextNode` property of the current node is set to `headNode` with a property value of **1**. The previous node of the `headNode` property is set to the current node:

```
Add To Head method
linked list's headNode property value 1
current node's property value 3
current node's next Node property value <nil>
current node's next Node set to headNode 1
linked list's headNode previous Node property value equal to currentNode property 1
linked list's headNode property value equal to current Node property 3
```

Let's take a look at the `AddAfter` method in the next section.

AddAfter method

The `AddAfter` method adds a node after a specific node to a double linked list. The `AddAfter` method of the double `LinkedList` class searches the node whose value is equal to `nodeProperty`. The found node is set as the `previousNode` of the node that was added with property. The `nextNode` of the added node will be the `nodeWith` property's `nextNode`. The `previousNode` of the added node will be the node that was found with value equal to `nodeProperty`. The `nodeWith` node will be updated to the current node. In the following code, the `AddAfter` method is shown:

```
//AddAfter method of LinkedList
func (linkedList *LinkedList) AddAfter(nodeProperty int,property int) {
 var node = &Node{}
 node.property = property
 node.nextNode = nil
 var nodeWith *Node
 nodeWith = linkedList.NodeWithValue(nodeProperty)
 if nodeWith != nil {

 node.nextNode = nodeWith.nextNode
 node.previousNode = nodeWith
 nodeWith.nextNode = node
 }
}
```

The example output after the `AddAfter` method is invoked with property 7 is as follows. A node with property value 7 is created. The `nextNode` property of the created node is `nil`. The `nextNode` property of the created node is set to `headNode` with property value 1. The `previousNode` property of `headNode` is set to the current node:

```
Add After method
current node property value 7
linked list's Node with value equal to property  1
 current node's next node property value <nil>
 current node's next node property value after adding current node 5
 current node's previous node property value after adding current node 1
 linked list's Node with value equal to property's next Node after adding current node 5
```

Let's take a look at the `AddToEnd` method in the next section.

The AddToEnd method

The `AddToEnd` method adds the node to the end of the double linked list. The `AddToEnd` method of the `LinkedList` class creates a node whose property is set as the integer parameter property. The method sets the `previousNode` property of the node that was added with the current `lastNode` property as follows. The `nextNode` of the current `lastNode` property is set to a node added with property at the end as follows:

```
//AddToEnd method of LinkedList
func (linkedList *LinkedList) AddToEnd(property int) {
 var node = &Node{}
 node.property = property
 node.nextNode = nil
 var lastNode *Node
 lastNode = linkedList.LastNode()
 if lastNode != nil {

 lastNode.nextNode = node
 node.previousNode = lastNode
 }
}
```

The example output after the `AddToEnd` method was invoked with property **5** is as follows. A node with property value **5** is created. The `lastNode` of the list has property value **1**. The `nextNode` property of the `lastNode` is `nil`. The `nextNode` of the `lastNode` is set to the node with property value **5**. The `previousNode` of the created node is set to the node with property value **1**:

```
Add To End method
linked list's lastNode property value 1
current node property value 5
 lastNode's next node property value <nil>
 lastNode's next node property value after adding the current node 5
 current node's previous node property value after setting to the current last node 1
```

Let's take a look at the `main` method in the next section.

The main method

In the following code snippet, the `main` method calls the `NodeBetweenValues` property with `firstProperty` and `secondProperty`. The node property between values `1` and `5` is printed:

```
// main method
func main() {
 var linkedList LinkedList
 linkedList = LinkedList{}
 linkedList.AddToHead(1)
 linkedList.AddToHead(3) linkedList.AddToEnd(5)
 linkedList.AddAfter(1,7)
 fmt.Println(linkedList.headNode.property)
 var node *Node
 node = linkedList.NodeBetweenValues(1,5)
 fmt.Println(node.property)
}
```

The `main` method creates a linked list. The nodes are added to the head and end. The node between values `1` and `5` is searched and its property is printed.

Run the following command to execute the `doubly_linked_list.go` file:

```
go run doubly_linked_list.go
```

After executing the preceding command, we get the following output:

```
chapter3 — -bash — 80×24
Bhagvans-MacBook-Pro:chapter3 bhagvankommadi$ go run doubly_linked_list.go
3
7
Bhagvans-MacBook-Pro:chapter3 bhagvankommadi$
```

The next section talks about sets, which are linear data structures.

Sets

A Set is a linear data structure that has a collection of values that are not repeated. A set can store unique values without any particular order. In the real world, sets can be used to collect all tags for blog posts and conversation participants in a chat. The data can be of Boolean, integer, float, characters, and other types. Static sets allow only query operations, which means operations related to querying the elements. Dynamic and mutable sets allow for the insertion and deletion of elements. Algebraic operations such as union, intersection, difference, and subset can be defined on the sets. The following example shows the `Set` integer with a `map` integer key and `bool` as a value:

```
//main package has examples shown
// in Hands-On Data Structures and algorithms with Go book
package main
// importing fmt package
import (
 "fmt"
)
//Set class
type Set struct {
 integerMap map[int]bool
}
//create the map of integer and bool
func (set *Set) New(){
 set.integerMap = make(map[int]bool)
}
```

The `AddElement`, `DeleteElement`, `ContainsElement`, `Intersect`, `Union`, and `main` methods are discussed in the following sections.

The AddElement method

The AddElement method adds the element to a set. In the following code snippet, the AddElement method of the Set class adds the element to integerMap if the element is not in the Set. The integerMap element has the key integer and value as bool, as shown in the following code:

```
// adds the element to the set
func (set *Set) AddElement(element int){
 if !set.ContainsElement(element) {
  set.integerMap[element] = true
 }
}
```

The example output after invoking the AddElement method with parameter **2** is as follows. The check is done if there is an element with value **2**. If there is no element, the map is set to true with the key as **2**:

```
Add Element method
does the set  have the element: false
set has the current element true
initial set &{map[1:true 2:true]}
true
```

Let's take a look at the DeleteElement method in the next section.

The DeleteElement method

The DeleteElement method deletes the element from integerMap using the delete method. This method removes the element from the integerMap of the set, as follows:

```
//deletes the element from the set
func (set *Set) DeleteElement(element int) {
    delete(set.integerMap,element)
}
```

The ContainsElement method

The `ContainsElement` method of the `Set` class checks whether or not the element exists in `integerMap`. The `integerMap` element is looked up with a key integer element, as shown in the following code example:

```
//checks if element is in the set
func (set *Set) ContainsElement(element int) bool{
 var exists bool
 _, exists = set.integerMap[element]
 return exists
}
```

The main method – contains element

In the following code snippet, the `main` method creates `Set`, invokes the `New` method, and adds elements `1` and `2`. The check is done if element `1` exists in the set:

```
// main method
func main() {
     var set *Set
     set = &Set{}
     set.New()
     set.AddElement(1)
     set.AddElement(2)
     fmt.Println(set)
     fmt.Println(set.ContainsElement(1))
}
```

Run the following command to execute the `set.go` file:

```
go run set.go
```

After executing the preceding command, we get the following output:

```
chapter3 — -bash — 80×24
Bhagvans-MacBook-Pro:chapter3 bhagvankommadi$ go run set.go
&{map[1:true 2:true]}
true
Bhagvans-MacBook-Pro:chapter3 bhagvankommadi$
```

Let's take a look at the `InterSect` method in the next section.

The InterSect method

In the following code, the `InterSect` method on the `Set` class returns an `intersectionSet` that consists of the intersection of `set` and `anotherSet`. The `set` class is traversed through `integerMap` and checked against another `Set` to see if any elements exist:

```
//Intersect method returns the set which intersects with anotherSet

func (set *Set) Intersect(anotherSet *Set) *Set{
 var intersectSet = & Set{}
 intersectSet.New()
 var value int
 for(value,_ = range set.integerMap){
   if anotherSet.ContainsElement(value) {
    intersectSet.AddElement(value)
   }
 }
 return intersectSet
}
```

The example output after invoking the intersect with the parameter of another `Set` is as follows. A new `intersectSet` is created. The current `set` is iterated and every value is checked to see if it is in another `set`. If the value is in another `set`, it is added to the `set` intersect:

```
Intersect method
intersect set does have the element false
Add Element method
does the set  have the element: false
set has the current element true
after adding to the intersect set does have the element true
intersection of sets  &{map[2:true]}
```

Let's take a look at the `Union` method in the next section.

The Union method

The `Union` method on the `Set` class returns a `unionSet` that consists of a union of `set` and `anotherSet`. Both sets are traversed through `integerMap` keys, and union set is updated with elements from the sets, as follows:

```
//Union method returns the set which is union of the set with anotherSet

func (set *Set) Union(anotherSet *Set) *Set{
 var unionSet = & Set{}
```

```
    unionSet.New()
    var value int
    for(value,_ = range set.integerMap){
      unionSet.AddElement(value)
    }

    for(value,_ = range anotherSet.integerMap){
      unionSet.AddElement(value)
    }

    return unionSet
}
```

The example output after invoking the union method with the `anotherSet` parameter is as follows. A new `unionSet` is created. The current set and another set values are iterated. Every value is added to the union set:

```
Union method
Add Element method
does the set  have the element: false
set has the current element true
adding element to union set 1
Add Element method
does the set  have the element: false
set has the current element true
adding element to union set 2
Add Element method
adding element to union set 2
Add Element method
does the set  have the element: false
set has the current element true
```

Let's take a look at the `main` method in the next section.

The main method – intersection and union

In the following code snippet, the `main` method calls intersect and union on the set class, passing the `anotherSet` parameter. The intersection and union sets are printed as follows:

```
// main method
func main() {
  var set *Set
  set = &Set{}
  set.New()
  set.AddElement(1)
  set.AddElement(2)
  fmt.Println("initial set", set)
  fmt.Println(set.ContainsElement(1))
  var anotherSet *Set
```

```
    anotherSet = &Set{}
    anotherSet.New()
    anotherSet.AddElement(2)
    anotherSet.AddElement(4)
    anotherSet.AddElement(5) fmt.Println(set.Intersect(anotherSet))
    fmt.Println(set.Union(anotherSet))
}
```

The main method takes two sets and finds the intersection and union of the sets.

Run the following command to execute the `set.go` file:

```
go run set.go
```

After executing the preceding command, we get the following output:

```
chapter3 — -bash — 80×24
Bhagvans-MacBook-Pro:chapter3 bhagvankommadi$ go run set.go
initial set &{map[1:true 2:true]}
true
another set &{map[1:true 2:true]}
intersection of sets  &{map[2:true]}
union of sets  &{map[1:true 2:true 4:true 5:true]}
Bhagvans-MacBook-Pro:chapter3 bhagvankommadi$
```

The next section talks about tuples, which are finite ordered sequences of objects.

Tuples

Tuples are finite ordered sequences of objects. They can contain a mixture of other data types and are used to group related data into a data structure. In a relational database, a tuple is a row of a table. Tuples have a fixed size compared to lists, and are also faster. A finite set of tuples in the relational database is referred to as a relation instance. A tuple can be assigned in a single statement, which is useful for swapping values. Lists usually contain values of the same data type, while tuples contain different data. For example, we can store a name, age, and favorite color of a user in a tuple. Tuples were covered in `Chapter 1`, *Data Structures and Algorithms*. The following sample shows a multi-valued expression from a function's call (`tuples.go`):

```
//main package has examples shown
 // in Hands-On Data Structures and algorithms with Go book
 package main
 // importing fmt package
 import (
 "fmt"
 )
```

```
//h function which returns the product of parameters x and y
func h(x int, y int) int {
return x*y
}
// g function which returns x and y parameters after modification
func g(l int, m int) (x int, y int) {
x=2*l
y=4*m
return
}
// main method
func main() {
fmt.Println(h(g()))
}
```

The `main` function calls the `h` function with the `g` function as its parameter. The `g` function returns the tuple `x` and `y` integers.

Run the following command to execute the `tuples.go` file:

```
go run tuples.go
```

After executing the preceding command, we get the following output:

```
chapter3 — -bash — 80×24
Bhagvans-MacBook-Pro:chapter3 bhagvankommadi$ go run tuples.go
16
Bhagvans-MacBook-Pro:chapter3 bhagvankommadi$
```

The next section talks about queues, which are linear data structures.

Queues

A queue consists of elements to be processed in a particular order or based on priority. A priority-based queue of orders is shown in the following code, structured as a heap. Operations such as enqueue, dequeue, and peek can be performed on queue. A queue is a linear data structure and a sequential collection. Elements are added to the end and are removed from the start of the collection. Queues are commonly used for storing tasks that need to be done, or incoming HTTP requests that need to be processed by a server. In real life, handling interruptions in real-time systems, call handling, and CPU task scheduling are good examples for using queues.

The following code shows the queue of Orders and how the `Queue` type is defined:

```
// Queue—Array of Orders Type
type Queue []*Order

// Order class
type Order struct {
    priority int
    quantity int
    product string
    customerName string
}
```

The following sections in the chapter discuss the `New`, `Add`, and `main` methods of queue.

The New method

The `New` method on the `Order` class assigns the properties from the `priority`, `quantity`, and `product` parameters for name and `customerName`. The method initializes the properties of the order as follows:

```
// New method initializes with Order with priority, quantity, product,
customerName
func (order *Order) New(priority int, quantity int, product string,
customerName string ){
 order.priority = priority
 order.quantity = quantity
 order.product = product
 order.customerName = customerName
 }
```

The Add method

In the following code snippet, the `Add` method on the `Queue` class takes the `order` parameter and adds it to `Queue` based on the priority. Based on this, the location of the `order` parameter is found by comparing it with the `priority` parameter:

```
//Add method adds the order to the queue
func (queue *Queue) Add(order *Order){
 if len(*queue) == 0 {
 *queue = append(*queue,order)
 } else{
 var appended bool
```

```
    appended = false
    var i int
    var addedOrder *Order
    for i, addedOrder = range *queue {
    if order.priority > addedOrder.priority {
    *queue = append((*queue)[:i], append(Queue{order}, (*queue)[i:]...)...)
    appended = true
    break
    }
    }
    if !appended {
    *queue = append(*queue, order)
    }
    }
}
```

The example output after the add method is invoked with the order parameter is as follows. The order is checked to see whether or not it exists in the queue. The order is then appended to the queue:

```
Add method
before adding the order to the queue false
after adding the order to the queue false
```

Let's take a look at the Main method in the next section.

The main method – queues

The main method creates two orders, and the priority of the orders is set to 2 and 1. In the following code, the queue will first process the order with the higher number on the priority value:

```
// main method
func main() {
    var queue Queue
    queue = make(Queue,0)
    var order1 *Order = &Order{}
    var priority1 int = 2
    var quantity1 int = 20
    var product1 string = "Computer"
    var customerName1 string = "Greg White"
    order1.New(priority1,quantity1,product1, customerName1)
    var order2 *Order = &Order{}
    var priority2 int = 1
    var quantity2 int = 10
```

```
    var product2 string = "Monitor"
    var customerName2 string = "John Smith"
    order2.New(priority2,quantity2,product2, customerName2)
    queue.Add(order1)

    queue.Add(order2)
   var i int
   for i=0; i< len(queue); i++ {
   fmt.Println(queue[i])
   }
   }
```

Run the following commands to execute the `queue.go` file:

```
go run queue.go
```

After executing the preceding command, we get the following output:

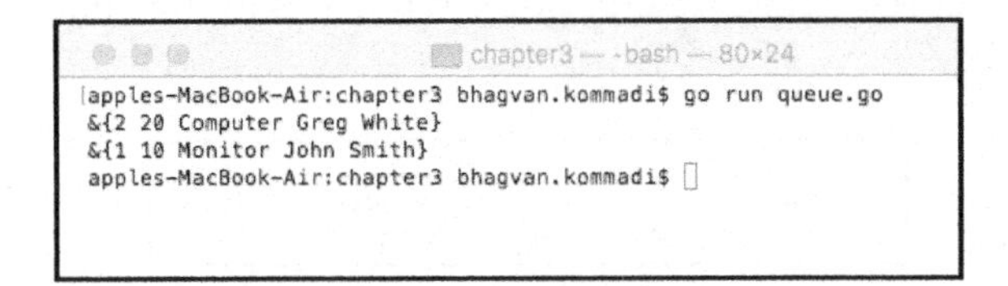

Let's take a look at *Synchronized queue* in the next section.

Synchronized queue

A synchronized queue consists of elements that need to be processed in a particular sequence. Passenger queue and ticket processing queues are types of synchronized queues, as follows:

```
//main package has examples shown
// in Hands-On Data Structures and algorithms with Go book
package main
// importing fmt package
import (
 "fmt"
 "time"
 "math/rand"
)
// constants
const (
 messagePassStart = iota
 messageTicketStart
```

```
 messagePassEnd
 messageTicketEnd
)
//Queue class
type Queue struct {
 waitPass int
 waitTicket int
 playPass bool
 playTicket bool
 queuePass chan int
 queueTicket chan int
 message chan int
}
```

We will discuss the different methods of synchronized queue in the following sections.

The New method

The `New` method on `Queue` initializes `message`, `queuePass`, and `queueTicket` with `nil` values. The `make` method creates a `Queue` with a `chan` integer parameter, as follows:

```
// New method initializes queue
func (queue *Queue) New() {
 queue.message = make(chan int)
 queue.queuePass= make(chan int)
 queue.queueTicket= make(chan int)
 }
```

In the following code example, the `Go` routine handles selecting the message based on the type of message and the respective queue to process it:

```
go func() {
 var message int
 for {
 select {
 case message = <-queue.message:
 switch message {
 case messagePassStart:
 queue.waitPass++
 case messagePassEnd:
 queue.playPass = false
 case messageTicketStart:
 queue.waitTicket++
 case messageTicketEnd:
 queue.playTicket = false
 }
 if queue.waitPass > 0 && queue.waitTicket > 0 && !queue.playPass &&
```

```
!queue.playTicket {
 queue.playPass = true
 queue.playTicket = true
 queue.waitTicket--
 queue.waitPass--
 queue.queuePass <- 1
 queue.queueTicket <- 1
 }
 }
 }
 }()
}
```

The StartTicketIssue method

The `StartTicketIssue` method starts the issuing of a ticket for passengers standing in a queue. The `StartTicketIssue` method on `Queue` sends `messageTicketStart` to the message queue and `queueTicket` receives the message. The ticket issue is started by sending messages to the queue, as follows:

```
// StartTicketIssue starts the ticket issue
func (Queue *Queue) StartTicketIssue() {
 Queue.message <- messageTicketStart
 <-Queue.queueTicket
}
```

The EndTicketIssue method

The `EndTicketIssue` method finishes the issuing of a ticket to a passenger standing in the queue. In the following code, the `EndTicketIssue` method on `Queue` sends `messageTicketEnd` to the message queue. The ticket issue is ended by sending the message:

```
// EndTicketIssue ends the ticket issue
func (Queue *Queue) EndTicketIssue() {
 Queue.message <- messageTicketEnd
}
```

The ticketIssue method

The `ticketIssue` method starts and finishes the issuing of a ticket to the passenger. The `ticketIssue` method invokes the `StartTicketIssue` and `EndTicketIssue` methods after `Sleep` calls for 10 seconds and two seconds. The ticket is issued after the ticket is processed, as shown in the following code:

```
//ticketIssue starts and ends the ticket issue
func ticketIssue(Queue *Queue) {
 for {
 // Sleep up to 10 seconds.
 time.Sleep(time.Duration(rand.Intn(10000)) * time.Millisecond)
 Queue.StartTicketIssue()
 fmt.Println("Ticket Issue starts")
 // Sleep up to 2 seconds.
 time.Sleep(time.Duration(rand.Intn(2000)) * time.Millisecond)
 fmt.Println("Ticket Issue ends")
 Queue.EndTicketIssue()
 }
}
```

The StartPass method

The `StartPass` method starts the passenger queue moving toward the ticket counter. The `StartPass` method on `Queue` sends `messagePassStart` to the message queue and `queuePass` receives the message. Passengers are moved into the queue as follows:

```
//StartPass ends the Pass Queue
func (Queue *Queue) StartPass() {
    Queue.message <- messagePassStart
    <-Queue.queuePass
}
```

The EndPass method

The `EndPass` method stops the passenger queue moving toward the ticket counter. The `EndPass` method on `Queue` sends `messagePassEnd` to the message queue in the following code. The passenger is moved to the counter for ticket processing, and the passenger is then out of the queue:

```
//EndPass ends the Pass Queue
func (Queue *Queue) EndPass() {
    Queue.message <- messagePassEnd
}
```

The passenger method

The passenger methods starts and ends passenger movement to the queue. The passenger method invokes the StartPass method, and the EndPass method ends after sleep calls for 10 seconds and two seconds. The passenger moves into the queue and reaches the ticket counter, as shown in the following code:

```
//passenger method starts and ends the pass Queue
func passenger(Queue *Queue) {
 //fmt.Println("starting the passenger Queue")
 for {
 // fmt.Println("starting the processing")
 // Sleep up to 10 seconds.
 time.Sleep(time.Duration(rand.Intn(10000)) * time.Millisecond)
 Queue.StartPass()
 fmt.Println(" Passenger starts")
 // Sleep up to 2 seconds.
 time.Sleep(time.Duration(rand.Intn(2000)) * time.Millisecond)
 fmt.Println( " Passenger ends")
 Queue.EndPass()
 }
}
```

The main method

The main method calls the passenger and ticketIssue methods after creating a queue. The passenger enters into the queue and a ticket is issued at the counter in the processing queue, as explained in the following code:

```
// main method
func main() {
 var Queue *Queue = & Queue{}
 //fmt.Println(Queue)
 Queue.New()
 fmt.Println(Queue)
 var i int
 for i = 0; i < 10; i++ {
 // fmt.Println(i, "passenger in the Queue")
 go passenger(Queue)
 }
 //close(Queue.queuePass)
 var j int
 for j = 0; j < 5; j++ {
 // fmt.Println(i, "ticket issued in the Queue")
 go ticketIssue(Queue)
 }
```

```
  select {}
}
```

Run the following command to execute the `sync_queue.go` file:

```
go run sync_queue.go
```

After executing the preceding command, we get the following output:

```
chapter3 — sync_queue ‹ go run sync_queue.go — 80×24
apples-MacBook-Air:chapter3 bhagvan.kommadi$ go run sync_queue.go
&{0 0 false false 0xc4200780c0 0xc420078120 0xc420078060}
  Passenger starts
Ticket Issue starts
Ticket Issue ends
 Passenger ends
Ticket Issue starts
  Passenger starts
 Passenger ends
Ticket Issue ends
Ticket Issue starts
  Passenger starts
 Passenger ends
Ticket Issue ends
Ticket Issue starts
  Passenger starts
 Passenger ends
Ticket Issue ends
Ticket Issue starts
  Passenger starts
Ticket Issue ends
```

The next section talks about `Stacks`, which are linear data structures.

Stacks

A stack is a last in, first out structure in which items are added from the top. Stacks are used in parsers for solving maze algorithms. `Push`, `pop`, `top`, and `get size` are the typical operations that are allowed on stack data structures. Syntax parsing, backtracking, and compiling time memory management are some real-life scenarios where stacks can be used. An example of stack implementation is as follows (`stack.go`):

```
//main package has examples shown
// in Hands-On Data Structures and algorithms with Go book
package main
// importing fmt package
import (
 "fmt"
 "strconv"
```

```
)
//Element class
type Element struct {
 elementValue int
}
// String method on Element class
func (element *Element) String() string {
 return strconv.Itoa(element.elementValue)
}
```

The `Element` class has `elementValue` as an attribute. The `String` method returns the element's `elementValue`.

Stacks methods, such as `New`, `Push`, `Pop`, and `main` are presented in the following sections.

The New method

The `New` method on the `Stack` class creates a dynamic array of elements. The `Stack` class has the count and array pointer of elements. The code snippet with the `Stack` class definition and the `New` method is as follows:

```
// NewStack returns a new stack.
func (stack *Stack) New() {
 stack.elements = make(*Element[] elements,0)
}
// Stack is a basic LIFO stack that resizes as needed.
type Stack struct {
 elements []*Element
 elementCount int
}
```

The Push method

The `Push` method adds the node to the top of the `stack` class. In the following code sample, the `Push` method on the `Stack` class adds the element to the elements array and increases the `Count` element, while the `append` method adds the element to the elements of the `stack` class:

```
// Push adds a node to the stack.
func (stack *Stack) Push(element *Element) {
 stack.elements = append(stack.elements[:stack.elementCount], element)
 stack.elementCount = stack.elementCount + 1
}
```

The example output after the push method is invoked with parameter elements as follows. The element with the value **7** is pushed to the stack. The count of the elements before pushing to the stack is **2**, and, after pushing to the stack, this figure is **3**:

```
Push method
before appending the element with value 7 the element Count 2
after appending the element with value 7 the element Count 3
```

Let's take a look at the `Pop` method in the next section.

The Pop method

The `Pop` method on the `Stack` implementation removes the last element from the element array and returns the element, as shown in the following code. The `len` method returns the length of the elements array:

```
// Pop removes and returns a node from the stack in last to first order.
func (stack *Stack) Pop() *Element {
 if stack.elementCount == 0 {
 return nil
 }
 var length int = len(stack.elements)
 var element *Element = stack.elements[length -1]
 //stack.elementCount = stack.elementCount - 1
 if length > 1 {
 stack.elements = stack.elements[:length-1]
 } else {
 stack.elements = stack.elements[0:]
 }
 stack.elementCount = len(stack.elements)
 return element
}
```

The example output after the `Pop` method is invoked is as follows. The element value **5** is passed and added to the `Pop` method. The count of elements before invoking the `Pop` method is **2**. The count of the elements after calling the `Pop` method is **1**:

```
Pop method
before removing the element with value 5 the element Count 2
after removing the element with value 5 the element Count 1
```

Let's take a look at the `main` method in the next section.

The main method

In the following code section, the `main` method creates a `stack`, calls the `New` method, and pushes the elements after initializing them. The popped-out element value and the order is printed:

```
// main method
func main() {
 var stack *Stack = & Stack{}
 stack.New()
 var element1 *Element = &Element{3}
 var element2 *Element = &Element{5}
 var element3 *Element = &Element{7}
 var element4 *Element = &Element{9}
 stack.Push(element1)
 stack.Push(element2)
 stack.Push(element3)
 stack.Push(element4)
 fmt.Println(stack.Pop(), stack.Pop(), stack.Pop(), stack.Pop())
}
```

Run the following commands to execute the `stack.go` file:

```
go run stack.go
```

After executing the preceding command, we get the following output:

```
chapter3 — -bash — 80×24
Bhagvans-MacBook-Pro:chapter3 bhagvankommadi$ go run stack.go
9 7 5 3
Bhagvans-MacBook-Pro:chapter3 bhagvankommadi$
```

Summary

This chapter covered the definition of `LinkedList`, double `LinkedList`, `Tuples`, `Sets`, `Queues`, and `Stacks`. The `LinkedList` methods – `AddToHead`, `AddToEnd`, `LastNode`, and `iterateList`—were also covered in this chapter. In addition, a priority queue was modeled as a heap of orders to be processed, sync queue was presented as passenger and ticket processing queues, and tuples were explained in a context in which a function returns a multivalued expression. The `new`, `push`, `pop`, and `string` methods for `Stack` were explained with code samples.

In the next chapter, we will cover areas such as the `Trees`, `Tables`, `Containers`, and `Hash` functions.

Questions

1. Where can you use double linked list? Please provide an example.
2. Which method on linked list can be used for printing out node values?
3. Which queue was shown with channels from the Go language?
4. Write a method that returns multiple values. What data structure can be used for returning multiple values?
5. Can set have duplicate elements?
6. Write a code sample showing the union and intersection of two sets.
7. In a linked list, which method is used to find the node between two values?
8. We have elements that are not repeated and unique. What is the correct data structure that represents the collection?
9. In Go, how do you generate a random integer between the values 3 and 5?
10. Which method is called to check if an element of value 5 exists in the Set?

Further reading

To read more about `LinkedLists`, `Sets`, `Tuples`, and `Stacks`, consult the following sources:

- *Design Patterns*, by Erich Gamma, Richard Helm, Ralph Johnson, and John Vlissides
- *Introduction to Algorithms – Third Edition*, by Thomas H. Cormen, Charles E. Leiserson, Ronald L. Rivest, and Clifford Stein
- *Data structures and Algorithms: An Easy Introduction*, by Rudolph Russell

4
Non-Linear Data Structures

Non-linear data structures are used in cryptography and other areas. A non-linear data structure is an arrangement in which an element is connected to many elements. These structures use memory quickly and efficiently. Free contiguous memory is not required for adding new elements.

The length of the data structures is not important before adding new elements. A non-linear data structure has multiple levels and a linear one has a single level. The values of the elements are not organized in a non-linear data structure. The data elements in a non-linear data structure cannot be iterated in one step. The implementation of these data structures is complicated.

Tree types such as binary search trees, treaps, and symbol tables are explained in this chapter.

This chapter covers the following non-linear data structures:

- Trees
- Tables
- Containers
- Hash functions

Technical requirements

Install Go version 1.10 from `https://golang.org/doc/install` for your OS.

The GitHub URL for the code in this chapter is as follows: `https://github.com/PacktPublishing/Learn-Data-Structures-and-Algorithms-with-Golang/tree/master/Chapter04`.

Trees

A tree is a non-linear data structure. Trees are used for search and other use cases. A binary tree has nodes that have a maximum of two children. A binary search tree consists of nodes where the property values of the left node are less than the property values of the right node. The root node is at level zero of a tree. Each child node could be a leaf.

Trees and binary trees were introduced in `Chapter 1`, *Data Structures and Algorithms*, while we were discussing logarithmic complexity. Let's take a closer look at them in the next section.

Binary search tree

A binary search tree is a data structure that allows for the quick lookup, addition, and removal of elements. It stores the keys in a sorted order to enable a faster lookup. This data structure was invented by P. F. Windley, A. D. Booth, A. J. T. Colin, and T. N. Hibbard. On average, space usage for a binary search tree is of the order $O(n)$, whereas the insert, search, and delete operations are of the order $O(\log n)$. A binary search tree consists of nodes with properties or attributes:

- A `key` integer
- A `value` integer
- The `leftNode` and `rightNode` instances of `TreeNode`

They can be represented in the following code:

```
// TreeNode class
type TreeNode struct {
 key int
 value int
 leftNode *TreeNode
 rightNode *TreeNode
}
```

In the next section, the `BinarySearchTree` class implementation is discussed. For this section, please refer to the `binary_search_tree.go` file.

The BinarySearchTree class

In the following code snippet, the BinarySearchTree class consists of a rootNode that's of the TreeNode type, and lock, which is of the sync.RWMutex type. The binary search tree is traversed from rootNode by accessing the nodes to the left and right of rootNode:

```
// BinarySearchTree class
type BinarySearchTree struct {
 rootNode *TreeNode
 lock sync.RWMutex
}
```

Now that we know what BinarySearchTree is, let's take a look at its different methods in the next section.

The InsertElement method

The InsertElement method inserts the element with the given key and value in the binary search tree. The tree's lock() instance is locked first and the unlock() method is deferred before inserting the element. The InsertTreeNode method is invoked by passing rootNode and the node to be created with the key and value, as shown here:

```
// InsertElement method
func (tree *BinarySearchTree) InsertElement(key int, value int) {
 tree.lock.Lock()
 defer tree.lock.Unlock()
 var treeNode *TreeNode
 treeNode= &TreeNode{key, value, nil, nil}
 if tree.rootNode == nil {
 tree.rootNode = treeNode
 } else {
 insertTreeNode(tree.rootNode, treeNode)
 }
}
```

The example output for inserting an element with key and value 3 is shown as follows. The insert element method calls insertTreeNode with rootNode with key 8 and the new treeNode with key 3:

```
insert element method key 3 value 3
insert TreeNode method rootNode 8 new Treenode 3
```

The insertTreeNode method

The `insertTreenode` method inserts the new `TreeNode` in the binary search tree. In the following code, the `insertTreeNode` method takes `rootNode` and `newTreeNode`, both of the `TreeNode` type, as parameters. Note that `newTreeNode` is inserted at the right place in the binary search tree by comparing the key values:

```
// insertTreeNode function
func insertTreeNode(rootNode *TreeNode, newTreeNode *TreeNode) {
 if newTreeNode.key < rootNode.key {
 if rootNode.leftNode == nil {
 rootNode.leftNode = newTreeNode
 } else {
 insertTreeNode(rootNode.leftNode, newTreeNode)
 }
 } else {
 if rootNode.rightNode == nil{
 rootNode.rightNode = newTreeNode
 } else {
 insertTreeNode(rootNode.rightNode, newTreeNode)
 }
 }
}
```

The inOrderTraverse method

The `inOrderTraverse` method visits all nodes in order. The `RLock()` method on the tree `lock` instance is called first. The `RUnLock()` method is deferred on the tree `lock` instance before invoking the `inOrderTraverseTree` method, as presented in the following code snippet:

```
// InOrderTraverseTree method
func (tree *BinarySearchTree) InOrderTraverseTree(function func(int)) {
 tree.lock.RLock()
 defer tree.lock.RUnlock()
 inOrderTraverseTree(tree.rootNode, function)
}
```

The inOrderTraverseTree method

The inOrderTraverseTree method traverses the left, the root, and the right tree. The inOrderTraverseTree method takes treeNode of the TreeNode type and function as parameters. The inOrderTraverseTree method is called on leftNode and rightNode with function as a parameter. A function is passed with treeNode.value, as shown in the following code snippet:

```
//  inOrderTraverseTree method
func inOrderTraverseTree(treeNode *TreeNode, function func(int)) {
 if treeNode != nil {
 inOrderTraverseTree(treeNode.leftNode, function)
 function(treeNode.value)
 inOrderTraverseTree(treeNode.rightNode, function)
 }
}
```

The PreOrderTraverseTree method

The PreOrderTraverseTree method visits all the tree nodes with preorder traversing. The tree lock instance is locked first and the Unlock method is deferred before preOrderTraverseTree is called. In the following code snippet, the preOrderTraverseTree method is passed with rootNode and function as parameters:

```
// PreOrderTraverseTree method
func (tree *BinarySearchTree) PreOrderTraverseTree(function func(int)) {
 tree.lock.Lock()
 defer tree.lock.Unlock()
 preOrderTraverseTree(tree.rootNode, function)
}
```

The preOrderTraverseTree method

The preOrderTraverseTree method is passed with treeNode of the TreeNode type and function as parameters. The preOrderTraverseTree method is called by passing leftNode and rightNode with function as parameters. The function is invoked with treeNode.value, as shown here:

```
//  preOrderTraverseTree method
func preOrderTraverseTree(treeNode *TreeNode, function func(int)) {
 if treeNode != nil {
 function(treeNode.value)
 preOrderTraverseTree(treeNode.leftNode, function)
 preOrderTraverseTree(treeNode.rightNode, function)
 }
```

```
}
```

The PostOrderTraverseTree method

The `PostOrderTraverseTree` method traverses the nodes in a post order (left, right, current node). In the following code snippet, the `PostOrderTraverseTree` method of the `BinarySearchTree` class visits all nodes with post-order traversing. The `function` method is passed as a parameter to the method. The `tree.lock` instance is locked first and the `Unlock` method is deferred on the tree `lock` instance before calling the `postOrderTraverseTree` method:

```
// PostOrderTraverseTree method
func (tree *BinarySearchTree) PostOrderTraverseTree(function func(int)) {
 tree.lock.Lock()
 defer tree.lock.Unlock()
 postOrderTraverseTree(tree.rootNode, function)
}
```

The postOrderTraverseTree method

The `postOrderTraverseTree` method is passed with `treeNode` of the `TreeNode` type and `function` as parameters. The `postOrderTraverseTree` method is called by passing `leftNode` and `rightNode` with `function` as parameters. In the following code snippet, `function` is invoked with `treeNode.value` as a parameter:

```
//  postOrderTraverseTree method
func postOrderTraverseTree(treeNode *TreeNode, function func(int)) {
 if treeNode != nil {
 postOrderTraverseTree(treeNode.leftNode, function)
 postOrderTraverseTree(treeNode.rightNode, function)
 function(treeNode.value)
 }
}
```

The MinNode method

`MinNode` finds the node with the minimum value in the binary search tree. In the following code snippet, the `RLock` method of the tree `lock` instance is invoked first and the `RUnlock` method on the tree `lock` instance is deferred. The `MinNode` method returns the element with the lowest value by traversing from `rootNode` and checking whether the value of `leftNode` is `nil`:

```
// MinNode method
func (tree *BinarySearchTree) MinNode() *int {
```

```
 tree.lock.RLock()
 defer tree.lock.RUnlock()
 var treeNode *TreeNode
 treeNode = tree.rootNode
 if treeNode == nil {
 //nil instead of 0
 return (*int)(nil)
 }
 for {
 if treeNode.leftNode == nil {
 return &treeNode.value
 }
 treeNode = treeNode.leftNode
 }
}
```

The MaxNode method

`MaxNode` finds the node with maximum property in the binary search tree. The `RLock` method of the tree `lock` instance is called first and the `RUnlock` method on the tree `lock` instance is deferred. The `MaxNode` method returns the element with the highest value after traversing from `rootNode` and finding a `rightNode` with a `nil` value. This is shown in the following code:

```
// MaxNode method
func (tree *BinarySearchTree) MaxNode() *int {
 tree.lock.RLock()
 defer tree.lock.RUnlock()
 var treeNode *TreeNode
 treeNode = tree.rootNode
 if treeNode == nil {
 //nil instead of 0
 return (*int)(nil)
 }
 for {
 if treeNode.rightNode == nil {
 return &treeNode.value
 }
 treeNode = treeNode.rightNode
 }
}
```

The SearchNode method

The `SearchNode` method searches the specified node in the binary search tree. First, the `RLock` method of the tree lock instance is called. Then, the `RUnlock` method on the tree `lock` instance is deferred. The `SearchNode` method of the `BinarySearchTree` class invokes the `searchNode` method with the `rootNode` and the `key` integer value as parameters, as shown here:

```
// SearchNode method
func (tree *BinarySearchTree) SearchNode(key int) bool {
 tree.lock.RLock()
 defer tree.lock.RUnlock()
 return searchNode(tree.rootNode, key)
}
```

The searchNode method

In the following code, the `searchNode` method takes `treeNode`, a pointer of the `TreeNode` type, and a `key` integer value as parameters. The method returns `true` or `false` after checking whether `treeNode` with the same value as `key` exists:

```
//  searchNode method
func searchNode(treeNode *TreeNode, key int) bool {
 if treeNode == nil {
 return false
 }
 if key < treeNode.key {
 return searchNode(treeNode.leftNode, key)
 }
 if key > treeNode.key {
 return searchNode(treeNode.rightNode, key)
 }
 return true
}
```

The RemoveNode method

The `RemoveNode` method of the `BinarySearchTree` class removes the element with `key` that's passed in. The method takes the `key` integer value as the parameter. The `Lock()` method is invoked on the tree's `lock` instance first. The `Unlock()` method of the tree `lock` instance is deferred, and `removeNode` is called with `rootNode` and the `key` value as parameters, as shown here:

```
// RemoveNode method
func (tree *BinarySearchTree) RemoveNode(key int) {
```

```
tree.lock.Lock()
defer tree.lock.Unlock()
removeNode(tree.rootNode, key)
}
```

The removeNode method

The `removeNode` method takes `treeNode` of the `TreeNode` type and a `key` integer value as parameters. In the following code snippet, the method recursively searches the `leftNode` instance of `treeNode` and the `key` value of `rightNode` if it matches the parameter value:

```
// removeNode method
func removeNode(treeNode *TreeNode, key int) *TreeNode {
if treeNode == nil {
return nil
}
if key < treeNode.key {
treeNode.leftNode = removeNode(treeNode.leftNode, key)
return treeNode
}
if key > treeNode.key {
treeNode.rightNode = removeNode(treeNode.rightNode, key)
return treeNode
}
// key == node.key
if treeNode.leftNode == nil && treeNode.rightNode == nil {
treeNode = nil
return nil
}
if treeNode.leftNode == nil {
treeNode = treeNode.rightNode
return treeNode
}
if treeNode.rightNode == nil {
treeNode = treeNode.leftNode
return treeNode
}
var leftmostrightNode *TreeNode
leftmostrightNode = treeNode.rightNode
for {
//find smallest value on the right side
if leftmostrightNode != nil && leftmostrightNode.leftNode != nil {
leftmostrightNode = leftmostrightNode.leftNode
} else {
break
}
}
```

```
 treeNode.key, treeNode.value = leftmostrightNode.key,
leftmostrightNode.value
 treeNode.rightNode = removeNode(treeNode.rightNode, treeNode.key)
 return treeNode
}
```

The String method

The `String` method turns the `tree` into a string format. At first, the `Lock()` method is invoked on the tree `lock` instance. Then, the `Unlock()` method of the tree `lock` instance is deferred. The `String` method prints a visual representation of `tree`:

```
// String method
func (tree *BinarySearchTree) String() {
 tree.lock.Lock()
 defer tree.lock.Unlock()
 fmt.Println("------------------------------------------------")
 stringify(tree.rootNode, 0)
 fmt.Println("------------------------------------------------")
}
```

The stringify method

In the following code snippet, the `stringify` method takes a `treeNode` instance of the `TreeNode` type and `level` (an integer) as parameters. The method recursively prints the tree based on the level:

```
// stringify method
func stringify(treeNode *TreeNode, level int) {
 if treeNode != nil {
 format := ""
 for i := 0; i < level; i++ {
 format += " "
 }
 format += "---[ "
 level++
 stringify(treeNode.leftNode, level)
 fmt.Printf(format+"%d\n", treeNode.key)
 stringify(treeNode.rightNode, level)
 }
}
```

The main method

In the following code, the `main` method creates the binary search tree and inserts the elements `8`, `3`, `10`, `1`, and `6` into it. `tree` is printed by invoking the `String` method:

```
// main method
func main() {
 var tree *BinarySearchTree = &BinarySearchTree{}
 tree.InsertElement(8,8)
 tree.InsertElement(3,3)
 tree.InsertElement(10,10)
 tree.InsertElement(1,1)
 tree.InsertElement(6,6)
 tree.String()
}
```

Run the following command to execute the `binary_search_tree.go` file:

```
go run binary_search_tree.go
```

The output is as follows:

```
chapter4 — -bash — 80×24
Bhagvans-MacBook-Pro:chapter4 bhagvankommadi$ go run binary_search_tree.go
************************************************
            ***> 1
      ***> 3
            ***> 6
***> 8
      ***> 10
************************************************
Bhagvans-MacBook-Pro:chapter4 bhagvankommadi$
```

The next section talks about AVL tree implementation.

Adelson, Velski, and Landis (AVL) tree

Adelson, Velski, and Landis pioneered the AVL tree data structure and hence it is named after them. It consists of height adjusting binary search trees. The balance factor is obtained by finding the difference between the heights of the left and right sub-trees. Balancing is done using rotation techniques. If the balance factor is greater than one, rotation shifts the nodes to the opposite of the left or right sub-trees. The search, addition, and deletion operations are processed in the order of $O(log\ n)$.

The following sections talks about the `KeyValue` interface definition and the `TreeNode` class. For this section, please refer to the `avl_tree.go` file.

The KeyValue interface

The `KeyValue` interface has the `LessThan` and `EqualTo` methods. The `LessThan` and `EqualTo` methods take `KeyValue` as a parameter and return a Boolean value after checking the less than or equal to condition. This is shown in the following code:

```
// KeyValue type
type KeyValue interface {
  LessThan(KeyValue) bool
  EqualTo(KeyValue) bool
}
```

The TreeNode class

The `TreeNode` class has `KeyValue`, `BalanceValue`, and `LinkedNodes` as properties. The AVL tree is created as a tree of nodes of the `TreeNode` type, as shown here:

```
// TreeNode class
type TreeNode struct {
 KeyValue     KeyValue
 BalanceValue int
 LinkedNodes [2]*TreeNode
}
```

Now, let's take a look at the different methods of the `TreeNode` class.

The opposite method

The `opposite` method takes a node value and returns the opposite node's value. In the following code snippet, the `opposite` method takes the `nodeValue` integer as a parameter and returns the opposite node's value:

```
//opposite method
func opposite(nodeValue int) int {
 return 1 - nodeValue
}
```

The singleRotation method

The `singleRotation` method rotates the node opposite to the specified sub-tree. As shown in the following snippet, the `singleRotation` function rotates the node opposite the left or right sub-tree. The method takes the pointer to `rootNode` and a `nodeValue` integer as parameters and returns a `TreeNode` pointer:

```
// single rotation method
func singleRotation(rootNode *TreeNode, nodeValue int) *TreeNode {
var saveNode *TreeNode
 saveNode = rootNode.LinkedNodes[opposite(nodeValue)]
 rootNode.LinkedNodes[opposite(nodeValue)] =
saveNode.LinkedNodes[nodeValue]
 saveNode.LinkedNodes[nodeValue] = rootNode
 return saveNode
}
```

The doubleRotation method

Here, the `doubleRotation` method rotates the node twice. The method returns a `TreeNode` pointer, taking parameters such as `rootNode`, which is a `treeNode` pointer, and `nodeValue`, which is an integer. This is shown in the following code:

```
// double rotation
func doubleRotation(rootNode *TreeNode, nodeValue int) *TreeNode {
var saveNode *TreeNode
 saveNode =
rootNode.LinkedNodes[opposite(nodeValue)].LinkedNodes[nodeValue]
rootNode.LinkedNodes[opposite(nodeValue)].LinkedNodes[nodeValue] =
saveNode.LinkedNodes[opposite(nodeValue)]
 saveNode.LinkedNodes[opposite(nodeValue)] =
rootNode.LinkedNodes[opposite(nodeValue)]
 rootNode.LinkedNodes[opposite(nodeValue)] = saveNode
saveNode = rootNode.LinkedNodes[opposite(nodeValue)]
 rootNode.LinkedNodes[opposite(nodeValue)] =
```

```
saveNode.LinkedNodes[nodeValue]
 saveNode.LinkedNodes[nodeValue] = rootNode
 return saveNode
}
```

The implementation of this method is shown in *The InsertNode method* section, as follows.

The adjustBalance method

The `adjustBalance` method adjusts the balance of the tree. In the following code snippet, the `adjustBalance` method does a double rotation given the balance factor, `rootNode`, and `nodeValue`. The `adjustBalance` method takes `rootNode`, which is an instance of the `TreeNode` type, `nodeValue`, and `balanceValue` (which are both integers) as parameters:

```
// adjust balance method
func adjustBalance(rootNode *TreeNode, nodeValue int, balanceValue int) {
 var node *TreeNode
 node = rootNode.LinkedNodes[nodeValue]
 var oppNode *TreeNode
 oppNode = node.LinkedNodes[opposite(balanceValue)]
 switch oppNode.BalanceValue {
 case 0:
 rootNode.BalanceValue = 0
 node.BalanceValue = 0
 case balanceValue:
 rootNode.BalanceValue = -balanceValue
 node.BalanceValue = 0
 default:
 rootNode.BalanceValue = 0
 node.BalanceValue = balanceValue
 }
 oppNode.BalanceValue= 0
}
```

The BalanceTree method

The `BalanceTree` method changes the balance factor by a single or double rotation. The method takes `rootNode` (a `TreeNode` pointer) and `nodeValue` (an integer) as parameters. The `BalanceTree` method returns a `TreeNode` pointer, as shown here:

```
// BalanceTree method
func BalanceTree(rootNode *TreeNode, nodeValue int) *TreeNode {
 var node *TreeNode
 node = rootNode.LinkedNodes[nodeValue]
 var balance int
 balance = 2*nodeValue - 1
```

```
    if node.BalanceValue == balance {
    rootNode.BalanceValue = 0
    node.BalanceValue = 0
    return singleRotation(rootNode, opposite(nodeValue))
    }
    adjustBalance(rootNode, nodeValue, balance)
    return doubleRotation(rootNode, opposite(nodeValue))
}
```

The insertRNode method

The `insertRNode` method inserts the node and balances the tree. This method inserts `rootNode` with the `KeyValue` key, as presented in the following code snippet. The method takes `rootNode`, which is a `TreeNode` pointer, and the `key` as an integer as parameters. The method returns a `TreeNode` pointer and a Boolean value if the `rootNode` is inserted:

```
//insertRNode method
func insertRNode(rootNode *TreeNode, key KeyValue) (*TreeNode, bool) {
 if rootNode == nil {
 return &TreeNode{KeyValue: key}, false
 }
 var dir int
 dir = 0
 if rootNode.KeyValue.LessThan(key) {
 dir = 1
 }
 var done bool
 rootNode.LinkedNodes[dir], done = insertRNode(rootNode.LinkedNodes[dir],
key)
 if done {
 return rootNode, true
 }
 rootNode.BalanceValue = rootNode.BalanceValue+(2*dir - 1)
 switch rootNode.BalanceValue {
 case 0:
 return rootNode, true
 case 1, -1:
 return rootNode, false
 }
 return BalanceTree(rootNode, dir), true
}
```

The InsertNode method

The `InsertNode` method inserts a node into the AVL tree. This method takes `treeNode`, which is a double `TreeNode` pointer, and the `key` value as parameters:

```
// InsertNode method
func InsertNode(treeNode **TreeNode, key KeyValue) {
 *treeNode, _ = insertRNode(*treeNode, key)
}
```

The example output of the `InsertNode` method is shown in the following screenshot. The `InsertNode` method calls the `insertRNode` method with the `rootNode` parameters and node to be inserted. `rootNode` has a key value of `5` and the node to be inserted has a key value of `6`. The tree needs to be balanced.

Hence, the next call will be `rootNode` with key `8` and node to be inserted. The next step calls `rootnode` with `key` value `7` and node to be inserted. The last call will be with `rootNode nil` and node to be inserted. The balance value is checked and the balance tree method returns the balanced tree:

```
Insert Node method
InsertRNode method rootnodekey 5 insert Node key 6
InsertRNode method rootnodekey 8 insert Node key 6
InsertRNode method rootnodekey 7 insert Node key 6
InsertRNode method rootnode nil insert Node key 6
balance Value -1
balance Value -2
Balance Tree method
```

The RemoveNode method

In the following code, the `RemoveNode` method removes the element from the AVL tree by invoking the `removeRNode` method. The method takes `treeNode`, which is a double `TreeNode` pointer, and `KeyValue` as parameters:

```
// RemoveNode method
func RemoveNode(treeNode **TreeNode, key KeyValue) {
 *treeNode, _ = removeRNode(*treeNode, key)
}
```

The removeBalance method

The `removeBalance` method removes the balance factor in a tree. This method adjusts the balance factor after removing the node and returns a `treeNode` pointer and a Boolean if the balance is removed. The method takes `rootNode` (an instance of `TreeNode`) and `nodeValue` (an integer) as parameters. This is shown in the following code:

```
// removeBalance method
func removeBalance(rootNode *TreeNode, nodeValue int) (*TreeNode, bool) {
 var node *TreeNode
 node = rootNode.LinkedNodes[opposite(nodeValue)]
 var balance int
 balance = 2*nodeValue - 1
 switch node.BalanceValue {
 case -balance:
 rootNode.BalanceValue = 0
 node.BalanceValue = 0
 return singleRotation(rootNode, nodeValue), false
 case balance:
 adjustBalance(rootNode, opposite(nodeValue), -balance)
 return doubleRotation(rootNode, nodeValue), false
 }
 rootNode.BalanceValue = -balance
 node.BalanceValue = balance
 return singleRotation(rootNode, nodeValue), true
}
```

The removeRNode method

The `removeRNode` method removes the node from the tree and balances the tree. This method takes `rootNode`, which is a `TreeNode` pointer, and the `key` value. This method returns a `TreeNode` pointer and Boolean value if `RNode` is removed, as shown in the following code snippet:

```
//removeRNode method
func removeRNode(rootNode *TreeNode, key KeyValue) (*TreeNode, bool) {
 if rootNode == nil {
 return nil, false
 }
 if rootNode.KeyValue.EqualTo(key) {
 switch {
 case rootNode.LinkedNodes[0] == nil:
 return rootNode.LinkedNodes[1], false
 case rootNode.LinkedNodes[1] == nil:
 return rootNode.LinkedNodes[0], false
 }
```

```
    var heirNode *TreeNode
    heirNode = rootNode.LinkedNodes[0]
    for heirNode.LinkedNodes[1] != nil {
    heirNode = heirNode.LinkedNodes[1]
    }
    rootNode.KeyValue = heirNode.KeyValue
    key = heirNode.KeyValue
    }
    var dir int
    dir = 0
    if rootNode.KeyValue.LessThan(key) {
    dir = 1
    }
    var done bool
    rootNode.LinkedNodes[dir], done = removeR(rootNode.LinkedNodes[dir], key)
    if done {
    return rootNode, true
    }
    rootNode.BalanceValue = rootNode.BalanceValue + (1 - 2*dir)
    switch rootNode.BalanceValue {
    case 1, -1:
    return rootNode, true
    case 0:
    return rootNode, false
    }
    return removeBalance(rootNode, dir)
  }
  type integerKey int
  func (k integerKey) LessThan(k1 KeyValue) bool { return k < k1.(integerKey)
  }
  func (k integerKey) EqualTo(k1 KeyValue) bool { return k == k1.(integerKey)
  }
```

The example output of the `removeRNode` method is shown as follows. The `RemoveNode` method calls the `removeRNode` method. The `removeRNode` method takes the parameters, such as `rootNode` and `KeyValue`, of the node:

```
inside Remove Node method
inside removeRNode method
inside removeRNode method
inside removeRNode method
rootNode balance value 1
```

The main method

In the following code snippet, the `main` method creates an AVL tree by inserting nodes with the `5`, `3`, `8`, `7`, `6`, and `10` keys. Nodes with the `3` and `7` keys are removed. The tree data structure is converted in to JSON in bytes. The JSON bytes are printed after being changed to a string:

```
//main method
func main() {
  var treeNode *TreeNode
  fmt.Println("Tree is empty")
  var avlTree []byte
  avlTree, _ = json.MarshalIndent(treeNode, "", " ")
  fmt.Println(string(avlTree))

  fmt.Println("\n Add Tree")
  InsertNode(&treeNode, integerKey(5))
  InsertNode(&treeNode, integerKey(3))
  InsertNode(&treeNode, integerKey(8))
  InsertNode(&treeNode, integerKey(7))
  InsertNode(&treeNode, integerKey(6))
  InsertNode(&treeNode, integerKey(10))
  avlTree, _ = json.MarshalIndent(treeNode, "", " ")
  fmt.Println(string(avlTree))

  fmt.Println("\n Delete Tree")
  RemoveNode(&treeNode, integerKey(3))
  RemoveNode(&treeNode, integerKey(7))
  avlTree, _ = json.MarshalIndent(treeNode, "", " ")
  fmt.Println(string(avlTree))
}
```

Run the following command to execute the `avl_tree.go` file:

```
go run avl_tree.go
```

The output is as follows:

```
chapter4 — -bash — 80×56
apples-MacBook-Air:chapter4 bhagvan.kommadi$ go run avl_tree.go
Empty Tree:
null

Insert Tree:
{
   "KeyValue": 7,
   "BalanceValue": 0,
   "LinkedNodes": [
      {
         "KeyValue": 5,
         "BalanceValue": 0,
         "LinkedNodes": [
            {
               "KeyValue": 3,
               "BalanceValue": 0,
               "LinkedNodes": [
                  null,
                  null
               ]
            },
            {
               "KeyValue": 6,
               "BalanceValue": 0,
               "LinkedNodes": [
                  null,
                  null
               ]
            }
         ]
      },
      {
         "KeyValue": 8,
         "BalanceValue": 1,
         "LinkedNodes": [
            null,
            {
               "KeyValue": 10,
               "BalanceValue": 0,
               "LinkedNodes": [
                  null,
                  null
               ]
            }
         ]
      }
   ]
}

Remove Tree:
{
   "KeyValue": 6,
   "BalanceValue": 1,
   "LinkedNodes": [
      {
         "KeyValue": 5,
```

In the next section, B+ tree implementation is discussed and code snippets are presented.

B+ tree

The B+ tree contains a list of keys and pointers to the next-level nodes in trees. During a search, recursion is used to search for an element by looking for the the adjacent node keys. B+ trees are used to store data in filesystems. B+ trees require fewer I/O operations to search for a node in the tree. Fan-out is defined as the number of nodes pointing to the child nodes of a node in a B+ tree. B+ trees were first described in a technical paper by Rudolf Bayer and Edward M. McCreight.

The block-oriented storage context in B+ trees helps with the storage and efficient retrieval of data. The space efficiency of a B+ tree can be enhanced by using compression techniques. B+ trees belong to a family of multiway search trees. For a b-order B+ tree, space usage is of the order $O(n)$. Inserting, finding, and removing operations are of the order $O(log_b n)$.

B-tree

The B-tree is a search tree with non-leaf nodes that only have keys, and the data is in the leaves. B-trees are used to reduce the number of disk accesses. The B-tree is a self-adjusting data structure that keeps data sorted. B-trees store keys in a sorted order for easy traversal. They can handle multiple insertions and deletions.

Knuth initially came up with the concept of this data structure. B-trees consist of nodes that have at most n children. Every non-leaf node in the tree has at least $n/2$ child nodes. Rudolf Bayer and Edward M. McCreight were the first to implement this data structure in their work. B-trees are used in HFS and Reiser4 filesystems to allow for quick access to any block in a file. On average, space usage is in the order of $O(n)$. Insert, search, and delete operations are in the order of $O(log\ n)$.

T-tree

The T-tree is a balanced data structure that has both the index and actual data in memory. They are used in in-memory databases. T refers to the shape of the node. Each node consists of pointers to the parent node and the left and right child nodes. Each node in the tree node will have an ordered array of data pointers and extra control data.

T-trees have similar performance benefits to in-memory tree structures. A T-tree is implemented on top of a self-balancing binary search tree. This data structure is good for ordered scanning of data. It supports various degrees of isolation.

Tables

As we already know, tables are used in data management and other areas. A table has a name and a header with the column names. Let's take a look at the different classes in tables such as the `Table` class, the `Row` class, the `Column` class, and the `PrintTable` method in the following sections.

For this section, please refer to the `table.go` file.

The Table class

A `Table` class has an array of rows and column names. The table's `Name` is a string property in the `struct` class, as shown here:

```
// Table Class
type Table struct {
    Rows []Row
    Name string
    ColumnNames []string
}
```

The Row class

The `Row` class has an array of columns and an `Id` integer, as shown in the following code. The `Id` instance is a unique identifier for a row:

```
// Row Class
type Row struct {
 Columns []Column
 Id int
}
```

The Column class

A `Column` class has an `Id` integer and a `Value string` that's identified by a unique identifier, as presented in the following code snippet:

```
// Column Class
type Column struct {
 Id int
 Value string
```

```
}
```

The printTable method

In the following code snippet, the `printTable` method prints the rows and columns of a table. Rows are traversed, and then for every row the columns are printed:

```
//printTable
func printTable(table Table){
 var rows []Row = table.Rows
 fmt.Println(table.Name)
 for _,row := range rows {
 var columns []Column = row.Columns
 for i,column := range columns {
 fmt.Println(table.ColumnNames[i],column.Id,column.Value);
 }
 }
}
```

The main method

In this `main` method, we will instantiate the classes such as `Table`, `Row`, and `Column`, which we just took a look at. The `main` method creates a table and sets the name and column names. Columns are created with values. The columns are set on the rows after the rows are created. The table is printed by invoking the `printTable` method, as shown here:

```
// main method
func main() {
 var table Table = Table{}
 table.Name = "Customer"
 table.ColumnNames = []string{"Id", "Name","SSN"}
 var rows []Row = make([]Row,2)
 rows[0] = Row{}
 var columns1 []Column = make([]Column,3)
 columns1[0] = Column{1,"323"}
 columns1[1] = Column{1,"John Smith"}
 columns1[2] = Column{1,"3453223"}
 rows[0].Columns = columns1
 rows[1] = Row{}
 var columns2 []Column = make([]Column,3)
 columns2[0] = Column{2,"223"}
 columns2[1] = Column{2,"Curran Smith"}
 columns2[2] = Column{2,"3223211"}
 rows[1].Columns = columns2
```

```
    table.Rows = rows
    fmt.Println(table)
    printTable(table)
}
```

Run the following command to execute the `table.go` file:

```
go run table.go
```

The output is as follows:

```
chapter4 — -bash — 80×24
apples-MacBook-Air:chapter4 bhagvan.kommadi$ go run table.go
{[{[{1 323} {1 John Smith} {1 3453223}] 0} {[{2 223} {2 Curran Smith} {2 3223211
}] 0}] Customer [Id Name SSN]}
Customer
Id 1 323
Name 1 John Smith
SSN 1 3453223
Id 2 223
Name 2 Curran Smith
SSN 2 3223211
apples-MacBook-Air:chapter4 bhagvan.kommadi$
```

The next section talks about the symbol table data structure.

Symbol tables

A symbol table is present in memory during the program translation process. It can be present in program binaries. A symbol table contains the symbol's name, location, and address. In Go, the `gosym` package implements access to the Go symbol and line number tables. Go binaries generated by the GC compilers have the symbol and line number tables. A line table is a data structure that maps program counters to line numbers.

Containers

The containers package provides access to the heap, list, and ring functionalities in Go. Containers are used in social networks, knowledge graphs, and other areas. Containers are lists, maps, slices, channels, heaps, queues, and treaps. Lists were introduced in `Chapter 1`, *Data Structures and Algorithms*. Maps and slices are built-in containers in Go. Channels in Go are called queues. A heap is a tree data structure. This data structure satisfies the heap property. A queue is modeled as a heap in `Chapter 3`, *Linear Data Structures*. A treap is a mix of a tree and a heap. It is a binary tree with keys and values and a heap that maintains priorities.

A ring is called a circular linked list and is presented in the next section. For this section, please refer to the `circular_list.go` file.

Circular linked list

A circular linked list is a data structure in which the last node is followed by the first node. The `container/ring` structures are used to model circular linked lists. An example implementation of a circular linked list is shown as follows:

```
package main
import (
 "container/ring"
 "fmt"
)
func main() {
 var integers []int
 integers = []int{1,3,5,7}
 var circular_list *ring.Ring
 circular_list= ring.New(len(integers))
 var i int
 for i = 0; i < circular_list.Len(); i++ {
 circular_list.Value = integers[i]
 circular_list = circular_list.Next()
 }
```

The `ring.New` method with the `len` *n* as a parameter creates a circular list of length *n*. The circular linked list is initialized with an integer array by moving through `circular_list` with the `Next` method. The `Do` method of `ring.Ring` class takes the element as an interface, and the element is printed as follows:

```
circular_list.Do(func(element interface{}) {
 fmt.Print(element,",")
 })
 fmt.Println()
```

The reverse of the circular list is traversed using the `Prev` method, and the value is printed in the following code:

```
// reverse of the circular list
 for i = 0; i < circular_list.Len(); i++ {
 fmt.Print(circular_list.Value,",")
 circular_list = circular_list.Prev()
 }
 fmt.Println()
```

In the following code snippet, the circular list is moved two elements forward using the `Move` method, and the value is printed:

```
// move two elements forward in the circular list
 circular_list = circular_list.Move(2)
 circular_list.Do(func(element interface{}) {
 fmt.Print(element,",")
 })
 fmt.Println()
}
```

Run the following command to execute the `circular_list.go` file:

```
go run circular_list.go
```

The output is as follows:

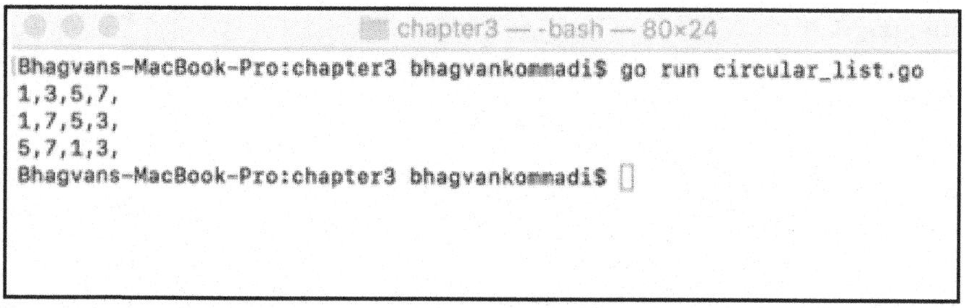

```
Bhagvans-MacBook-Pro:chapter3 bhagvankommadi$ go run circular_list.go
1,3,5,7,
1,7,5,3,
5,7,1,3,
Bhagvans-MacBook-Pro:chapter3 bhagvankommadi$
```

The next section talks about the `hash` function data structure.

The hash functions

Hash functions are used in cryptography and other areas. These data structures are presented with code examples related to cryptography. There are two ways to implement a `hash` function in Go: with `crc32` or `sha256`. Marshaling (changing the string to an encoded form) saves the internal state, which is used for other purposes later. A `BinaryMarshaler` (converting the string into binary form) example is explained in this section:

```
//main package has examples shown
// in Hands-On Data Structures and algorithms with Go book
package main
// importing bytes, crpto/sha256, encoding, fmt and log package
import (
 "bytes"
```

```
 "crypto/sha256"
 "encoding"
 "fmt"
 "log"
 "hash"
)
```

The `main` method creates a binary marshaled hash of two example strings. The hashes of the two strings are printed. The sum of the first hash is compared with the second hash using the equals method on bytes. This is shown in the following code:

```
//main method
func main() {
 const (
 example1 = "this is a example "
 example2 = "second example"
 )
 var firstHash hash.Hash
 firstHash = sha256.New()
 firstHash.Write([]byte(example1))
 var marshaler encoding.BinaryMarshaler
 var ok bool
 marshaler, ok = firstHash.(encoding.BinaryMarshaler)
 if !ok {
 log.Fatal("first Hash is not generated by encoding.BinaryMarshaler")
 }
 var data []byte
 var err error
 data, err = marshaler.MarshalBinary()
 if err != nil {
 log.Fatal("failure to create first Hash:", err)
 }
 var secondHash hash.Hash
 secondHash = sha256.New()
var unmarshaler encoding.BinaryUnmarshaler
 unmarshaler, ok = secondHash.(encoding.BinaryUnmarshaler)
 if !ok {
 log.Fatal("second Hash is not generated by encoding.BinaryUnmarshaler")
 }
 if err := unmarshaler.UnmarshalBinary(data); err != nil {
 log.Fatal("failure to create hash:", err)
 }
 firstHash.Write([]byte(example2))
 secondHash.Write([]byte(example2))
 fmt.Printf("%x\n", firstHash.Sum(nil))
 fmt.Println(bytes.Equal(firstHash.Sum(nil), secondHash.Sum(nil)))
}
```

Run the following command to execute the `hash.go` file:

```
go run hash.go
```

The output is as follows:

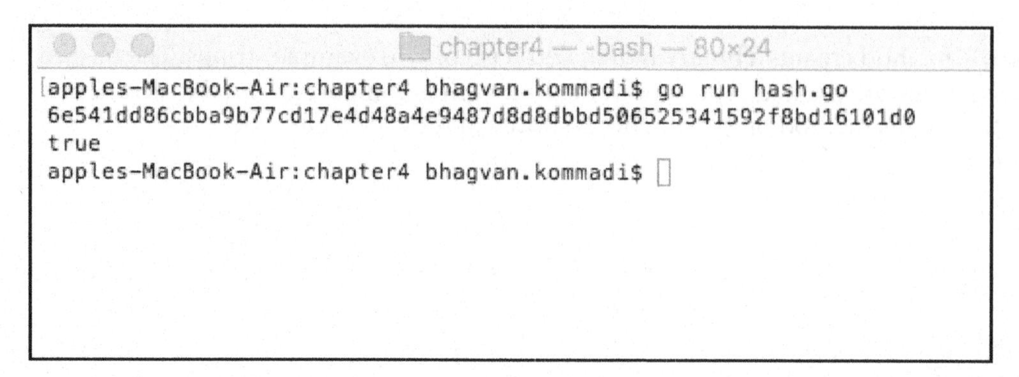

Summary

This chapter covered trees, binary search trees, and AVL trees. Treap, B-trees, and B+ trees were explained briefly. Operations such as insertion, deletion, and updating elements in trees were shown with various code examples. Tables, containers, and hash functions were presented in the last section. The complexity in time and space for operations such as insertion, deletion, and search were explained in each section.

In the next chapter, homogeneous data structures such as two-dimensional and multi-dimensional arrays will be covered.

Questions

1. Can you give an example where you can use a binary search tree?
2. Which method is used to search for an element in a binary search tree?
3. Which techniques are used to adjust the balance in an AVL tree?
4. What is a symbol table?

5. Which class and method are called to generate a binary marshaled hash on the hash class?
6. Which container in Go is used to model a circular linked list?
7. How do you create a JSON (indented) from a tree structure? Which class and method are used?
8. How do you compare the sum of hashes?
9. What is the balance factor in an AVL tree?
10. How do you identify a row and column in a table?

Further reading

The following books are recommended if you want to know more about trees, binary search trees, and AVL trees:

- *Design Patterns*, by Erich Gamma, Richard Helm, Ralph Johnson, and John Vlissides
- *Introduction to Algorithms – Third Edition*, by Thomas H. Cormen, Charles E. Leiserson, Ronald L. Rivest, and Clifford Stein
- *Data structures and Algorithms: An Easy Introduction*, by Rudolph Russell

5
Homogeneous Data Structures

Homogeneous data structures contain similar types of data, such as integers or double values. Homogeneous data structures are used in matrices, as well as tensor and vector mathematics. **Tensors** are mathematical structures for scalars and vectors. A first-rank tensor is a **vector**. A vector consists of a row or a column. A tensor with zero rank is a **scalar**. A **matrix** is a two-dimensional cluster of numbers. They are all used in scientific analysis.

Tensors are used in material science. They are used in mathematics, physics, mechanics, electrodynamics, and general relativity. Machine learning solutions utilize a tensor data structure. A tensor has properties such as position, shape, and a static size.

This chapter covers the following homogeneous data structures:

- **Two-dimensional arrays**
- **Multi-dimensional arrays**

The following scenarios are shown to demonstrate the usage of two-dimensional and multi-dimensional arrays:

- Matrix representation
- Multiplication
- Addition
- Subtraction
- Determinant calculation
- Inversion
- Transposition

Technical requirements

Install Go Version 1.10 from `https://golang.org/doc/install` for your OS.

The GitHub URL for the code in this chapter is as follows: `https://github.com/PacktPublishing/Learn-Data-Structures-and-Algorithms-with-Golang/tree/master/Chapter05`.

Two-dimensional arrays

Two-dimensional arrays were presented briefly in `Chapter 2`, *Getting Started with Go for Data Structures and Algorithms*. To recap, for dynamic allocation, we use **slice of slices,** which is a two-dimensional array. A two-dimensional array, is a list of single-dimensional arrays. Every element in a two-dimensional array `arr`, is identified as `arr[i][j]`, where `arr` is the name of the array and *i* and *j* represent rows and columns, and their values ranging from 0 to *m* and 0 to *n*, respectively. Traversing a two-dimensional array is of $O(m*n)$ complexity.

The following code shows how to initialize an array:

```
var arr = [4][5] int{
    {4,5,7,8,9},
    {1,2,4,5,6},
    {9,10,11,12,14},
    {3,5,6,8,9}
}
```

An element in a two-dimensional array is accessed with a row index and column index. In the following example, the array's value in row `2` and column `3` is retrieved as an integer value:

```
var value int = arr[2][3]
```

Arrays can store a sequential collection of data elements of the same type. Homogeneous data structure arrays consist of contiguous memory address locations.

Two-dimensional matrices are modeled as two-dimensional arrays. A scalar is an element of a field that defines a vector space. A matrix can be multiplied by a scalar. You can divide a matrix by any non-zero real number.

The order of a matrix is the number of rows, *m*, by the number of columns, *n*. A matrix with rows *m* and columns *n* is referred to as an ***m* x *n* matrix**. There are multiple types of matrices, such as a **row matrix**, **column matrix**, **triangular matrix**, **null matrix**, and **zero matrix**; let's discuss them in the following sections.

Row matrix

A row matrix is a 1 x *m* matrix consisting of a single row of *m* elements, as shown here:

```
var matrix = [1][3] int{
    {1, 2, 3}
}
```

Run the following command to execute the `row_matrix.go` file:

```
go run row_matrix.go
```

The output is as follows:

```
chapter5 — -bash — 80×24
apples-MacBook-Air:chapter5 bhagvan.kommadi$ go run row_matrix.go
[[1 2 3]]
apples-MacBook-Air:chapter5 bhagvan.kommadi$
```

The next section talks about the **column matrix** data structure.

Column matrix

A column matrix is an *m* x 1 matrix that has a single column of *m* elements. The following code snippet shows how to create a column matrix:

```
var matrix = [4][1] int{
    {1},
    {2},
    {3},
    {4}
}
```

Run the following command to execute the `column_matrix.go` file:

```
go run column_matrix.go
```

The output is as follows:

```
chapter5 — -bash — 80×24
apples-MacBook-Air:chapter5 bhagvan.kommadi$ go run column_matrix.go
[[1] [2] [3] [4]]
apples-MacBook-Air:chapter5 bhagvan.kommadi$
```

The next section talks about the lower triangular matrix data structure.

Lower triangular matrix

A **lower triangular matrix** consists of elements that have a value of zero above the main diagonal. The following code snippet shows how to create a lower triangular matrix:

```
var matrix = [3][3] int{
    {1,0,0},
    {1,1,0},
    {2,1,1}
}
```

Run the following command to execute the `lower_triangular.go` file:

```
go run lower_triangular.go
```

The output is as follows:

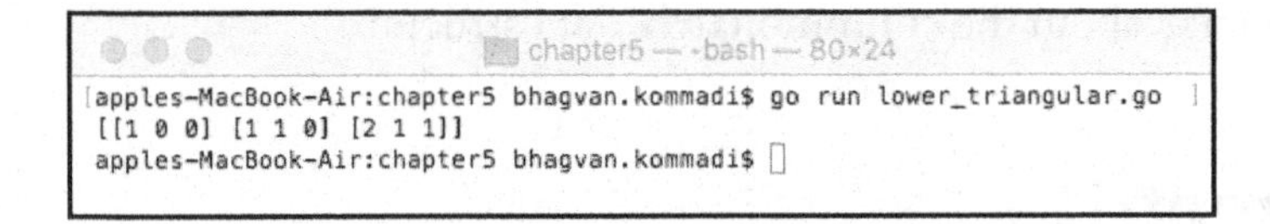

The next section talks about the upper triangular matrix data structure.

Upper triangular matrix

An upper triangular matrix consists of elements with a value of zero below the main diagonal. The following code creates an upper triangular matrix:

```
var matrix = [3][3] int{
    {1,2,3},
    {0,1,4},
    {0,0,1}
}
```

Run the following command to execute the `upper_triangular.go` file:

```
go run upper_triangular.go
```

The output is as follows:

```
chapter5 — -bash — 80×24
apples-MacBook-Air:chapter5 bhagvan.kommadi$ go run upper_triangular.go
[[1 2 3] [0 1 4] [0 0 1]]
apples-MacBook-Air:chapter5 bhagvan.kommadi$
```

The next section talks about the **null matrix data** structure.

Null matrix

A null or a zero matrix is a matrix entirely consisting of zero values, as shown in the following code snippet:

```
var matrix = [3][3] int{
      {0,0,0},
      {0,0,0},
      {0,0,0}
}
```

Run the following command to execute the `null_matrix.go` file:

```
go run null_matrix.go
```

The output is as follows:

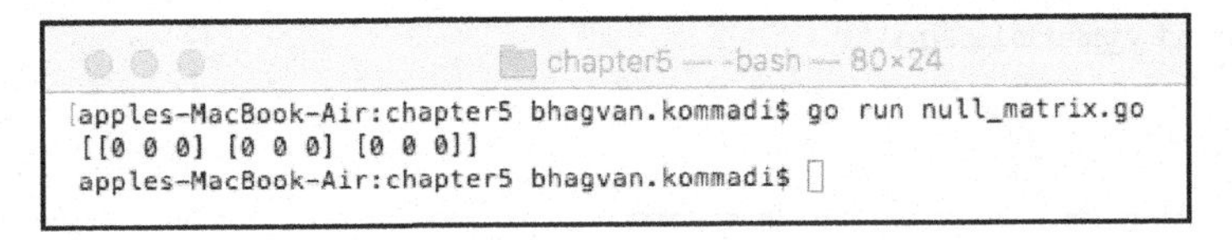

The next section talks about the **identity matrix** data structure.

Identity matrix

An identity matrix is a unit matrix with ones are on the main diagonal and zeros are elsewhere. The following code snippet creates an identity matrix:

```
///main package has examples shown
// in Go Data Structures and algorithms book
package main

// importing fmt package
import (
    "fmt"
)
// identity method
func Identity(order int) [][]float64 {
var matrix [][]float64
    matrix = make([][]float64, order)
var i int
    for i = 0; i < order; i++ {
var temp []float64
        temp = make([]float64, order)
        temp[i] = 1
        matrix[i] = temp
    }
    return matrix
}
// main method
func main() {
    fmt.Println(Identity(4))
}
```

Run the following command to execute the preceding code snippet:

```
go run identity_matrix.go
```

The output is as follows:

```
chapter5 — -bash — 80×24
apples-MacBook-Air:chapter5 bhagvan.kommadi$ go run identity_matrix.go
[[1 0 0 0] [0 1 0 0] [0 0 1 0] [0 0 0 1]]
apples-MacBook-Air:chapter5 bhagvan.kommadi$
```

The next section talks about the **symmetric matrix** data structure.

Symmetric matrix

A symmetric matrix is a matrix whose transpose is equal to itself. Symmetric matrices include other types of matrices such as **antimetric**, **centrosymmetric**, **circulant**, **covariance**, **coxeter**, **hankel**, **hilbert**, **persymmetric**, **skew-symmetric**, and **toeplitz matrices**. A **negative matrix** is a matrix in which each element is a negative number.

Basic 2D matrix operations

In this section, we will look at the basic operations on the **two-dimensional matrix**. Let's start with initializing the matrices.

`matrix1` and `matrix2` are initialized in the following code snippet:

```
var matrix1 = [2][2] int{
    {4,5},
    {1,2}
}
var matrix2 = [2][2] int{
    {6,7},
    {3,4}
}
```

The `add`, `subtract`, `multiply`, `transpose`, and `inversion` operations are presented in the next few sections. For this section, please refer to the `binary_search_tree.go` file.

The add method

The `add` method adds the elements of two 2 x 2 matrices. The following code returns the created matrix by adding the two matrices:

```
// add method
func add(matrix1 [2][2]int, matrix2 [2][2]int) [2][2]int {
    var m int
    var l int
    var sum [2][2]int
    for l = 0; l < 2; l++ {
        for m=0; m <2; m++ {
            sum[l][m] = matrix1[l][m] +matrix2[l][m]
        }
    }
    return sum
}
```

The sum between the two matrices is the result of calling the `add` method. The parameters that are passed are the matrices to be added, as shown here:

```
var sum [2][2]int
sum = add(matrix1, matrix2)
```

The example output of the add method is as follows. Adding `matrix1` and `matrix2` gives a **sum matrix**:

```
add method
adding matrix1 [[4 5] [1 2]] matrix2 [[6 7] [3 4]]
after addition - sum [[10 12] [4 6]]
[[10 12] [4 6]]
```

The subtract method

The `subtract` method subtracts the elements of two 2 x 2 matrices. The `subtract` method in the following snippet subtracts the elements of `matrix1` and `matrix2`. This method returns the resulting matrix after subtraction:

```
// subtract method
func subtract(matrix1 [2][2]int, matrix2 [2][2]int) [2][2]int {
    var m int
    var l int
    var difference [2][2]int
    for l = 0; l < 2; l++ {
        for m=0; m <2; m++ {
            difference[l][m] = matrix1[l][m] -matrix2[l][m]
        }
    }
    return difference
}
```

The difference between two matrices is the result of calling the `subtract` method. The parameters that are passed are the matrices to be subtracted, as shown here:

```
var difference [2][2]int
difference = subtract(matrix1, matrix2)
```

The example output of the subtract method is as follows:

```
subtract method
difference of matrix1 [[4 5] [1 2]] and matrix2 [[6 7] [3 4]]
after subtraction - difference [[-2 -2] [-2 -2]]
[[-2 -2] [-2 -2]]
```

The multiply method

The multiply method multiplies the elements of two 2 x 2 matrices. The multiplication of two matrices, matrix1 and matrix2, is shown in the following snippet. The matrix that's generated after the multiplication is returned by the multiply method:

```
// multiply method
func multiply(matrix1 [2][2]int, matrix2 [2][2]int) [2][2]int {
     var m int
    var l int
    var n int
    var product [2][2]int
    for l = 0; l < 2; l++ {
        for m=0; m <2; m++ {
            var productSum int = 0
            for n=0; n< 2; n++ {
                productSum = productSum + matrix1[l][n]*matrix2[n][m]
            }
            product[l][m] = productSum;
        }
    }
    return product
}
```

The product of two matrices is calculated using the multiply method in the following code snippet, which takes the two matrices as parameters:

```
var product [2][2]int
product = multiply(matrix1, matrix2)
```

The example output of the multiply method is as follows. The product of matrix1 and matrix2 is the **product matrix**:

```
multiply method
product of matrix1 [[4 5] [1 2]] and matrix2 [[6 7] [3 4]]
after multiplication  product [[39 48] [12 15]]
[[39 48] [12 15]]
```

The transpose method

The transpose of a matrix is achieved using the `transpose` method. This method takes the matrix as a parameter and returns the transposed matrix:

```
// transpose method
func transpose(matrix1 [2][2]int) [2][2]int {
    var m intvar l int
    var transMatrix [2][2]int
    for l = 0; l < 2; l++ {
        for m=0; m <2; m++ {
            transMatrix[l][m] = matrix1[m][l]
        }
    }
    return transMatrix
}
```

The determinant method

The `determinant` method calculates the determinant of the matrix. The `determinant` method in the following code snippet calculates the `determinant` value of a matrix. The method takes the matrix and returns a `float32` value, which is the `determinant` of the matrix:

```
// determinant method
func determinant(matrix1 [2][2]int) float32 {
    var m int
    var l int
    var det float32
    det = det + ( (matrix1[0][0]*matrix1[1][1])-
(matrix1[0][1]*matrix1[1][0]));
    return det
}
```

The inverse method

The `inverse` method returns the inverse of the matrix, which is passed as a parameter. This is shown in the following snippet:

```
//inverse method
func inverse(matrix [2][2]int) [][]float64 {
  var det float64
  det = determinant(matrix)
  var invmatrix float64
```

```
    invmatrix[0][0] = matrix[1][1]/det
    invmatrix[0][1] = -1*matrix[0][1]/det
    invmatrix[1][0] = -1*matrix[1][0]/det
    invmatrix[1][1] = matrix[0][0]/det
    return invmatrix
}
```

Run the following command to execute the `twodmatrix.go` file:

```
go run twodmatrix.go
```

The output is as follows:

```
Bhagvans-MacBook-Pro:chapter5 bhagvankommadi$ go run twodmatrix.go
[[10 12] [4 6]]
[[-2 -2] [-2 -2]]
[[39 48] [12 15]]
Bhagvans-MacBook-Pro:chapter5 bhagvankommadi$
```

The next section talks about the zig-zag matrix data structure.

Zig-zag matrix

A zig-zag matrix is a square arrangement of *n* x *n* integers. The integers are arranged on anti-diagonals in sequentially increasing order. The following code explains how to create a zig-zag matrix and also how to traverse it. The `PrintZigZag` method creates the matrix in a zig-zag fashion with the elements in a sequentially increasing order. The method takes the integer `n` as a parameter and returns the integer array, which is the zig-zag matrix:

```
///main package has examples shown
// in Go Data Structures and algorithms book
package main
// importing fmt package
import (
    "fmt"
)
//prints the matrix in zig-zag fashion
func PrintZigZag(n int) []int {
    var zigzag []int
    zigzag = make([]int, n*n)
    var i int
    i = 0
    var m int
    m = n * 2
    var  p int
```

```
        for p = 1; p <= m; p++ {
            var x int
            x = p - n
            if x < 0 {
               x = 0
            }
            var y int
            y = p - 1
            if y > n-1 {
                y = n - 1
           }
           var j int
           j = m - p
            if j > p {
                j = p
            }
            var k int
            for k = 0; k < j; k++ {
               if p&1 == 0 {
                   zigzag[(x+k)*n+y-k] = i
               } else {
                   zigzag[(y-k)*n+x+k] = i
                }
               i++
            }
       }
       return zigzag
   }
```

The main method invokes the PrintZigZag method, which takes the parameter n and prints the matrix first from left to right, then from right to left for the second level, and so on. The number of integers is 5 and the field width is 2:

```
   // main method
   func main() {
     var n int
     n = 5
     var length int
       length = 2
       var i int
       var sketch int
       for i, sketch = range PrintZigZag(n) {
          fmt.Printf("%*d ", length, sketch)
           if i%n == n-1 {
               fmt.Println("")
          }
      }
   }
```

Run the following command to execute the `zigzagmatrix.go` file:

```
go run zigzagmatrix.go
```

The output is as follows:

```
Bhagvans-MacBook-Pro:chapter5 bhagvankommadi$ go run zigzagmatrix.go
 0  1  5  6 14
 2  4  7 13 15
 3  8 12 16 21
 9 11 17 20 22
10 18 19 23 24
Bhagvans-MacBook-Pro:chapter5 bhagvankommadi$
```

The next section talks about the spiral matrix data structure.

Spiral matrix

A spiral matrix is an arrangement of *n* x *n* integers in which integers are arranged spirally in sequentially increasing order. A spiral matrix is an **old toy algorithm**. The spiral order is maintained using four loops, one for each corner of the matrix. The `PrintSpiral` method in the following code snippet creates a matrix with elements arranged spirally in increasing order. The method takes a parameter, `n`, and returns an integer array:

```
///main package has examples shown
// in Go Data Structures and algorithms book
package main
// importing fmt package
import (
    "fmt"
)
//PrintSpiral method
func PrintSpiral(n int) []int {

    var left int
    var top int
    var right int
    var bottom int

    left =0
    top =0
    right = n-1
    bottom = n-1
    var size int
```

```
    size = n * n
    var s []int
    s = make([]int, size)

    var i int
    i = 0
    for left < right {
        var c int
        for c = left; c <= right; c++ {
            s[top*n+c] = i
            i++
        }
        top++
        var r int
        for r = top; r <= bottom; r++ {
            s[r*n+right] = i
            i++
        }
        right--
        if top == bottom {
            break
        }
        for c = right; c >= left; c-- {
            s[bottom*n+c] = i
            i++
        }
        bottom--
        for r = bottom; r >= top; r-- {
            s[r*n+left] = i
            i++
        }
        left++
    }
    s[top*n+left] = i

    return s
}
```

In the following code snippet, the `main` method invokes the `PrintSpiral` method, which takes the integer `n` and prints the integer values of the matrix spirally. The values returned from the `PrintSpiral` method are printed as fields with a width of `2`:

```
func main() {
   var n int
    n = 5
  var length int
    length = 2
    var i int
```

```
        var sketch int
        for i, sketch = range PrintSpiral(n) {
            fmt.Printf("%*d ", length, sketch)
            if i%n == n-1 {
                fmt.Println("")
            }
        }
    }
```

Run the following command to execute the `spiralmatrix.go` file:

```
go run spiralmatrix.go
```

The output is as follows:

```
Bhagvans-MacBook-Pro:chapter5 bhagvankommadi$ go run spiralmatrix.go
 0  1  2  3  4
15 16 17 18  5
14 23 24 19  6
13 22 21 20  7
12 11 10  9  8
Bhagvans-MacBook-Pro:chapter5 bhagvankommadi$
```

The next section talks about the **Boolean matrix** data structure.

Boolean matrix

A Boolean matrix is a matrix that consists of elements in the mth row and the nth column with a value of 1. A matrix can be modified to be a Boolean matrix by making the values in the mth row and the nth column equal to 1. In the following code, the Boolean matrix transformation and print methods are shown in detail. The `changeMatrix` method transforms the input matrix in to a Boolean matrix by changing the row and column values from 0 to 1 if the cell value is 1. The method takes the input matrix as the parameter and returns the changed matrix, as shown in the following code:

```
///main package has examples shown
// in Go Data Structures and algorithms book
package main

// importing fmt package
import (
    "fmt"
)
//changeMatrix method
```

```
func changeMatrix(matrix [3][3]int) [3][3]int {
    var i int
    var j int
    var Rows [3]int
    var Columns [3]int

    var matrixChanged [3][3]int

    for i=0; i<3; i++{
      for j=0; j < 3; j++{
          if matrix[i][j]==1 {
             Rows[i] =1
             Columns[j] =1
          }

      }
     }

    for i=0; i<3; i++ {
     for j=0; j<3; j++{
       if Rows[i]==1 || Columns[j]==1{
       matrixChanged[i][j] = 1
       }

     }
   }

   return matrixChanged

}
```

The example output of the change matrix method is shown the following screenshot. The elements with **1** in the row or column are checked and the row elements are updated to **1**:

```
inside changeMatrix method
before initializing the elements to 1 if the row or column contains 1
100
000
000
after initializing the elements to 1 if the row or column contains 1
111
100
100
```

Let's take a look at the `printMatrix` method and the `main` method.

The printMatrix method

In the following code snippet, the `printMatrix` method takes the input matrix and prints the matrix values by row and traverses the columns for every row:

```
//printMatrix method
func printMatrix(matrix [3][3]int) {
   var i int
   var j int
   //var k int
   for i=0; i< 3; i++ {

     for j=0; j < 3;j++ {

          fmt.Printf("%d",matrix[i][j])

     }
     fmt.Printf("\n")
   }


}
```

The main method

The `main` method in the following code snippet invokes the `changeMatrix` method after initializing the matrix. The changed matrix is printed after the invocation of the `changeMatrix` method:

```
//main method
func main() {

 var matrix = [3][3] int {{1,0,0},{0,0,0},{0,0,0}}

 printMatrix(matrix)


 matrix = changeMatrix(matrix)

 printMatrix(matrix)


}
```

Run the following command to execute the `boolean_matrix.go` file:

```
go run boolean_matrix.go
```

The output is as follows:

```
chapter5 — -bash — 80×24
Bhagvans-MacBook-Pro:chapter5 bhagvankommadi$ go run boolean_matrix.go
100
000
000
111
100
100
Bhagvans-MacBook-Pro:chapter5 bhagvankommadi$
```

The next section talks about multi-dimensional arrays.

Multi-dimensional arrays

An **array** is a homogeneous collection of data elements. An array's indexes range from index 0 to index *m*-1, where *m* is the fixed length of the array. An array with multiple dimensions is an array of an array. The following code initializes a multi-dimensional array. A three-dimensional array is printed:

```
///main package has examples shown
// in Go Data Structures and algorithms book
package main

// importing fmt package
import (
    "fmt"
    "math/rand"
)
//main method
func main() {

var threedarray [2][2][2]int

var i int

var j int

var k int
```

```
    for i=0; i < 2; i++ {

        for j=0; j < 2; j++ {

            for k=0; k < 2; k++ {

                threedarray[i][j][k] = rand.Intn(3)
            }
        }
    }

    fmt.Println(threedarray)
}
```

Run the following command to execute the preceding code snippet:

```
go run multidarray.go
```

The output is as follows:

```
chapter5 — -bash — 80×24
Bhagvans-MacBook-Pro:chapter5 bhagvankommadi$ go run multidarray.go
[[[2 0] [2 2]] [[1 0] [1 2]]]
Bhagvans-MacBook-Pro:chapter5 bhagvankommadi$
```

The next section talks about **tensor** data structures.

Tensors

A tensor is a multi-dimensional array of components that are spatial coordinates. Tensors are used extensively in physics and biological studies in topics such as electromagnetism and diffusion tensor imaging. William Rowan Hamilton was the first to come up with the term *tensor*. Tensors play a basic role in abstract algebra and algebraic topology.

The tensor order is the sum of the order of its arguments, plus the order of the result tensor. For example, an inertia matrix is a second-order tensor. Spinors are also multi-dimensional arrays, but the values of their elements change via coordinate transformations.

The initialization of a tensor is shown here. The array is initialized with integer values ranging from 0 to 3:

```
var array [3][3][3]int
var i int
var j int
```

```
var k int
for i=0; i < 3; i++ {
   for j=0; j < 3; j++ {
     for k=0; k < 3; k++ {

          array[i][j][k] = rand.Intn(3)
     }
   }
}
```

Unfolding a tensor is done along the first dimension. Rearranging the tensor mode's *n* vectors is referred to as mode *n*-unfolding of a tensor. 0-mode unfolding of a tensor array is shown here:

```
for j=0; j < 3; j++ {
  for k=0; k < 3; k++ {
      fmt.Printf("%d ",array[0][j][k])
  }
  fmt.Printf("\n")
}
```

1-mode unfolding of a tensor array is shown here. The array's first dimension index is set to 1:

```
for j=0; j < 3; j++ {
     for k=0; k < 3; k++ {
         fmt.Printf("%d ",array[1][j][k])
     }
     fmt.Printf("\n")
   }
```

The 2-mode unfolding of a tensor array is shown here. The array's first dimension row index is set to 2:

```
for j=0; j < 3; j++ {
           for k=0; k < 3; k++ {
               fmt.Printf("%d ",array[2][j][k])
           }
           fmt.Printf("\n")
         }
```

Run the following command to execute the `tensor.go` file:

```
go run tensor.go
```

The output is as follows:

```
chapter5 — -bash — 80×24
Bhagvans-MacBook-Pro:chapter5 bhagvankommadi$ go run tensor.go
[[[2 0 2] [2 1 0] [1 2 1]] [[0 2 1] [0 2 1] [2 0 2]] [[2 2 2] [0 2 1] [0 1 1]]]
zero mode unfold
2 0 2
2 1 0
1 2 1
1-mode unfold
0 2 1
0 2 1
2 0 2
2-mode unfold
2 2 2
0 2 1
0 1 1
Bhagvans-MacBook-Pro:chapter5 bhagvankommadi$
```

Summary

This chapter covered homogeneous data structures such as two-dimensional arrays and multi-dimensional arrays. Matrix operations such as sum, subtraction, multiplication, inverse, and determinant have been explained with code examples. Spiral matrices, zig-zag matrices, and Boolean matrices have been explained using two-dimensional arrays. Tensors and operations such as folding were also covered.

In the next chapter, heterogeneous data structures such as linked lists, ordered lists, and unordered lists will be covered.

Questions

1. What is 2-mode unfolding of a tensor array?
2. Write a two-dimensional array of strings and initialize it. Print the strings.
3. Give an example of a multi-dimensional array and traverse through it.
4. For a 3 x 3 matrix, write code that calculates the determinant of the matrix.
5. What is a transpose of a 3 x 3 matrix?
6. What is a zig-zag matrix?
7. Write code with an example of a spiral matrix.
8. Which dimension is typically unfolded for tensor arrays?
9. How do you define a Boolean matrix?
10. Choose two 3 x 3 matrices and find the product of the matrices.

Further reading

The following books are recommended if you want to learn more about arrays, matrices, and tensors:

- *Advanced Data Structures*, by Peter Brass
- *Dynamic Data Structures: Lists, Stacks, Queues, and Trees*, by Bogdan Patrut, and Tiberiu Socaciu
- *Data structures and Algorithms: An Easy Introduction*, by Rudolph Russell

6
Heterogeneous Data Structures

Heterogeneous data structures are data structures that contain diverse types of data, such as integers, doubles, and floats. **Linked lists** and **ordered lists** are good examples of these data structures. They are used for memory management. A linked list is a chain of elements that are associated together by means of pointers. Each element's pointer links to the following item, which connects the chain together. Linked lists don't have to take up a block of memory. The memory that they utilize can be allocated dynamically. It comprises a progression of nodes, which are the components of the list. Ordered lists and unordered lists from HTML are shown to demonstrate the usage of lists and storage management. We will cover linked lists, ordered lists, and unordered lists in this chapter and show the implementation of their methods with appropriate examples. This chapter covers the following heterogeneous data structures:

- Linked lists
- Ordered lists
- Unordered lists

We covered singly linked lists and doubly linked lists with code examples in `Chapter 3`, *Linear Data Structures*. Circular-linked lists were covered in `Chapter 4`, *Non-Linear Data Structures*.

Technical requirements

Install Go Version 1.10 for your OS from the following link: `https://golang.org/doc/install`.

The GitHub URL for the code in this chapter is as follows: `https://github.com/PacktPublishing/Learn-Data-Structures-and-Algorithms-with-Golang/tree/master/Chapter06`.

Linked lists

A linked list is a linear collection of elements with information. The linked list shrinks or expands based on whether the components are to be included or removed. This list can be small or enormous, yet, regardless of the size, the elements that make it up are straightforward. Linked lists were covered in `Chapter 3`, *Linear Data Structures*. They consume more memory than arrays. Reverse traversing is a problem for singly linked lists because a singly linked list points to the next node forward. The next section explains how to reverse a singly linked list with a code example.

Singly, doubly, and circular-linked lists will be covered in this chapter.

Singly linked lists

A singly linked list is a dynamic data structure in which addition and removal operations are easy; this is because it's a dynamic data structure and not fixed. Stack and queue data structures are implemented with linked lists. More memory is consumed when elements are dynamically added because dynamic data structures aren't fixed. Random retrieval is not possible with a singly linked list because you will need to traverse the nodes for a positioned node. Insertion into a singly linked list can be at the beginning or end of the list, and after a specified node. Deletion can happen at the beginning or end of the list and after a specified node.

Reversing a singly linked list is shown in this section. The methods that are explained in this section are a part of the `linked_list.go` file that's provided in the code bundle.

The `Node` class is defined in this snippet with a node pointer, `nextNode`, and a `rune` property:

```
//main package has examples shown
// in Go Data Structures and algorithms book
package main

// importing fmt package
import (
    "fmt"
)

// Node struct
type Node struct {
    nextNode *Node
    property rune
}
```

The methods of singly linked lists are discussed in the following sections.

The CreateLinkedList method

The `CreateLinkedList` method creates a linked list of runes from *a* to *z*:

```
// create List method
func CreateLinkedList() *Node {
    var headNode *Node
    headNode = &Node{nil, 'a'}
    var currNode *Node
    currNode = headNode
    var i rune
    for i= 'b'; i <= 'z'; i++ {
        var node *Node
        node = &Node{nil, i}
        currNode.nextNode = node
        currNode = node
    }
    return headNode
}
```

The example output for the create linked list is shown as follows. The `headNode` is created with a value of `97`. The linked list is created with nodes starting from *a* to *z*:

```
Create Linked List method
head Node after creation &{<nil> 97}
head Node &{0xc00000e200 97}
abcdefghijklmnopqrstuvwxyz
```

The ReverseLinkedList method

The `ReverseLinkedList` function takes a node pointer, `nodeList`, and returns a node pointer to a reversed linked list.

The following code snippet shows how the linked list is reversed:

```
// Reverse List method
func ReverseLinkedList(nodeList *Node) *Node {
    var currNode *Node
    currNode = nodeList
    var topNode *Node = nil
    for {
        if currNode == nil {
            break
```

```
        }
        var tempNode *Node
        tempNode = currNode.nextNode
        currNode.nextNode = topNode
        topNode = currNode
        currNode = tempNode
    }
    return topNode
}
```

The example output for the reverse linked list method is as follows. The method takes the parameter of a linked string starting from *a* to *z*. The reversed list is from *z* to *a* nodes:

```
Reverse Linked List method
after reverse &{0xc00000e370 122}
zyxwvutsrqponmlkjihgfedcba
apples-MacBook-Air:ch6 bhagvan.kommadi$
```

The main method

The `main` method creates the linked list, and prints the linked list and the reversed list in string format:

```
// main method
func main() {
    var linkedList = CreateLinkedList()
    StringifyList(linkedList)
    StringifyList(ReverseLinkedList(linkedList))
}
```

Run the following command to execute the `linked_list.go` file:

```
go run linked_list.go
```

This is the output:

```
chapter6 — -bash — 80×24
apples-MacBook-Air:chapter6 bhagvan.kommadi$ go run linked_list.go
abcdefghijklmnopqrstuvwxyz
zyxwvutsrqponmlkjihgfedcba
apples-MacBook-Air:chapter6 bhagvan.kommadi$
```

The next section talks about the doubly linked list data structure.

Doubly linked lists

A doubly linked list is a data structure that consists of nodes that have links to the previous and the next nodes. Doubly linked lists were presented with code examples in `Chapter 3`, *Linear Data Structures*. Lists in Go are implemented as doubly linked lists. The elements `14` and `1` are pushed backward and forward, respectively. The elements `6` and `5` are inserted before and after. The doubly linked list is iterated and the elements are printed. The code in this section shows how lists can be used:

```
//main package has examples shown
// in Go Data Structures and algorithms book
package main

// importing fmt and list package
import (
    "container/list"
    "fmt"
)

// main method
func main() {
    var linkedList *list.List
    linkedList = list.New()
    var element *list.Element
    element = linkedList.PushBack(14)
    var frontElement *list.Element
    frontElement = linkedList.PushFront(1)
    linkedList.InsertBefore(6, element)
    linkedList.InsertAfter(5, frontElement)

    var currElement *list.Element
    for currElement = linkedList.Front(); currElement != nil; currElement =
    currElement.Next() {
        fmt.Println(currElement.Value)
    }
}
```

Run the following command to execute the `double_linked_list.go` file:

```
go run double_linked_list.go
```

This is the output:

```
apples-MacBook-Air:chapter6 bhagvan.kommadi$ go run double_linked_list.go
1
5
6
14
apples-MacBook-Air:chapter6 bhagvan.kommadi$
```

The next section talks about the circular-linked list data structure.

Circular-linked lists

A circular-linked list is a collection of nodes in which the last node is connected to the first node. Circular-linked lists were briefly covered in `Chapter 4`, *Non-Linear Data Structures*. Circular-linked lists are used to create a circular queue.

In the following section, a circular queue struct is defined and implemented. The methods that are explained in this section are part of the `circular_queue.go` file given in the code bundle.

The CircularQueue class

The `CircularQueue` class has `size`, `head`, and last integer properties, as well as a `nodes` array. The class is defined in the following code snippet:

```
//main package has examples shown
// in Go Data Structures and algorithms book
package main

// importing fmt package
import (
    "fmt"
)

//Circular Queue
type CircularQueue struct {
    size int
    nodes []interface{}
    head int
    last int
}
```

Let's discuss the different methods of the `CircularQueue` class in the following sections.

The NewQueue method

The `NewQueue` method creates a new instance of the circular queue. The `NewQueue` function takes the `num` parameter, which is the `size` of the queue. The function returns the circular queue of nodes, as shown in the following code:

```
// NewCircularQueue method
func NewQueue(num int) *CircularQueue {
    var circularQueue CircularQueue
    circularQueue = CircularQueue{size: num + 1, head: 0, last: 0}
    circularQueue.nodes = make([]interface{}, circularQueue.size)
    return &circularQueue
}
```

The IsUnUsed method

The `IsUnUsed` method of the `CircularQueue` class in the following snippet checks whether `head` is equal to the `last` node and returns `true` if so; otherwise, it returns `false`:

```
// IsUnUsed method
func (circularQueue CircularQueue) IsUnUsed() bool {
    return circularQueue.head == circularQueue.last
}
```

The IsComplete method

The `IsComplete` function of the `CircularQueue` class returns `true` if the head node's position is the same as the `last` node position `+1`; otherwise, it returns `false`:

```
// IsComplete method
func (circularQueue CircularQueue) IsComplete() bool {
    return circularQueue.head == (circularQueue.last+1)%circularQueue.size
}
```

The Add method

This method adds the given element to the circular queue. In the following code snippet, the `Add` method takes an `element` parameter of the interface type and adds the `element` to the circular queue:

```
// Add method
func (circularQueue *CircularQueue) Add(element interface{}) {
    if circularQueue.IsComplete() {
        panic("Queue is Completely Utilized")
    }
    circularQueue.nodes[circularQueue.last] = element
    circularQueue.last = (circularQueue.last + 1) % circularQueue.size
}
```

The example output for the `Add` method is as follows. The `Add` method takes the `element` with value `1` and updates the queue:

```
Add method element 1
before adding queue [<nil> <nil> <nil> <nil> <nil> <nil>]
after adding queue [1 <nil> <nil> <nil> <nil> <nil>]
```

The MoveOneStep method

The `MoveOnestep` method moves the `element` one step forward in the circular queue. The `MoveOneStep` method takes the `element` parameter of the interface type and moves the `head` node to position two after setting the `element` as the `head` node:

```
//MoveOneStep method
func (circularQueue *CircularQueue) MoveOneStep() (element interface{}) {
    if circularQueue.IsUnUsed() {
        return nil
    }
    element = circularQueue.nodes[circularQueue.head]
    circularQueue.head = (circularQueue.head + 1) % circularQueue.size
    return
}
```

The main method

The `main` method creates the queue and adds elements to the circular queue:

```
// main method
func main() {
   var circularQueue *CircularQueue
```

```
    circularQueue = NewQueue(5)
    circularQueue.Add(1)
    circularQueue.Add(2)
    circularQueue.Add(3)
    circularQueue.Add(4)
    circularQueue.Add(5)
    fmt.Println(circularQueue.nodes)

}
```

Run the following command to execute the `circular_queue.go` file:

```
go run circular_queue.go
```

This is the output:

```
chapter6 — -bash — 80×24
apples-MacBook-Air:chapter6 bhagvan.kommadi$ go run circular_queue.go
[1 2 3 4 5 <nil>]
apples-MacBook-Air:chapter6 bhagvan.kommadi$
```

In the following sections, ordered lists and unordered lists are explained with code examples.

Ordered lists

Lists in Go can be sorted in two ways:

- **Ordered list**: By creating a group of methods for the slice data type and calling `sort`
- **Unordered list**: The other way is to invoke `sort.Slice` with a custom `less` function

The only difference between an ordered list and an unordered list is that, in an ordered list, the order in which the items are displayed is mandatory.

An ordered list in HTML starts with an `<ol>` tag. Each item in the list is written in `<li>` tags. Here's an example:

```
<ol>
    <li>Stones</li>
    <li>Branches</li>
    <li>Smoke</li>
</ol>
```

An example of an ordered list using Golang is shown in the following code snippet. The `Employee` class has `Name`, `ID`, `SSN`, and `Age` properties:

```
///main package has examples shown
// in Go Data Structures and algorithms book
package main

// importing fmt and sort package
import (
    "fmt"
    "sort"
)

// class Employee
type Employee struct {
    Name string
    ID string
    SSN int
    Age int
}
```

The methods that are explained in the following sections are a part of the `linked_list.go` file that's provided in the code bundle.

The ToString method

The `ToString` method of the `Employee` class returns a `string` version of employee. The `string` version consists of a comma-separated `Name`, `Age`, `ID`, and `SSN`. This is shown in the following code snippet:

```
// ToString method
func (employee Employee) ToString() string {
    return fmt.Sprintf("%s: %d,%s,%d", employee.Name,
employee.Age,employee.ID,
    employee.SSN)
}
```

The SortByAge type

The `SortByAge` method sorts the elements concerned by `Age`. The `SortByAge` interface operates on the `Employee` array. This is shown in the following code snippet:

```
// SortByAge type
type SortByAge []Employee

// SortByAge interface methods
func (sortIntf SortByAge) Len() int { return len(sortIntf) }
func (sortIntf SortByAge) Swap(i int, j int) { sortIntf[i], sortIntf[j] =
sortIntf[j], sortIntf[i] }
func (sortIntf SortByAge) Less(i int, j int) bool { return sortIntf[i].Age
< sortIntf[j].Age }
```

The `main` method initializes the employees array and sorts the array by age:

```
func main() {
    var employees = []Employee{
        {"Graham","231",235643,31},
        {"John", "3434",245643,42},
        {"Michael","8934",32432, 17},
        {"Jenny", "24334",32444,26},
    }
    fmt.Println(employees)
    sort.Sort(SortByAge(employees))
    fmt.Println(employees)
    sort.Slice(employees, func(i int, j int) bool {
        return employees[i].Age > employees[j].Age
    })
    fmt.Println(employees)
}
```

Run the following command to execute the `sort_slice.go` snippet:

```
go run sort_slice.go
```

This is the output:

```
chapter6 — -bash — 80×24
apples-MacBook-Air:chapter6 bhagvan.kommadi$ go run sort_slice.go
[{Graham 231 235643 31} {John 3434 245643 42} {Michael 8934 32432 17} {Jenny 243
34 32444 26}]
[{Michael 8934 32432 17} {Jenny 24334 32444 26} {Graham 231 235643 31} {John 343
4 245643 42}]
[{John 3434 245643 42} {Graham 231 235643 31} {Jenny 24334 32444 26} {Michael 89
34 32432 17}]
apples-MacBook-Air:chapter6 bhagvan.kommadi$
```

An ordered list is sorted using the sort criteria as follows. The `sort_keys.go` code snippet shows how things are sorted by various criteria, such as `name`, `mass`, and `distance`. The `Mass` and `Miles` units are defined as `float64`:

```
///main package has examples shown
// in Go Data Structures and algorithms book
package main

// importing fmt and sort package
import (
    "fmt"
    "sort"
)

// Mass and Miles Types
type Mass float64
type Miles float64
```

The next section talks about the `Thing` struct definition.

The Thing class

A `Thing` class is defined in the following code with `name`, `mass`, `distance`, `meltingpoint`, and `freezingpoint` properties:

```
// Thing class
type Thing struct {
    name string
    mass Mass
    distance Miles
    meltingpoint int
    freezingpoint int
}
```

The next section talks about the `ByFactor` function type.

The ByFactor function type

`ByFactor` is a type of `less` function. The following code snippet shows the `ByFactor` type:

```
// ByFactor function type
type ByFactor func(Thing1 *Thing, Thing2 *Thing) bool
```

The Sort method

The `Sort` method is a function with the `byFactor` parameter, as shown here:

```
// Sort method
func (byFactor ByFactor) Sort(Things []Thing) {
    var sortedThings *ThingSorter
    sortedThings = &ThingSorter{
        Things: Things,
        byFactor: byFactor,
    }
    sort.Sort(sortedThings)
}
```

Thing sorter class

The `Thing` sorter sorts the elements by their properties. The `ThingSorter` class has an array of things and a `byFactor` method:

```
// ThingSorter class
type ThingSorter struct {
    Things []Thing
    byFactor func(Thing1 *Thing, Thing2 *Thing) bool
}
```

The next section talks about the implementation of the `len`, `swap`, and `less` methods.

The len, swap, and less methods

The `sort.Interface` has the `len`, `swap`, and `less` methods, as shown in the following code:

```
// Len method
func (ThingSorter *ThingSorter) Len() int {
    return len(ThingSorter.Things)
}

// Swap method
func (ThingSorter *ThingSorter) Swap(i int, j int) {
    ThingSorter.Things[i], ThingSorter.Things[j] = ThingSorter.Things[j],
    ThingSorter.Things[i]
}

// Less method
func (ThingSorter *ThingSorter) Less(i int, j int) bool {
    return ThingSorter.byFactor(&ThingSorter.Things[i],
&ThingSorter.Things[j])
}
```

The main method

The `main` method creates things and initializes them with values. This method shows things that are sorted by `mass`, `distance`, and `name` in decreasing order of distance:

```
// Main method
func main() {
  var Things = []Thing{
    {"IronRod", 0.055, 0.4, 3000, -180},
    {"SteelChair", 0.815, 0.7, 4000, -209},
    {"CopperBowl", 1.0, 1.0, 60, -30},
    {"BrassPot", 0.107, 1.5, 10000, -456},
  }

  var name func(*Thing, *Thing) bool
  name = func(Thing1 *Thing, Thing2 *Thing) bool {
    return Thing1.name < Thing2.name
  }
  var mass func(*Thing, *Thing) bool
  mass = func(Thing1 *Thing, Thing2 *Thing) bool {
    return Thing1.mass < Thing2.mass
  }
  var distance func(*Thing, *Thing) bool
  distance = func(Thing1 *Thing, Thing2 *Thing) bool {
```

```
    return Thing1.distance < Thing2.distance
  }
  var decreasingDistance func(*Thing, *Thing) bool
  decreasingDistance = func(p1, p2 *Thing) bool {
    return distance(p2, p1)
  }

  ByFactor(name).Sort(Things)
  fmt.Println("By name:", Things)
  ByFactor(mass).Sort(Things)
  fmt.Println("By mass:", Things)
  ByFactor(distance).Sort(Things)
  fmt.Println("By distance:", Things)
  ByFactor(decreasingDistance).Sort(Things)
  fmt.Println("By decreasing distance:", Things)
}
```

Run the following command to execute the `sort_keys.go` file:

```
go run sort_keys.go
```

This is the output:

```
chapter6 — -bash — 80×24
apples-MacBook-Air:chapter6 bhagvan.kommadi$ go run sort_keys.go
By name: [{BrassPot 0.107 1.5 10000 -456} {CopperBowl 1 1 60 -30} {IronRod 0.055
 0.4 3000 -180} {SteelChair 0.815 0.7 4000 -209}]
By mass: [{IronRod 0.055 0.4 3000 -180} {BrassPot 0.107 1.5 10000 -456} {SteelCh
air 0.815 0.7 4000 -209} {CopperBowl 1 1 60 -30}]
By distance: [{IronRod 0.055 0.4 3000 -180} {SteelChair 0.815 0.7 4000 -209} {Co
pperBowl 1 1 60 -30} {BrassPot 0.107 1.5 10000 -456}]
By decreasing distance: [{BrassPot 0.107 1.5 10000 -456} {CopperBowl 1 1 60 -30}
 {SteelChair 0.815 0.7 4000 -209} {IronRod 0.055 0.4 3000 -180}]
apples-MacBook-Air:chapter6 bhagvan.kommadi$
```

The next section talks about the `struct` data structure.

The struct type

A `struct` type (class) can be sorted using different sets of multiple fields. In the `sort_multi_keys.go` code, we show how to sort `struct` types. A class called `Commit` consists of the `username`, `lang`, and `numlines` properties. `username` is a string, `lang` is a string, and `numlines` is an integer. In the following code, the `Commit` class is sorted by commits and lines:

```
///main package has examples shown
// in Go Data Structures and algorithms book
package main

// importing fmt and sort package
import (
  "fmt"
  "sort"
)

// A Commit is a record of code checkin
type Commit struct {
  username string
  lang string
  numlines int
}
```

In the next section, the implementation of the `multiSorter` class is discussed.

The multiSorter class

The `multiSorter` class consists of the commits and `lessFunction` array properties. The `multiSorter` class implements the `Sort` interface to sort the commits, as shown in the following code:

```
type lessFunc func(p1 *Commit, p2 *Commit) bool
// multiSorter class
type multiSorter struct {
 Commits []Commit
 lessFunction    []lessFunc
}
```

The different methods of the `multiSorter` class are discussed in the following sections.

The Sort method

In the following code snippet, the `Sort` method of `multiSorter` sorts the `Commits` array by invoking `sort.Sort` and passing the `multiSorter` argument:

```
// Sort method
func (multiSorter *multiSorter) Sort(Commits []Commit) {
    multiSorter.Commits = Commits
    sort.Sort(multiSorter)
}
```

The OrderBy method

The `OrderedBy` method takes the `less` function and returns `multiSorter`. The `multisorter` instance is initialized by the `less` function, as shown in the following code snippet:

```
// OrderedBy method
func OrderedBy(lessFunction ...lessFunc) *multiSorter {
  return &multiSorter{
    lessFunction: lessFunction,
  }
}
```

The len method

The `len` method of the `multiSorter` class returns the length of the `Commits` array. The `Commits` array is a property of `multiSorter`:

```
// Len method
func (multiSorter *multiSorter) Len() int {
 return len(multiSorter.Commits)
}
```

The Swap method

The `Swap` method of `multiSorter` takes the integers `i` and `j` as input. This method swaps the array elements at index `i` and `j`:

```
// Swap method
func (multiSorter *multiSorter) Swap(i int, j int) {
  multiSorter.Commits[i] = multiSorter.Commits[j]
  multiSorter.Commits[j] = multiSorter.Commits[i]
}
```

The less method

The `Less` method of the `multiSorter` class takes the integers *i* and *j* and compares the element at index *i* to the element at index *j*:

```
func (multiSorter *multiSorter) Less(i int, j int) bool {

  var p *Commit
  var q *Commit
  p = &multiSorter.Commits[i]
  q = &multiSorter.Commits[j]

  var k int
  for k = 0; k < len(multiSorter.lessFunction)-1; k++ {
    less := multiSorter.lessFunction[k]
    switch {
    case less(p, q):
      return true
    case less(q, p):
      return false
    }
  }
  return multiSorter.lessFunction[k](p, q)
}
```

The main method

The `main` method creates a `Commit` array and initializes the array with values. Functions are created for sorting by `user`, `language`, and `lines`. `OrderedBy` returns a `multiSorter`, and its `sort` method is called by `user`, `language`, `increasingLines`, and `decreasingLines`:

```
//main method
func main() {
  var Commits = []Commit{
    {"james", "Javascript", 110},
    {"ritchie", "python", 250},
    {"fletcher", "Go", 300},
    {"ray", "Go", 400},
    {"john", "Go", 500},
    {"will", "Go", 600},
    {"dan", "C++", 500},
    {"sam", "Java", 650},
    {"hayvard", "Smalltalk", 180},
  }
  var user func(*Commit, *Commit) bool
  user = func(c1 *Commit, c2 *Commit) bool {
```

```
    return c1.username < c2.username
  }
  var language func(*Commit, *Commit) bool
  language = func(c1 *Commit, c2 *Commit) bool {
    return c1.lang < c2.lang
  }
  var increasingLines func(*Commit, *Commit) bool
  increasingLines = func(c1 *Commit, c2 *Commit) bool {
    return c1.numlines < c2.numlines
  }
  var decreasingLines func(*Commit, *Commit) bool
  decreasingLines = func(c1 *Commit, c2 *Commit) bool {
    return c1.numlines > c2.numlines // Note: > orders downwards.
  }
  OrderedBy(user).Sort(Commits)
  fmt.Println("By username:", Commits)
  OrderedBy(user, increasingLines).Sort(Commits)
  fmt.Println("By username,asc order", Commits)
  OrderedBy(user, decreasingLines).Sort(Commits)
  fmt.Println("By username,desc order", Commits)
  OrderedBy(language, increasingLines).Sort(Commits)
  fmt.Println("By lang,asc order", Commits)
  OrderedBy(language, decreasingLines, user).Sort(Commits)
  fmt.Println("By lang,desc order", Commits)
}
```

Run the following command to execute the `sort_multi_keys.go` file:

```
go run sort_multi_keys.go
```

This is the output:

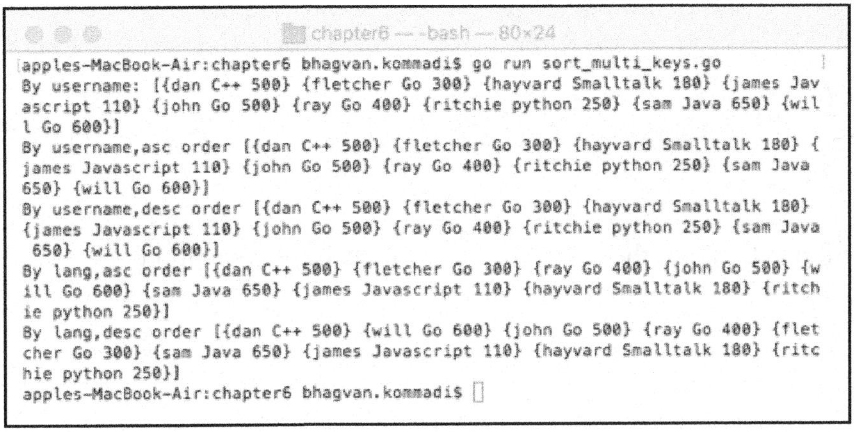

```
chapter6 — -bash — 80×24
apples-MacBook-Air:chapter6 bhagvan.kommadi$ go run sort_multi_keys.go
By username: [{dan C++ 500} {fletcher Go 300} {hayvard Smalltalk 180} {james Jav
ascript 110} {john Go 500} {ray Go 400} {ritchie python 250} {sam Java 650} {wil
l Go 600}]
By username,asc order [{dan C++ 500} {fletcher Go 300} {hayvard Smalltalk 180} {
james Javascript 110} {john Go 500} {ray Go 400} {ritchie python 250} {sam Java
650} {will Go 600}]
By username,desc order [{dan C++ 500} {fletcher Go 300} {hayvard Smalltalk 180}
{james Javascript 110} {john Go 500} {ray Go 400} {ritchie python 250} {sam Java
 650} {will Go 600}]
By lang,asc order [{dan C++ 500} {fletcher Go 300} {ray Go 400} {john Go 500} {w
ill Go 600} {sam Java 650} {james Javascript 110} {hayvard Smalltalk 180} {ritch
ie python 250}]
By lang,desc order [{dan C++ 500} {will Go 600} {john Go 500} {ray Go 400} {flet
cher Go 300} {sam Java 650} {james Javascript 110} {hayvard Smalltalk 180} {ritc
hie python 250}]
apples-MacBook-Air:chapter6 bhagvan.kommadi$
```

The next section talks about the HTML unordered list data structure.

Unordered lists

An **unordered list** is implemented as a linked list. In an unordered list, the relative positions of items in contiguous memory don't need to be maintained. The values will be placed in a random fashion.

An unordered list starts with a `<ul>` tag in HTML 5.0. Each list item is coded with `<li>` tags. Here's an example:

```
<ul>
    <li> First book </li>
    <li> Second book </li>
    <li> Third book </li>
</ul>
```

The following is an example of an unordered list in Golang. The `Node` class has a property and a `nextNode` pointer, as shown in the following code. The linked list will have a set of nodes with a property attribute. The unordered list is presented in the script called `unordered_list.go`:

```
//main package has examples shown
// in Hands-On Data Structures and algorithms with Go book
package main

// importing fmt package
import (
    "fmt"
)

//Node class
type Node struct {
    property int
    nextNode *Node
}
```

The next section talks about the `UnOrderedList` class implementation.

The UnOrderedList class

The unordered list consists of elements that are not ordered by numbers. An `UnOrderedList` class has a `headNode` pointer as the property. Traversing to the next node from the head node, you can iterate through the linked list:

```
// UnOrderedList class
type UnOrderedList struct {
    headNode *Node
}
```

The next section discusses the `AddtoHead` method and the `IterateList` method of the `UnOrderedList` struct.

The AddtoHead method

The `AddtoHead` method adds the node to the head of the unordered list. The `AddToHead` method of the `UnOrderedList` class has a property parameter that's an integer. It will make the `headNode` point to a new node created with `property`, and the `nextNode` points to the current `headNode` of the unordered list:

```
//AddToHead method of UnOrderedList class
func (UnOrderedList *UnOrderedList) AddToHead(property int) {
  var node = &Node{}
  node.property = property
  node.nextNode = nil
  if UnOrderedList.headNode != nil {
    node.nextNode = UnOrderedList.headNode
  }
  UnOrderedList.headNode = node
}
```

The IterateList method

The `IterateList` method of the `UnOrderedList` class prints the node property of the nodes in the list. This is shown in the following code:

```
//IterateList method iterates over UnOrderedList
func (UnOrderedList *UnOrderedList) IterateList() {
  var node *Node
  for node = UnOrderedList.headNode; node != nil; node = node.nextNode {
    fmt.Println(node.property)
  }
}
```

The main method

The `main` method creates an instance of a linked list, and integer properties `1`, `3`, `5`, and `7` are added to the head of the linked list. The linked list's `headNode` property is printed after the elements are added:

```
// main method
func main() {
  var unOrderedList UnOrderedList
  unOrderedList = UnOrderedList{}
  unOrderedList.AddToHead(1)
  unOrderedList.AddToHead(3)
  unOrderedList.AddToHead(5)
  unOrderedList.AddToHead(7)
  unOrderedList.IterateList()
}
```

Run the following command to execute the `unordered_list.go` file from the code bundle:

```
go run unordered_list.go
```

This is the output:

```
chapter6 — -bash — 80×24
apples-MacBook-Air:chapter6 bhagvan.kommadi$ go run unordered_list.go
7
5
3
1
apples-MacBook-Air:chapter6 bhagvan.kommadi$
```

Summary

This chapter covered heterogeneous data structures such as ordered lists and unordered lists with code examples. The *Ordered lists* section covered sorting slices by single key, multiple keys, and `sort.Slice`. Slices are sorted by making the array of struct elements implement the `sort.Sort` interface. Unordered lists were described as linked lists with values that are not ordered.

The next chapter will cover dynamic data structures such as **dictionaries**, **TreeSets**, **sequences**, **synchronized TreeSets**, and **mutable TreeSets**.

Questions

1. Which method of the `sort.Sort` interface returns the size of the elements to be sorted?
2. Which function needs to be passed to the `sort.Slice` method to sort a slice?
3. What does the `swap` method do to the elements at the *i* and *j* indices?
4. What is the default order for sorting elements using `sort.Sort`?
5. How do you implement ascending and descending sorting with `sort.Slice`?
6. How do you sort an array and keep the original order of the elements?
7. Which interface is used to reverse the order of the data?
8. Show an example of sorting a slice.
9. Which method is called to add elements to an unordered list?
10. Write a code example of an unordered list of floats.

Further reading

The following books are recommended if you want to know more about heterogeneous data structures:

- *Design Patterns*, by Erich Gamma, Richard Helm, Ralph Johnson, and John Vlissides
- *Introduction to Algorithms – Third Edition*, by Thomas H. Cormen, Charles E. Leiserson, Ronald L. Rivest, and Clifford Stein
- *Data structures and Algorithms: An Easy Introduction*, by Rudolph Russell

7
Dynamic Data Structures

A **dynamic data structure** is a set of elements in memory that has the adaptability to expand or shrink. This ability empowers a software engineer to control precisely how much memory is used. Dynamic data structures are used for handling generic data in a key-value store. They can be used in distributed caching and storage management. Dynamic data structures are valuable in many circumstances in which dynamic addition or deletion of elements occur. They are comparable in capacity to a smaller relational database or an in-memory database. These data structures are used in marketing and customer relationship management applications. Dictionaries, TreeSets, and sequences are examples of dynamic data structures.

In this chapter, we will explain what dictionaries, TreeSets, and sequences are and show you how they are implemented with the help of code examples.

This chapter covers the following dynamic data structures:

- Dictionaries
- TreeSets:
    - Synchronized TreeSets
    - Mutable TreeSets
- Sequences:
    - Farey
    - Fibonacci
    - Look-and-say
    - Thue–Morse

Technical requirements

Install Go Version 1.10 from `https://golang.org/doc/install` for your OS.

The GitHub URL for the code in this chapter is as follows: `https://github.com/PacktPublishing/Learn-Data-Structures-and-Algorithms-with-Golang/tree/master/Chapter07`.

Dictionaries

A **dictionary** is a collection of unique key and value pairs. A dictionary is a broadly useful data structure for storing a set of data items. It has a key, and each key has a solitary item associated with it. When given a key, the dictionary will restore the item associated with that key. These keys can be of any type: strings, integers, or objects. Where we need to sort a list, an element value can be retrieved utilizing its key. Add, remove, modify, and lookup operations are allowed in this collection. A dictionary is similar to other data structures, such as hash, map, and HashMap. The key/value store is used in distributed caching and in memory databases. Arrays differ from dictionaries in how the data is accessed. A set has unique items, whereas a dictionary can have duplicate values.

Dictionary data structures are used in the following streams:

- Phone directories
- Router tables in networking
- Page tables in operating systems
- Symbol tables in compilers
- Genome maps in biology

The following code shows how to initialize and modify a dictionary. In this snippet, the dictionary has the key `DictKey` and is a string:

```
//main package has examples shown
// in Go Data Structures and algorithms book
package main

// importing fmt package
import (
"fmt"
  "sync"
)

// DictKey type
```

```
type DictKey string
```

The following sections talk about the type and methods in dictionaries.

DictVal type

The dictionary has the value `DictVal` of type `string` mapped to `DictKey`:

```
// DictVal type
type DictVal string
```

Dictionary class

The dictionary in the following code is a class with dictionary elements, with `DictKey` as the key and `DictVal` as the value. It has a `sync.RWMutex` property, `lock`:

```
// Dictionary class
type Dictionary struct {
    elements map[DictKey]DictVal
    lock sync.RWMutex
}
```

The `Put`, `Remove`, `Contain`, `Find`, `Rest`, `NumberofElements`, `GetKeys`, `GetValues`, and `Main` methods are discussed in the following sections.

Put method

A has a `Put` method, as shown in the following example, that takes the `key` and `value` parameters of the `DictKey` and `DictVal` types respectively. The `Lock` method of the dictionary's `lock` instance is invoked, and the `Unlock` method is deferred. If there are empty `map` elements in the dictionary, elements are initialized using `make`.
The `map` elements are set with a `key` and a `value` if they are not empty:

```
// Put method
func (dict *Dictionary) Put(key DictKey, value DictVal) {
    dict.lock.Lock()
    defer dict.lock.Unlock()
    if dict.elements == nil {
        dict.elements = make(map[DictKey]DictVal)
    }
    dict.elements[key] = value
}
```

The example output of the `put` method is as follows. The `put` method takes the **key 1** and **value 1**. The `map` is updated with `key` and `value`:

```
Put method key 1 value 1
before putting the element dictionary map[]
after putting the element dictionary map[1:1]
```

Remove method

A dictionary has a `remove` method, as shown in the following code, which has a `key` parameter of the `DictKey` type. This method returns a `bool` value if the value associated with `Dictkey` is removed from the map:

```
// Remove method
func (dict *Dictionary) Remove(key DictKey) bool {
    dict.lock.Lock()
    defer dict.lock.Unlock()
    var exists bool
    _, exists = dict.elements[key]
    if exists {
        delete(dict.elements, key)
    }
    return exists
}
```

Contains method

In the following code, the `Contains` method has an input parameter, `key`, of the `DictKey` type, and returns `bool` if `key` exists in the dictionary:

```
// Contains method
func (dict *Dictionary) Contains(key DictKey) bool {
    dict.lock.RLock()
    defer dict.lock.RUnlock()
    var exists bool
    _, exists = dict.elements[key]
    return exists
}
```

Find method

The `Find` method takes the `key` parameter of the `DictKey` type and returns the `DictVal` type associated with the key. The following code snippet explains the `Find` method:

```
// Find method
func (dict *Dictionary) Find(key DictKey) DictVal {
    dict.lock.RLock()
    defer dict.lock.RUnlock()
    return dict.elements[key]
}
```

Reset method

The `Reset` method of the `Dictionary` class is presented in the following snippet. The `Lock` method of the dictionary's `lock` instance is invoked and `Unlock` is deferred. The `elements` map is initialized with a `map` of the `DictKey` key and the `DictVal` value:

```
// Reset method
func (dict *Dictionary) Reset() {
    dict.lock.Lock()
    defer dict.lock.Unlock()
    dict.elements = make(map[DictKey]DictVal)
}
```

NumberOfElements method

The `NumberOfElements` method of the `Dictionary` class returns the length of the `elements` map. The `RLock` method of the `lock` instance is invoked. The `RUnlock` method of the `lock` instance is deferred before returning the length; this is shown in the following code snippet:

```
// NumberOfElements method
func (dict *Dictionary) NumberOfElements() int {
    dict.lock.RLock()
    defer dict.lock.RUnlock()
    return len(dict.elements)
}
```

GetKeys method

The GetKeys method of the Dictionary class is shown in the following code snippet. The method returns the array of the DictKey elements. The RLock method of the lock instance is invoked, and the RUnlock method is deferred. The dictionary keys are returned by traversing the element's map:

```
// GetKeys method
func (dict *Dictionary) GetKeys() []DictKey {
    dict.lock.RLock()
    defer dict.lock.RUnlock()
    var dictKeys []DictKey
    dictKeys = []DictKey{}
    var key DictKey
    for key = range dict.elements {
        dictKeys = append(dictKeys, key)
    }
    return dictKeys
}
```

GetValues method

The GetValues method of the Dictionary class returns the array of the DictVal elements. In the following code snippet, the RLock method of the lock instance is invoked and the RUnlock method is deferred. The array of dictionary values is returned after traversing the element's map:

```
// GetValues method
func (dict *Dictionary) GetValues() []DictVal {
    dict.lock.RLock()
    defer dict.lock.RUnlock()
    var dictValues []DictVal
    dictValues = []DictVal{}
    var key DictKey
    for key = range dict.elements {
        dictValues = append(dictValues, dict.elements[key])
    }
    return dictValues
}
```

The main method

The following code shows the main method, where the dictionary is initialized and printed:

```
// main method
func main() {
  var dict *Dictionary = &Dictionary{}
  dict.Put("1","1")
  dict.Put("2","2")
  dict.Put("3","3")
  dict.Put("4","4")
  fmt.Println(dict)
}
```

Run the following commands to execute the `dictionary.go` file:

```
go run dictionary.go
```

The output is as follows:

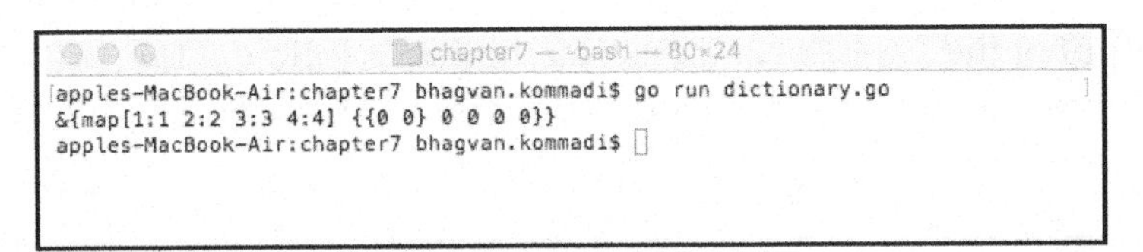

Let's take a look at the `TreeSet` data structure in the following section.

TreeSets

TreeSets are used in marketing and customer relationship management applications. `TreeSet` is a set that has a binary tree with unique elements. The elements are sorted in a natural order. In the following code snippet, `TreeSet` creation, insertion, search, and `stringify` operations are presented. `TreeSet` allows only one null value if the set is empty. The elements are sorted and stored as elements. The `add`, `remove`, and `contains` functions cost *log*(*n*) on `TreeSets`:

```
///main package has examples shown
// in Go Data Structures and algorithms book
package main

// TreeSet class
type TreeSet struct {
  bst *BinarySearchTree
```

```
}
```

We will discuss the different `TreeSet` methods in the following sections.

InsertTreeNode method

The `InsertTreeNode` method of the `TreeSet` class takes `treeNodes` variable arguments of the `TreeNode` type. In the following code, the elements with the `key` and `value` are inserted in the binary search tree of `TreeSet`:

```
// InsertTreeNode method
func (treeset *TreeSet) InsertTreeNode(treeNodes ...TreeNode) {
  var treeNode TreeNode
  for _, treeNode = range treeNodes {
    treeset.bst.InsertElement(treeNode.key, treeNode.value)
  }
}
```

The example output of the `InsertTreeNode` method is as follows. The `InsertTreeNode` method takes `treeNodes` as the parameter. `treeNodes` are inserted with `rootNode`, which has a value of `8`:

```
insert tree Node method tree Nodes [{8 8 <nil> <nil>} {3 3 <nil> <nil>} {10 10 <n
il> <nil>} {1 1 <nil> <nil>} {6 6 <nil> <nil>}]
insert element method key 8 value 8
rootnode 8
insert element method key 3 value 3
insert TreeNode method rootNode 8 new Treenode 3
insert element method key 10 value 10
insert TreeNode method rootNode 8 new Treenode 10
insert element method key 1 value 1
insert TreeNode method rootNode 8 new Treenode 1
insert TreeNode method rootNode 3 new Treenode 1
insert element method key 6 value 6
insert TreeNode method rootNode 8 new Treenode 6
insert TreeNode method rootNode 3 new Treenode 6
```

Delete method

The `Delete` method of the `TreeSet` class is shown in the following code snippet. In this method, `treeNodes` with the provided key are removed:

```
// Delete method
func (treeset *TreeSet) Delete(treeNodes ...TreeNode) {
  var treeNode TreeNode
  for _, treeNode = range treeNodes {
    treeset.bst.RemoveNode(treeNode.key)
  }
}
```

InOrderTraverseTree method

The `InOrderTraverseTree` method of the `BinarySearchTree` class takes `function` as a parameter. The `RLock` method of the `lock` instance is invoked. The `RUnlock` method of the tree's `lock` instance is deferred. `InOrderTraverseTree` is invoked with the `rootNode` of the tree and function as parameters:

```
//InOrderTraverseTree method
func (tree *BinarySearchTree) InOrderTraverseTree(function func(int)) {
  tree.lock.RLock()
  defer tree.lock.RUnlock()
  inOrderTraverseTree(tree.rootNode, function)
}
```

The inOrderTraverseTree method

The `inOrderTraverseTree` method traverses from the left of the tree to root of the node and then to the right of the tree. The `inOrderTraverseTree` method takes `treeNode` and `function` as parameters. The method recursively calls the `inOrderTraverseTree` method with `function` and then `leftNode` and `rightNode` in separate calls. The `function` method is invoked with the `value` of `treeNode`:

```
// inOrderTraverseTree method
func inOrderTraverseTree(treeNode *TreeNode, function func(int)) {
  if treeNode != nil {
    inOrderTraverseTree(treeNode.leftNode, function)
    function(treeNode.value)
    inOrderTraverseTree(treeNode.rightNode, function)
  }
}
```

PreOrderTraverseTree method

The `PreOrderTraverseTree` method of the `BinarySearchTree` class takes the function as its parameter. The `Lock` method on the tree's `lock` instance is invoked first, and the `Unlock` method is deferred. The `PreOrderTraverseTree` method is called with the `rootNode` of the tree and function as parameters:

```
// PreOrderTraverse method
func (tree *BinarySearchTree) PreOrderTraverseTree(function func(int)) {
  tree.lock.Lock()
  defer tree.lock.Unlock()
  preOrderTraverseTree(tree.rootNode, function)
}
```

The preOrderTraverseTree method

The `preOrderTraverseTree` method traverses the tree from the root, to the left and right of the tree. The `preOrderTraverseTree` method takes `treeNode` and `function` as parameters. If `treeNode` is not `nil`, `function` is invoked with the `value` of `treeNode`, and the `preOrderTraverseTree` method is invoked with `function` and `leftNode` and `rightNode` as parameters:

```
// preOrderTraverseTree method
func preOrderTraverseTree(treeNode *TreeNode, function func(int)) {
  if treeNode != nil {
    function(treeNode.value)
    preOrderTraverseTree(treeNode.leftNode, function)
    preOrderTraverseTree(treeNode.rightNode, function)
  }
}
```

Search method

The `Search` method of the `TreeSet` class takes a variable argument named `treeNodes` of the `TreeNode` type and returns true if one of those `treeNodes` exists; otherwise, it returns `false`. The code following snippet outlines the `Search` method:

```
// Search method
func (treeset *TreeSet) Search(treeNodes ...TreeNode) bool {
  var treeNode TreeNode
  var exists bool
  for _, treeNode = range treeNodes {
```

```
    if exists = treeset.bst.SearchNode(treeNode.key); !exists {
      return false
    }
  }
  return true
}
```

The String method

In the following code snippet, the `String` method of the `TreeSet` class returns the string version of `bst`:

```
// String method
func (treeset *TreeSet) String() {
  treeset.bst.String()
}
```

The main method

The `main` method in the `TreeSet` class creates a `TreeSet` with `TreeNodes`. The following snippet creates a `TreeSet` and invokes the `String` method:

```
// main method
func main() {
  var treeset *TreeSet = &TreeSet{}
  treeset.bst = &BinarySearchTree{}
  var node1 TreeNode = TreeNode{8,8, nil,nil}
  var node2 TreeNode = TreeNode{3,3,nil, nil}
  var node3 TreeNode = TreeNode{10,10,nil,nil}
  var node4 TreeNode = TreeNode{1,1,nil,nil}
  var node5 TreeNode = TreeNode{6,6,nil,nil}
  treeset.InsertTreeNode(node1,node2,node3, node4, node5)
  treeset.String()
}
```

Run the following commands to execute the `treeset.go` and `binarysearchtree.go` files:

```
$ go build treeset.go binarysearchtree.go
$ ./treeset
```

The output is as follows:

```
chapter7 — -bash — 80×24
apples-MacBook-Air:chapter7 bhagvan.kommadi$ go build treeset.go binarysearchtre
e.go
apples-MacBook-Air:chapter7 bhagvan.kommadi$ ./treeset
************************************************
                ***> 1
        ***> 3
                ***> 6
***> 8
        ***> 10
************************************************
apples-MacBook-Air:chapter7 bhagvan.kommadi$
```

The next section talks about the synchronized `TreeSet` data structure.

Synchronized TreeSets

Operations that are performed on synchronized TreeSets are synchronized across multiple calls that access the elements of TreeSets. Synchronization in TreeSets is achieved using a `sync.RWMutex` lock. The `lock` method on the tree's `lock` instance is invoked, and the unlock method is deferred before the `tree` nodes are inserted, deleted, or updated:

```
// InsertElement method
func (tree *BinarySearchTree) InsertElement(key int, value int) {
  tree.lock.Lock()
  defer tree.lock.Unlock()
  var treeNode *TreeNode
  treeNode = &TreeNode{key, value, nil, nil}
  if tree.rootNode == nil {
    tree.rootNode = treeNode
  } else {
    insertTreeNode(tree.rootNode, treeNode)
  }
}
```

Mutable TreeSets

Mutable TreeSets can use `add`, `update`, and `delete` operations on the tree and its nodes. `insertTreeNode` updates the tree by taking the `rootNode` and `treeNode` parameters to be updated. The following code snippet shows how to insert a `TreeNode` with a given `rootNode` and `TreeNode`:

```
// insertTreeNode method
func insertTreeNode(rootNode *TreeNode, newTreeNode *TreeNode) {
  if newTreeNode.key < rootNode.key {
    if rootNode.leftNode == nil {
      rootNode.leftNode = newTreeNode
    } else {
      insertTreeNode(rootNode.leftNode, newTreeNode)
    }
  } else {
    if rootNode.rightNode == nil {
      rootNode.rightNode = newTreeNode
    } else {
      insertTreeNode(rootNode.rightNode, newTreeNode)
    }
  }
}
```

Let's discuss the different mutable TreeSets in the following sections.

RemoveNode method

The `RemoveNode` method of a `BinarySearchTree` is as follows:

```
// RemoveNode method
func (tree *BinarySearchTree) RemoveNode(key int) {
  tree.lock.Lock()
  defer tree.lock.Unlock()
  removeNode(tree.rootNode, key)
}
```

Treeset.bst

The TreeNode's can be updated by accessing `treeset.bst` and traversing the binary search tree from the `rootNode` and the left and right nodes of `rootNode`, as shown here:

```
var treeset *TreeSet = &TreeSet{}
treeset.bst = &BinarySearchTree{}
var node1 TreeNode = TreeNode{8, 8, nil, nil}
var node2 TreeNode = TreeNode{3, 3, nil, nil}
var node3 TreeNode = TreeNode{10, 10, nil, nil}
var node4 TreeNode = TreeNode{1, 1, nil, nil}
var node5 TreeNode = TreeNode{6, 6, nil, nil}
treeset.InsertTreeNode(node1, node2, node3, node4, node5)
treeset.String()
```

In the next section, we will take a look at sequences.

Sequences

A **sequence** is a set of numbers that are grouped in a particular order. The number of elements in the stream can be infinite, and these sequences are called **streams**. A **subsequence** is a sequence that's created from another sequence. The relative positions of the elements in a subsequence will remain the same after deleting some of the elements in a sequence.

In the following sections, we will take a look at different sequences such as the Farey sequence, Fibonacci sequence, look-and-say, and Thue–Morse.

Farey sequence

A **Farey sequence** consists of reduced fractions with values between zero and one. The denominators of the fractions are less than or equal to *m*, and organized in ascending order. This sequence is called a **Farey series**. In the following code, reduced fractions are displayed:

```
///main package has examples shown
// in Go Data Structures and algorithms book
package main
// importing fmt package
import (
  "fmt"
)
```

```
// fraction class
type fraction struct {
  numerator int
  denominator int
}
```

Lets take a look at the different methods in a Farey sequence.

String method

The `fraction` class has the numerator and denominator integer properties. The `String` method of the `fraction` class, as shown in the following snippet, returns a `string` version of `fraction`:

```
// string method of fraction class
func (frac fraction) String() string {
  return fmt.Sprintf("%d/%d", frac.numerator, frac.denominator)
}
```

The g method

The `g` method takes two fractions and prints the series of reduced fractions. The `g` function takes an `l` or an `r` fraction, and `num` int as arguments to print the reduced fraction as a series. The following code snippet shows the `g` method:

```
// g method
func g(l fraction, r fraction, num int) {
  var frac fraction
  frac = fraction{l.numerator + r.numerator, l.denominator + r.denominator}
  if frac.denominator <= num {
    g(l, frac, num)
    fmt.Print(frac, " ")
    g(frac, r, num)
  }
}
```

The main method

The following snippet shows the `main` method. In the `main` method, reduced fraction series are printed using recursion:

```
// main method
func main() {
 var num int
 var l fraction
 var r fraction
 for num = 1; num <= 11; num++ {
 l = fraction{0, 1}
 r = fraction{1, 1}
 fmt.Printf("F(%d): %s ", num, l)
 g(l, r, num)
 fmt.Println(r)
 }
```

Run the following command to execute the `farey_sequence.go` file:

```
go run farey_sequence.go
```

The output is as follows:

```
chapter7 — -bash — 80×29
apples-MacBook-Air:chapter7 bhagvan.kommadi$ go run farey_sequence.go
F(1): 0/1 1/1
F(2): 0/1 1/2 1/1
F(3): 0/1 1/3 1/2 2/3 1/1
F(4): 0/1 1/4 1/3 1/2 2/3 3/4 1/1
F(5): 0/1 1/5 1/4 1/3 2/5 1/2 3/5 2/3 3/4 4/5 1/1
F(6): 0/1 1/6 1/5 1/4 1/3 2/5 1/2 3/5 2/3 3/4 4/5 5/6 1/1
F(7): 0/1 1/7 1/6 1/5 1/4 2/7 1/3 2/5 3/7 1/2 4/7 3/5 2/3 5/7 3/4 4/5 5/6 6/7 1/
1
F(8): 0/1 1/8 1/7 1/6 1/5 1/4 2/7 1/3 3/8 2/5 3/7 1/2 4/7 3/5 5/8 2/3 5/7 3/4 4/
5 5/6 6/7 7/8 1/1
F(9): 0/1 1/9 1/8 1/7 1/6 1/5 2/9 1/4 2/7 1/3 3/8 2/5 3/7 4/9 1/2 5/9 4/7 3/5 5/
8 2/3 5/7 3/4 7/9 4/5 5/6 6/7 7/8 8/9 1/1
F(10): 0/1 1/10 1/9 1/8 1/7 1/6 1/5 2/9 1/4 2/7 3/10 1/3 3/8 2/5 3/7 4/9 1/2 5/9
 4/7 3/5 5/8 2/3 7/10 5/7 3/4 7/9 4/5 5/6 6/7 7/8 8/9 9/10 1/1
F(11): 0/1 1/11 1/10 1/9 1/8 1/7 1/6 2/11 1/5 2/9 1/4 3/11 2/7 3/10 1/3 4/11 3/8
 2/5 3/7 4/9 5/11 1/2 6/11 5/9 4/7 3/5 5/8 7/11 2/3 7/10 5/7 8/11 3/4 7/9 4/5 9/
11 5/6 6/7 7/8 8/9 9/10 10/11 1/1
|F(100)|: 3045
|F(200)|: 12233
|F(300)|: 27399
|F(400)|: 48679
|F(500)|: 76117
|F(600)|: 109501
|F(700)|: 149019
|F(800)|: 194751
|F(900)|: 246327
|F(1000)|: 304193
apples-MacBook-Air:chapter7 bhagvan.kommadi$
```

The next section talks about the Fibonacci sequence data structure.

Fibonacci sequence

The **Fibonacci sequence** consists of a list of numbers in which every number is the sum of the two preceding numbers. Pingala, in 200 BC, was the first to come up with Fibonacci numbers. The Fibonacci sequence is as follows:

$$0, 1, 1, 2, 3, 5, 8, 13, 21, 34, 55, 89, 144....$$

The recurrence relation for the Fibonacci sequence is as follows:

$$F_n = F_{n-1} + F_{n-2}$$

The seed values are as follows:

$$F_0 = 0, F_1 = 1$$

A Fibonacci prime is a Fibonacci number that is a prime number. The Fibonacci prime series is as follows:

$$2, 3, 5, 13, 89, 233, 1, 597, 28, 657, 514, 229...$$

Computer algorithms such as the Fibonacci search technique, heap, and cubes are popular applications of Fibonacci numbers. Pseudorandom number generators use Fibonacci numbers.

The following code snippet shows the Fibonacci sequence and recursive Fibonacci number calculation. The `Series` function is presented as well. The `Series` function calculates the Fibonacci numbers in the sequence:

```
///main package has examples shown
// in Go Data Structures and algorithms book
package main

// importing fmt and strconv package
import (
  "fmt"
  "strconv"
)

// Series method
func Series(n int) int {
  var f []int
  f = make([]int, n+1, n+2)
  if n < 2 {
```

```
    f = f[0:2]
  }
  f[0] = 0
  f[1] = 1
  var i int
  for i = 2; i <= n; i++ {
    f[i] = f[i-1] + f[i-2]
  }
  return f[n]
}
```

The different methods of the Fibonacci sequence are discussed in the following sections.

FibonacciNumber method

The `FibonacciNumber` method takes the integer *n* and, by recursion, calculates the Fibonacci numbers. The following code snippet shows this recursion:

```
// FibonacciNumber method
func FibonacciNumber(n int) int {
  if n <= 1 {
    return n
  }
  return FibonacciNumber(n-1) + FibonacciNumber(n-2)
}
```

Main method

The `main` method in the following code snippet shows how the Fibonacci sequence is calculated:

```
// main method
func main() {
 var i int
 for i = 0; i <= 9; i++ {
 fmt.Print(strconv.Itoa(Series(i)) + " ")
 }
 fmt.Println("")
 for i = 0; i <= 9; i++ {
 fmt.Print(strconv.Itoa(FibonacciNumber(i)) + " ")
 }
 fmt.Println("")
}
```

Run the following command to execute the `fibonacci_sequence.go` file:

```
go run fibonacci_sequence.go
```

The output is as follows:

```
chapter7 — -bash — 83×28
apples-MacBook-Air:chapter7 bhagvan.kommadi$ go run fibonacci_sequence.go
0 1 1 2 3 5 8 13 21 34
0 1 1 2 3 5 8 13 21 34
apples-MacBook-Air:chapter7 bhagvan.kommadi$
```

The next section talks about the look-and-say data structure.

Look-and-say

The **look-and-say** sequence is a sequence of integers:

$$1, 11, 21, 1, 211, 111, 221, 312, 211 \ldots$$

The sequence is generated by counting the digits of the previous number in the group. John Conway initially coined the term *look-and-say sequence.*

The look-and-say sequence is shown in the following code. The `look_say` method takes a string as a parameter and returns a look-and-say sequence of integers:

```
//main package has examples shown
// in Go Data Structures and algorithms book
package main

// importing fmt and strconv package
import (
  "fmt"
  "strconv"
)

// look_say method
func look_say(str string) (rstr string) {
  var cbyte byte
  cbyte = str[0]
  var inc int
  inc = 1
```

```
    var i int
    for i = 1; i < len(str); i++ {
      var dbyte byte
      dbyte = str[i]
      if dbyte == cbyte {
        inc++
        continue
      }
      rstr = rstr + strconv.Itoa(inc) + string(cbyte)
      cbyte = dbyte
      inc = 1
    }
    return rstr + strconv.Itoa(inc) + string(cbyte)
  }
```

The `main` method initializes the string and invokes the `look_say` method. The look-and-say sequence that is returned from the method is printed:

```
// main method
func main() {
  var str string
  str = "1"
  fmt.Println(str)
  var i int
  for i = 0; i < 8; i++ {
    str = look_say(str)
    fmt.Println(str)
  }
}
```

Run the following command to execute the `look_say.go` file:

```
go run look_say.go
```

The output is as follows:

```
chapter7 — -bash — 80×24
apples-MacBook-Air:chapter7 bhagvan.kommadi$ go run look_say.go
1
11
21
1211
111221
312211
13112221
1113213211
31131211131221
apples-MacBook-Air:chapter7 bhagvan.kommadi$
```

The next section talks about the Thue–Morse data structure.

Thue–Morse

The **Thue–Morse** sequence is a binary sequence starting at zero that appends the Boolean complement of the current sequence.

The Thue–Morse sequence is as follows:

$$0, 01, 0110, 01101001, 0110100110010110, \ldots$$

The Thue–Morse sequence was applied by Eugene Prophet and used by Axel Thue in the study of combinatorics on words. The Thue–Morse sequence is used in the area of fractal curves, such as Koch snowflakes.

The following code snippet creates the Thue–Morse sequence. The `ThueMorseSequence` function takes a `bytes.Buffer` instance buffer and modifies the buffer to the Thue–Morse sequence by applying the `complement` operation on the `bytes`:

```
//main package has examples shown
// in Go Data Structures and algorithms book
package main

// importing fmt and bytes package
import (
 "bytes"
 "fmt"
)

// ThueMorseSequence method
func ThueMorseSequence(buffer *bytes.Buffer) {

 var b int
 var currLength int
 var currBytes []byte
 for b, currLength, currBytes = 0, buffer.Len(), buffer.Bytes(); b <
currLength; b++ {
 if currBytes[b] == '1' {
 buffer.WriteByte('0')
 } else {
 buffer.WriteByte('1')
 }
 }
}
```

The `main` method initializes the sequence number as `0`. The `ThueMorseSequence` method takes the pointer to the `bytes.Buffer` and modifies it by invoking the `ThueMorseSequence` method. The resulting sequence is printed on the Terminal:

```
// main method
func main() {
 var buffer bytes.Buffer
 // initial sequence member is "0"
 buffer.WriteByte('0')
 fmt.Println(buffer.String())
 var i int
 for i = 2; i <= 7; i++ {
 ThueMorseSequence(&buffer)
 fmt.Println(buffer.String())
 }
}
```

Run the following command to execute the `thue_morse.go` file:

```
go run thue_morse.go
```

The output is as follows:

```
chapter7 — -bash — 80×24
apples-MacBook-Air:chapter7 bhagvan.kommadi$ go run thue_morse.go
0
01
0110
01101001
0110100110010110
01101001100101101001011001101001
0110100110010110100101100110100110010110011010010110100110010110
apples-MacBook-Air:chapter7 bhagvan.kommadi$
```

Summary

This chapter covered the `contains`, `put`, `remove`, `find`, `reset`, `NumberOfElements`, `getKeys`, and `getValues` methods of the dictionary data structure. The `InsertTreeNode`, `Delete`, `Search`, and `stringify` TreeSet operations have been explained in detail, and code examples were provided. The `BinarySearchTree` structure has been presented in code, along with the `InsertElement`, `InOrderTraversal`, `PreOrderTraverseTree`, `SearchNode`, and `RemoveNode` functions.

The next chapter covers algorithms such as sorting, searching, recursion, and hashing.

Questions

1. How do you ensure a `BinarySearchTree` is synchronized?
2. Which method is called to postpone the invocation of a function?
3. How do you define dictionary keys and values with custom types?
4. How do you find the length of a map?
5. What keyword is used to traverse a list of `treeNodes` in a tree?
6. In a Farey sequence, what are the real numbers in the series called?
7. What is a Fibonacci number?
8. How do you convert an integer into a string?
9. What method is used to convert a byte into a string?
10. What method is called to add elements to a dictionary?

Further reading

The following books are recommended if you want to learn more about dynamic data structures:

- *Design Patterns*, by Erich Gamma, Richard Helm, Ralph Johnson, and John Vlissides
- *Introduction to Algorithms – Third Edition*, by Thomas H. Cormen, Charles E. Leiserson, Ronald L. Rivest, and Clifford Stein
- *Data structures and Algorithms: An Easy Introduction*, by Rudolph Russell

8
Classic Algorithms

Classic algorithms are used in the areas of data search and cryptography. Sorting, searching, recursing, and hashing algorithms are good examples of classic algorithms. Sorting algorithms are used to order elements into either an ascending or descending key arrangement. These algorithms are frequently used to canonicalize data and to create readable content. Search algorithms are used to find an element in a set. A recursive algorithm is one that calls itself with input items. A hashing algorithm is a cryptographic hash technique. It is a scientific calculation that maps data with a subjective size to a hash with a settled size. It's intended to be a single direction function, that you cannot alter.

In this chapter, we will cover the different classic algorithms and explain them with suitable examples.

This chapter covers the following algorithms:

- Sorting:
    - Bubble
    - Selection
    - Insertion
    - Shell
    - Merge
    - Quick
- Searching:
    - Linear
    - Sequential
    - Binary
    - Interpolation
- Recursion
- Hashing

Technical requirements

Install Go version 1.10 from `https://golang.org/doc/install` for your OS.

The GitHub URL for the code in this chapter is as follows: `https://github.com/PacktPublishing/Learn-Data-Structures-and-Algorithms-with-Golang/tree/master/Chapter08`.

Sorting

Sorting algorithms arrange the elements in a collection in ascending or descending order. Lexicographical order can be applied to a collection of characters and strings. The efficiency of these algorithms is in the performance of sorting the input data into a sorted collection. The best sorting algorithm time complexity is $O(n \log n)$. Sorting algorithms are classified by the following criteria:

- Computational complexity
- Memory usage
- Stability
- Type of sorting: serial/parallel
- Adaptability
- Method of sorting

In the following sections, we'll look at the different sorting algorithms, that is, bubble, selection, insertion, shell, merge, and quick.

Bubble

The bubble sort algorithm is a sorting algorithm that compares a pair of neighboring elements and swaps them if they are in the wrong order. The algorithm has a complexity of $O(n^2)$, where n is the number of elements to be sorted. The smallest or greatest value bubbles up to the top of the collection, or the smallest or greatest sinks to the bottom (depending on whether you're sorting into ascending or descending order).

The following code snippet shows the implementation of the bubble sort algorithm. The `bubbleSorter` function takes an integer array and sorts the array's elements in ascending order.

The `main` method initializes the array's integers and invokes the `bubbleSorter` function, as follows:

```
//main package has examples shown
// in Go Data Structures and algorithms book
package main

// importing fmt and bytes package
import (
  "fmt"
)

//bubble Sorter method
func bubbleSorter(integers [11]int) {

  var num int
  num = 11
  var isSwapped bool
  isSwapped = true
  for isSwapped {
    isSwapped = false
    var i int
    for i = 1; i < num; i++ {
      if integers[i-1] > integers[i] {

        var temp = integers[i]
        integers[i] = integers[i-1]
        integers[i-1] = temp
        isSwapped = true
      }
    }
  }
  fmt.Println(integers)
}

// main method
func main() {
  var integers [11]int = [11]int{31, 13, 12, 4, 18, 16, 7, 2, 3, 0, 10}
  fmt.Println("Bubble Sorter")
  bubbleSorter(integers)

}
```

Run the following command to execute the bubble_sort.go file:

```
go run bubble_sort.go
```

The output is as follows:

```
apples-MacBook-Air:chapter8 bhagvan.kommadi$ go run bubble_sort.go
Bubble Sorter
[0 2 3 4 7 10 12 13 16 18 31]
apples-MacBook-Air:chapter8 bhagvan.kommadi$
```

Let's take a look at the selection sort algorithm in the following section.

Selection

Selection sort is an algorithm that divides the input collection into two fragments. This sublist of elements is sorted by swapping the smallest or largest element from the left of the list to the right. The algorithm is of the order $O(n^2)$. This algorithm is inefficient for large collections, and it performs worse than the insertion sort algorithm.

The following code shows the implementation of the SelectionSorter function, which takes the collection to be sorted:

```
//main package has examples shown
// in Go Data Structures and algorithms book
package main

// importing fmt package
import (
  "fmt"
)

// Selection Sorter method
func SelectionSorter(elements []int) {

  var i int
  for i = 0; i < len(elements)-1; i++ {
    var min int
    min = i
    var j int
    for j = i + 1; j <= len(elements)-1; j++ {
      if elements[j] < elements[min] {
```

```
          min = j
        }
      }
      swap(elements, i, min)
    }
  }
```

Let's take a look at the different selection methods in the next sections.

The swap method

The `swap` method takes the elements array and the `i` and `j` indices as parameters. The method swaps the element at position `i` with the element at position `j`, as shown here:

```
// swap method
func swap(elements []int, i int, j int) {
  var temp int
  temp = elements[j]
  elements[j] = elements[i]
  elements[i] = temp
}
```

The main method

The `main` method initializes the `elements` array. The `elements` are printed before and after sorting in the following code snippet:

```
//main method
func main() {
  var elements []int
  elements = []int{11, 4, 18, 6, 19, 21, 71, 13, 15, 2}
  fmt.Println("Before Sorting ", elements)
  SelectionSorter(elements)
  fmt.Println("After Sorting", elements)
}
```

Run the following command to execute the `selection_sort.go` file:

```
go run selection_sort.go
```

The output is as follows:

```
chapter8 — -bash — 80×24
apples-MacBook-Air:chapter8 bhagvan.kommadi$ go run selection_sort.go
Before Sorting  [11 4 18 6 19 21 71 13 15 2]
After Sorting [2 4 6 11 13 15 18 19 21 71]
apples-MacBook-Air:chapter8 bhagvan.kommadi$
```

Let's take a look at the insertion sort algorithm in the following section.

Insertion

Insertion sort is an algorithm that creates a final sorted array one element at a time. The algorithm's performance is of the order $O(n^2)$. This algorithm is less efficient on large collections than other algorithms, such as quick, heap, and merge sort. In real life, a good example of insertion sort is the way cards are manually sorted by the players in a game of bridge.

The implementation of the insertion sort algorithm is shown in the following code snippet. The `RandomSequence` function takes the number of elements as a parameter and returns an array of random integers:

```
//main package has examples shown
// in Go Data Structures and algorithms book
package main

// importing fmt and bytes package
import (
  "fmt"
  "math/rand"
  "time"
)

// randomSequence method
func randomSequence(num int) []int {

    var sequence []int
    sequence = make([]int, num,num)
    rand.Seed(time.Now().UnixNano())
    var i int
    for i= 0; i < num; i++ {
        sequence[i] = rand.Intn(999) - rand.Intn(999)
    }
```

```
    return sequence
}
```

Let's take a look at the different insertion methods in the next sections.

InsertionSorter method

The implementation of the `InsertionSorter` method is shown in the following snippet. This method takes the array of integers as a parameter and sorts them:

```
//InsertionSorter method
func InsertionSorter(elements []int) {
    var n = len(elements)
    var i int

    for i = 1; i < n; i++ {
        var j int
        j = i
        for j > 0 {
            if elements[j-1] > elements[j] {
                elements[j-1], elements[j] = elements[j], elements[j-1]
            }
            j = j - 1
        }
    }
}
```

The main method

The `main` method initializes the `sequence` by invoking the `randomSequence` function, as shown in the following code. The `InsertionSorter` function takes the `sequence` and sorts it in ascending order:

```
//main method
func main() {

    var sequence []int
    sequence = randomSequence(24)
    fmt.Println("\n^^^^^^ Before Sorting ^^^ \n\n", sequence)
    InsertionSorter(sequence)
    fmt.Println("\n--- After Sorting ---\n\n", sequence, "\n")
}
```

Run the following command to execute the `insertion_sort.go` file:

```
go run insertion_sort.go
```

The output is as follows:

```
apples-MacBook-Air:chapter8 bhagvan.kommadi$ go run insertion_sort.go

^^^^^^ Before Sorting ^^^

 [162 -80 -274 -297 -565 -15 396 -329 -787 -50 -245 427 292 -903 -112 -492 603 3
73 76 281 -69 61 -73 -17]

--- After Sorting ---

 [-903 -787 -565 -492 -329 -297 -274 -245 -112 -80 -73 -69 -50 -17 -15 61 76 162
 281 292 373 396 427 603]

apples-MacBook-Air:chapter8 bhagvan.kommadi$
```

Let's take a look at the shell sort algorithm in the next section.

Shell

The shell sort algorithm sorts a pair of elements that are not in sequence in a collection. The distance between the elements to be compared is decreased sequentially. This algorithm performs more operations and has a greater cache miss ratio than the quick sort algorithm.

In the following code, we can see the implementation of the shell sort algorithm. The `ShellSorter` function takes an integer array as a parameter and sorts it:

```
//main package has examples shown
// in Go Data Structures and algorithms book
package main

// importing fmt and bytes package
import (
  "fmt"
)

// shell sorter method
func ShellSorter(elements []int) {
  var (
    n = len(elements)
    intervals = []int{1}
    k = 1
```

```
    )

    for {
      var interval int
      interval = power(2, k) + 1
      if interval > n-1 {
        break
      }
      intervals = append([]int{interval}, intervals...)
      k++
    }
    var interval int
    for _, interval = range intervals {
      var i int
      for i = interval; i < n; i += interval {
        var j int
        j = i
        for j > 0 {
          if elements[j-interval] > elements[j] {
            elements[j-interval], elements[j] = elements[j], elements[j-
interval]
          }
          j = j - interval
        }
      }
    }
  }
```

Let's take a look at the different shell methods in the following sections.

The power method

The `power` method takes `exponent` and `index` as parameters and returns the power of the exponent to the index, as follows:

```
//power function
func power(exponent int, index int) int {
  var power int
  power = 1
  for index > 0 {
    if index&1 != 0 {
      power *= exponent
    }
    index >>= 1
    exponent *= exponent
  }
  return power
```

```
}
```

The main method

The `main` method initializes the `elements` integer array and invokes the `ShellSorter` method, as follows:

```
// main method
func main() {
  var elements []int
  elements = []int{34, 202, 13, 19, 6, 5, 1, 43, 506, 12, 20, 28, 17, 100,
25, 4, 5, 97, 1000, 27}
  ShellSorter(elements)
  fmt.Println(elements)
}
```

Run the following command to execute the `shell_sort.go` file:

```
go run shell_sort.go
```

The output is as follows:

```
chapter8 — -bash — 80×24
apples-MacBook-Air:chapter8 bhagvan.kommadi$ go run shell_sort.go
[1 4 5 5 6 12 13 17 19 20 25 27 28 34 43 97 100 202 506 1000]
apples-MacBook-Air:chapter8 bhagvan.kommadi$
```

Let's take a look at the merge sort algorithm in the next section.

Merge

The merge sort algorithm is a comparison-based method that was invented by John Von Neumann. Each element in the adjacent list is compared for sorting. The performance of the algorithm is in the order of *O(n log n)*. This algorithm is the best algorithm for sorting a linked list.

The following code snippet demonstrates the merge sort algorithm. The `createArray` function takes `num int` as a parameter and returns an integer, `array`, that consists of randomized elements:

```
//main package has examples shown
// in Go Data Structures and algorithms book
package main

// importing fmt and bytes package
import (
  "fmt"
  "math/rand"
  "time"
)

// create array
func createArray(num int) []int {
  var array []int
  array = make([]int, num, num)
  rand.Seed(time.Now().UnixNano())
  var i int
  for i = 0; i < num; i++ {
    array[i] = rand.Intn(99999) - rand.Intn(99999)
  }
  return array
}
```

Let's take a look at the different merge methods in the following sections.

MergeSorter method

The `MergeSorter` method takes an array of integer elements as a parameter, and two sub-arrays of elements are recursively passed to the `MergeSorter` method. The resultant arrays are joined and returned as the collection, as follows:

```
// MergeSorter algorithm
func MergeSorter(array []int) []int {

  if len(array) < 2 {
    return array
  }
  var middle int
  middle = (len(array)) / 2
  return JoinArrays(MergeSorter(array[:middle]),
MergeSorter(array[middle:]))
}
```

JoinArrays method

The `JoinArrays` function takes the `leftArr` and `rightArr` integer arrays as parameters. The combined array is returned in the following code:

```
// Join Arrays method
func JoinArrays(leftArr []int, rightArr []int) []int {

  var num int
  var i int
  var j int
  num, i, j = len(leftArr)+len(rightArr), 0, 0
  var array []int
  array = make([]int, num, num)

  var k int
  for k = 0; k < num; k++ {
    if i > len(leftArr)-1 && j <= len(rightArr)-1 {
      array[k] = rightArr[j]
      j++
    } else if j > len(rightArr)-1 && i <= len(leftArr)-1 {
      array[k] = leftArr[i]
      i++
    } else if leftArr[i] < rightArr[j] {
      array[k] = leftArr[i]
      i++
    } else {
      array[k] = rightArr[j]
      j++
    }
  }
  return array
}
```

The main method

The `main` method initializes the integer array of `40` elements, and the elements are printed before and after sorting, as follows:

```
// main method
func main() {

  var elements []int
  elements = createArray(40)
  fmt.Println("\n Before Sorting \n\n", elements)
  fmt.Println("\n-After Sorting\n\n", MergeSorter(elements), "\n")
```

```
}
```

Run the following command to execute the `merge_sort.go` file:

```
go run merge_sort.go
```

The output is as follows:

```
apples-MacBook-Air:chapter8 bhagvan.kommadi$ go run merge_sort.go

 Before Sorting

 [39352 57110 -3150 12621 22464 -14792 -14706 2235 -23041 13456 19996 -62227 -10
89 54671 -17076 -11845 -30902 71964 35193 -56512 23260 -16191 6350 25010 -17747
-8953 -23844 -14690 -28506 22337 -5930 43571 37533 83694 -67673 -21766 2013 -152
14 74836 -15149]

-After Sorting

 [-67673 -62227 -56512 -30902 -28506 -23844 -23041 -21766 -17747 -17076 -16191 -
15214 -15149 -14792 -14706 -14690 -11845 -8953 -5930 -3150 -1089 2013 2235 6350
12621 13456 19996 22337 22464 23260 25010 35193 37533 39352 43571 54671 57110 71
964 74836 83694]

apples-MacBook-Air:chapter8 bhagvan.kommadi$
```

Let's take a look at the quick sort algorithm in the following section.

Quick

Quick sort is an algorithm for sorting the elements of a collection in an organized way. Parallelized quick sort is two to three times faster than merge sort and heap sort. The algorithm's performance is of the order $O(n \log n)$. This algorithm is a space-optimized version of the binary tree sort algorithm.

In the following code snippet, the quick sort algorithm is implemented. The `QuickSorter` function takes an array of integer `elements`, `upper int`, and `below int` as parameters. The function divides the array into parts, which are recursively divided and sorted:

```
//main package has examples shown
// in Go Data Structures and algorithms book
package main

// importing fmt package
import (
  "fmt"
)
```

```
//Quick Sorter method
func QuickSorter(elements []int, below int, upper int) {
  if below < upper {
    var part int
    part = divideParts(elements, below, upper)
    QuickSorter(elements, below, part-1)
    QuickSorter(elements, part+1, upper)
  }
}
```

Let's take a look at the different quick methods in the following sections.

The divideParts method

The `divideParts` method takes an array of integer `elements`, `upper int`, and `below int` as parameters. The method sorts the elements in ascending order, as shown in the following code:

```
// divideParts method
func divideParts(elements []int, below int, upper int) int {
  var center int
  center = elements[upper]
  var i int
  i = below
  var j int
  for j = below; j < upper; j++ {
    if elements[j] <= center {
      swap(&elements[i], &elements[j])
      i += 1
    }
  }
  swap(&elements[i], &elements[upper])
  return i
}
```

The swap method

In the following code snippet, the swap method exchanges elements by interchanging the values:

```
//swap method
func swap(element1 *int, element2 *int) {
  var val int
  val = *element1
  *element1 = *element2
  *element2 = val
}
```

The main method

The main method asks the user to input the number of elements and the elements to be read. The array is initialized and printed before and after sorting, as follows:

```
// main method
func main() {
  var num int

  fmt.Print("Enter Number of Elements: ")
  fmt.Scan(&num)

  var array = make([]int, num)

  var i int
  for i = 0; i < num; i++ {
    fmt.Print("array[", i, "]: ")
    fmt.Scan(&array[i])
  }

  fmt.Print("Elements: ", array, "\n")
  QuickSorter(array, 0, num-1)
  fmt.Print("Sorted Elements: ", array, "\n")
}
```

Run the following command to execute the quick_sort.go file:

```
go run quick_sort.go
```

The output is as follows:

```
chapter8 — -bash — 80×24
apples-MacBook-Air:chapter8 bhagvan.kommadi$ go run quick_sort.go
Enter Number of Elements: 10
array[0]: 34
array[1]: 3
array[2]: 6
array[3]: 14
array[4]: 21
array[5]: 28
array[6]: 87
array[7]: 56
array[8]: 45
array[9]: 34
Elements: [34 3 6 14 21 28 87 56 45 34]
Sorted Elements: [3 6 14 21 28 34 34 45 56 87]
apples-MacBook-Air:chapter8 bhagvan.kommadi$
```

Now that we are done with sort algorithms, let's take a look at the search algorithms in the next section.

Searching

Search algorithms are used to retrieve information that's stored in a data source or a collection. The algorithm is given the key of the element in question, and the associated value will be found. Search algorithms return a true or a false Boolean value based on the availability of the information. They can be enhanced to display multiple values related to the search criteria. Different types of search algorithms include linear, binary, and interpolation. These algorithms are categorized by the type of search. Search algorithms include brute force and heuristic methods. The algorithms are chosen for their efficiency. Different factors for choosing these algorithms are as follows:

- Input type
- Output type
- Definiteness
- Correctness
- Finiteness
- Effectiveness
- Generality

In this section, we will discuss the different types of search algorithms.

Linear

The linear search method finds a given value within a collection by sequentially checking every element in the collection. The time complexity of the linear search algorithm is *O(n)*. The binary search algorithm and hash tables perform better than this search algorithm.

The implementation of the linear search method is shown in the following code snippet. The `LinearSearch` function takes an array of integer `elements` and `findElement int` as parameters. The function returns a Boolean `true` if the `findElement` is found; otherwise, it returns `false`:

```
//main package has examples shown
// in Go Data Structures and algorithms book
package main

// importing fmt package
import (
  "fmt"
)

// Linear Search method
func LinearSearch(elements []int, findElement int) bool {
  var element int
  for _, element = range elements {
    if element == findElement {
      return true
    }
  }
  return false
}
```

The `main` method initializes the array of integer `elements` and invokes the `LinearSearch` method by passing an integer that needs to be found, as follows:

```
// main method
func main() {
  var elements []int
  elements = []int{15, 48, 26, 18, 41, 86, 29, 51, 20}
  fmt.Println(LinearSearch(elements, 48))
}
```

Run the following command to execute the `linear_search.go` file:

```
go run linear_search.go
```

The output is as follows:

```
apples-MacBook-Air:chapter8 bhagvan.kommadi$ go run linear_search.go
true
apples-MacBook-Air:chapter8 bhagvan.kommadi$
```

Let's take a look at the binary search algorithm in the following section.

Binary

The binary search algorithm compares the input value to the middle element of the sorted collection. If the values are not equal, the half in which the element is not found is eliminated. The search continues on the remaining half of the collection. The time complexity of this algorithm is in the order of *O(log n)*.

The following code snippet shows an implementation of the binary search algorithm using the `sort.Search` function from the `sort` package. The `main` method initializes the `elements` array and invokes the `sort.Search` function to find an integer element:

```
//main package has examples shown
// in Go Data Structures and algorithms book
package main

// importing fmt package
import (
  "fmt"
  "sort"
)

// main method
func main() {
  var elements []int
  elements = []int{1, 3, 16, 10, 45, 31, 28, 36, 45, 75}
  var element int
  element = 36

  var i int

  i = sort.Search(len(elements), func(i int) bool { return elements[i] >=
element })
  if i < len(elements) && elements[i] == element {
    fmt.Printf("found element %d at index %d in %v\n", element, i,
elements)
```

```
    } else {
      fmt.Printf("element %d not found in %v\n", element, elements)
    }
  }
```

Run the following command to execute the `binary_search.go` file:

```
go run binary_search.go
```

The output is as follows:

```
chapter8 — -bash — 80×24
apples-MacBook-Air:chapter8 bhagvan.kommadi$ go run binary_search.go
found element 36 at index 7 in [1 3 16 10 45 31 28 36 45 75]
apples-MacBook-Air:chapter8 bhagvan.kommadi$
```

Let's take a look at the interpolation search algorithm in the following section.

Interpolation

The interpolation search algorithm searches for the element in a sorted collection. The algorithm finds the input element at an estimated position by diminishing the search space before or after the estimated position. The time complexity of the search algorithm is of the order $O(log\ log\ n)$.

The following code snippet implements the interpolation search algorithm. The `InterpolationSearch` function takes the array of integer elements and the integer element to be found as parameters. The function finds the element in the collection and returns the Boolean and the index for the found element:

```
//main package has examples shown
// in Go Data Structures and algorithms book
package main

// importing fmt package
import (
  "fmt"
)

//interpolation search method
func InterpolationSearch(elements []int, element int) (bool, int) {
  var mid int
  var low int
  low = 0
```

```
    var high int
    high = len(elements) - 1

    for elements[low] < element && elements[high] > element {
      mid = low + ((element-elements[low])*(high-low))/(elements[high]-
  elements[low])

      if elements[mid] < element {
        low = mid + 1
      } else if elements[mid] > element {
        high = mid - 1
      } else {
        return true, mid
      }
    }

    if elements[low] == element {
      return true, low
    } else if elements[high] == element {
      return true, high
    } else {
      return false, -1
    }

    return false, -1
  }
```

The `main` method initializes the array of integer elements and invokes the `InterpolationSearch` method with the `elements` array and the `element` parameters, as follows:

```
// main method
func main() {
  var elements []int
  elements = []int{2, 3, 5, 7, 9}
  var element int
  element = 7
  var found bool
  var index int
  found, index = InterpolationSearch(elements, element)
  fmt.Println(found, "found at", index)
}
```

Run the following command to execute the `interpolation_search.go` file:

```
go run interpolation_search.go
```

The output is as follows:

```
chapter8 — -bash — 80×24
apples-MacBook-Air:chapter8 bhagvan.kommadi$ go run interpolation_search.go
true found at 3
apples-MacBook-Air:chapter8 bhagvan.kommadi$
```

Now that we are done with search algorithms, let's take a look at the recursion algorithms in the next section.

Recursion

Recursion is an algorithm in which one of the steps invokes the currently running method or function. This algorithm acquires the outcome for the input by applying basic tasks and then returns the value. This method was briefly discussed in the *Divide and conquer algorithms* section of `Chapter 1`, *Data Structures and Algorithms*. During recursion, if the base condition is not reached, then a stack overflow condition may arise.

A recursion algorithm is implemented in the following code snippet. The `Factor` method takes the `num` as a parameter and returns the factorial of **num**. The method uses recursion to calculate the factorial of the number:

```
//main package has examples shown
// in Go Data Structures and algorithms book
package main

// importing fmt and bytes package
import (
  "fmt"
)

//factorial method
func Factor(num int) int {
  if num <= 1 {
    return 1
  }
  return num * Factor(num-1)
}
```

The `main` method defines the integer with a value of `12` and invokes the `Factor` method. The factorial of the number `12` is printed, as shown in the following code:

```
//main method
func main() {
  var num int = 12
  fmt.Println("Factorial: %d is %d", num, Factor(num))
}
```

Run the following command to execute the `recurse_factorial.go` file:

```
go run recurse_factorial.go
```

The output is as follows:

```
apples-MacBook-Air:chapter8 bhagvan.kommadi$ go run recurse_factorial.go
Factorial of %d is %d 12 479001600
apples-MacBook-Air:chapter8 bhagvan.kommadi$
```

Now that we are done with recursive algorithms, let's take a look at the hash algorithms in the next section.

Hashing

Hash functions were introduced in `Chapter 4`, *Non-Linear Data Structures*. Hash implementation in Go has `crc32` and `sha256` implementations. An implementation of a hashing algorithm with multiple values using an XOR transformation is shown in the following code snippet. The `CreateHash` function takes a `byte` array, `byteStr`, as a parameter and returns the `sha256` checksum of the byte array:

```
//main package has examples shown
// in Go Data Structures and algorithms book
package main

// importing fmt package
import (
  "fmt"
  "crypto/sha1"
  "hash"
)
```

```
//CreateHash method
func CreateHash(byteStr []byte) []byte {
  var hashVal hash.Hash
  hashVal = sha1.New()
  hashVal.Write(byteStr)

  var bytes []byte

  bytes = hashVal.Sum(nil)
  return bytes
}
```

In the following sections, we will discuss the different methods of hash algorithms.

The CreateHashMutliple method

The `CreateHashMutliple` method takes the `byteStr1` and `byteStr2` byte arrays as parameters and returns the XOR-transformed bytes value, as follows:

```
// Create hash for Multiple Values method
func CreateHashMultiple(byteStr1 []byte, byteStr2 []byte) []byte {
  return xor(CreateHash(byteStr1), CreateHash(byteStr2))
}
```

The XOR method

The `xor` method takes the `byteStr1` and `byteStr2` byte arrays as parameters and returns the XOR-transformation result, as follows:

```
// XOR method
func xor(byteStr1 []byte, byteStr2 []byte) []byte {
  var xorbytes []byte
  xorbytes = make([]byte, len(byteStr1))
  var i int
  for i = 0; i < len(byteStr1); i++ {
    xorbytes[i] = byteStr1[i] ^ byteStr2[i]
  }
  return xorbytes
}
```

The main method

The `main` method invokes the `createHashMutliple` method, passing `Check` and `Hash` as string parameters, and prints the hash value of the strings, as follows:

```
// main method
func main() {

  var bytes []byte
  bytes = CreateHashMultiple([]byte("Check"), []byte("Hash"))

  fmt.Printf("%x\n", bytes)
}
```

Run the following command to execute the `hash.go` file:

```
go run hash.go
```

The output is as follows:

```
chapter8 — -bash — 80×24
apples-MacBook-Air:chapter8 bhagvan.kommadi$ go run hash.go
cc6b831e2cf05c16a6b0f9c4c9e66b40677b9e7e
apples-MacBook-Air:chapter8 bhagvan.kommadi$
```

Summary

This chapter covered sorting algorithms such as bubble, selection, insertion, shell, merge, and quick sort. Search algorithms such as linear, binary, and interpolation were the discussed. Finally, the recursion and hashing algorithms were explained with code snippets. All of the algorithms were discussed alongside code examples and performance analysis.

In the next chapter, network representation using graphs and sparse matrix representation using list of lists will be covered, along with appropriate examples.

Questions

1. What is the order of complexity of bubble sort?
2. Which sorting algorithm takes one element at a time to create a final sorted collection?
3. What sorting method sorts pairs of elements that are far apart from each other?
4. What is the complexity of using the merge sort algorithm?
5. Which is better: the quick, merge, or heap sort algorithm?
6. What are the different types of search algorithms?
7. Provide a code example of the recursion algorithm.
8. Who was the first person to describe the interpolation search?
9. Which sorting algorithm is based on a comparison-based method of an adjacent list of elements?
10. Who was the person to publish the shell sort algorithm?

Further reading

The following books are recommended if you want to know more about algorithms such as sorting, selecting, searching, and hashing:

- *Design Patterns*, by Erich Gamma, Richard Helm, Ralph Johnson, and John Vlissides
- *Introduction to Algorithms – Third Edition*, by Thomas H. Cormen, Charles E. Leiserson, Ronald L. Rivest, and Clifford Stein
- *Data structures and Algorithms: An Easy Introduction*, by Rudolph Russell

3
Section 3: Advanced Data Structures and Algorithms using Go

Network representation, sparse matrix representation, memory management, instance based learning, compiler translation, and process scheduling-related data structures and algorithms are presented in this section. The data structures shown in the algorithms are graphs, list of lists, AVL trees, K-D trees, ball trees, Van Emde Boas trees, buffer trees, and red-black trees. Cache-oblivious data structures and data flow analysis are covered with code examples and efficiency analysis.

This section contains the following chapters:

- `Chapter 9`, *Network and Sparse Matrix Representation*
- `Chapter 10`, *Memory Management*

9
Network and Sparse Matrix Representation

A **sparse matrix** is a matrix in which most of the values are zero. The ratio of zero values to non-zero values is known as the **sparsity**. An estimation of a matrix's sparsity can be helpful when creating hypotheses about the availability of networks. Extensive big sparse matrices are commonly used in machine learning and natural language parsing. It is computationally costly to work with them. Recommendation engines use them for representing products inside a catalog. Computer vision uses sparse matrices and network data structures when working with pictures that contain sections with dark pixels. Network and sparse matrix data structures are also used in social graphs and map layouts. In this chapter, we will cover the following topics:

- Network representations using graphs:
    - Social network representation
    - Map layouts
    - Knowledge graphs
- Sparse matrix representation using a list of lists

A social graph that connects people is implemented in this chapter, and a code example shows how the graph can be traversed. Map layouts are explained with geographic locations with latitude and longitude. Knowledge graphs are explained via the use of a car and its parts.

Technical requirements

Install Go version 1.10 from `https://golang.org/doc/install for your OS.`

The GitHub URL for the code in this chapter is as follows: `https://github.com/PacktPublishing/Learn-Data-Structures-and-Algorithms-with-Golang/tree/master/Chapter09`.

Network representation using graphs

A graph is a representation of a set of objects that's connected by links. The links connect vertices, which are points. The basic operations on a graph are the addition and removal of links and vertices. These are some different types of graphs:

- Directed graph
- Non-directed graph
- Connected graph
- Non-connected graph
- Simple graph
- Multi-graph

An **adjacency list** consists of adjacent vertices of a graph that have objects or records. An adjacency matrix consists of source and destination vertices. An incidence matrix is a two-dimensional Boolean matrix. The matrix has rows of vertices and columns that represent the links (edges).

Network representation using a graph is shown in the following code. A social graph consists of an array of links:

```
///main package has examples shown
// in Go Data Structures and algorithms book
package main

// importing fmt package
import (
  "fmt"
)
// Social Graph
type SocialGraph struct {
  Size int
  Links [][]Link
}
```

The `Link` struct is defined and implemented in the next section.

The Link class

The `Link` class consists of the `vertex1` and `vertex2` vertices and the `LinkWeight` integer property:

```
// Link class
type Link struct {
  Vertex1 int
  Vertex2 int
  LinkWeight int
}
```

The next section talks about the implementation of the different `Link` class methods.

The NewSocialGraph method

The `NewSocialGraph` function creates a social graph given `num`, which is the size of the graph. `Size` is the number of links in the graph:

```
// NewSocialGraph method
func NewSocialGraph(num int) *SocialGraph {
  return &SocialGraph{
    Size: num,
    Links: make([][]Link, num),
  }
}
```

The AddLink method

The `AddLink` method adds the link between two vertices. The `AddLink` method of a social graph takes `vertex1`, `vertex2`, and `weight` as parameters. The method adds the link from `vertex1` to `vertex2`, as shown in the following code:

```
// AddLink method
func (socialGraph *SocialGraph) AddLink(vertex1 int, vertex2 int, weight
int) {
  socialGraph.Links[vertex1] = append(socialGraph.Links[vertex1],
Link{Vertex1: vertex1, Vertex2: vertex2, LinkWeight: weight})
}
```

The PrintLinks method

The `PrintLinks` method of the `SocialGraph` class prints the links from `vertex = 0` and all the links in the graph:

```
// Print Links Example
func (socialGraph *SocialGraph) PrintLinks() {

  var vertex int
  vertex = 0

  fmt.Printf("Printing all links from %d\n", vertex)
  var link Link
  for _, link = range socialGraph.Links[vertex] {
    fmt.Printf("Link: %d -> %d (%d)\n", link.Vertex1, link.Vertex2,
link.LinkWeight)
  }

  fmt.Println("Printing all links in graph.")
  var adjacent []Link
  for _, adjacent = range socialGraph.Links {
    for _, link = range adjacent {
      fmt.Printf("Link: %d -> %d (%d)\n", link.Vertex1, link.Vertex2,
link.LinkWeight)
    }
  }
}
```

The main method

The `main` method creates a social graph by invoking the `NewSocialGraph` method. The links from `0` to `1`, `0` to `2`, `1` to `3`, and `2` to `4` are added to the social graph. The links are printed using the `printLinks` method:

```
// main method
func main() {

  var socialGraph *SocialGraph

  socialGraph = NewSocialGraph(4)

  socialGraph.AddLink(0, 1, 1)
  socialGraph.AddLink(0, 2, 1)
  socialGraph.AddLink(1, 3, 1)
  socialGraph.AddLink(2, 4, 1)
```

```
  socialGraph.PrintLinks()

}
```

Run the following command to execute the `social_graph.go` file:

```
go run social_graph.go
```

The output is as follows:

```
apples-MacBook-Air:chapter9 bhagvan.kommadi$ go run social_graph.go
Printing all links from 0
Link: 0 -> 1 (1)
Link: 0 -> 2 (1)
Printing all links in graph.
Link: 0 -> 1 (1)
Link: 0 -> 2 (1)
Link: 1 -> 3 (1)
Link: 2 -> 4 (1)
apples-MacBook-Air:chapter9 bhagvan.kommadi$
```

In the next section, we will take a look at the unit test for the social graph method.

Test

Here, we have written a unit test for the social graph method. The code is as follows:

```
///main package has examples shown
// in Go Data Structures and algorithms book
package main

// importing testing package
import (
  "fmt"
  "testing"
)
// NewSocialGraph test method
func TestNewSocialGraph(test *testing.T) {

  var socialGraph *SocialGraph

  socialGraph = NewSocialGraph(1)

  if socialGraph == nil {
```

```
        test.Errorf("error in creating a social Graph")
    }

}
```

Run the following command to execute the preceding code snippet:

```
go test -run NewSocialGraph -v
```

The output is as follows:

```
test — -bash — 80×24
apples-MacBook-Air:test bhagvan.kommadi$ go test -run NewSocialGraph -v
=== RUN   TestNewSocialGraph
--- PASS: TestNewSocialGraph (0.00s)
PASS
ok      _/Users/bhagvan.kommadi/desktop/packt/GoBook/Book/code/chapter9/test    0
.007s
apples-MacBook-Air:test bhagvan.kommadi$
```

In the next section, a social network representation will be implemented with code examples. The preceding graph will be enhanced with nodes. Each node will represent a social entity.

Representing a social network

A **social network** consists of social links that contain social entities such as people, friends, discussions, shares, beliefs, trust, and likes. This graph is used to represent the social network.

Metrics related to the proximity of entities can be calculated based on the graph. Social graphs consist of graph nodes and links, which are maps with a key name and multiple keys names, respectively:

```
///Main package has examples shown
// in Go Data Structures and algorithms book
package main

// importing fmt package
import (
  "fmt"
)


type Name string
```

```
type SocialGraph struct {
  GraphNodes map[Name]struct{}
  Links map[Name]map[Name]struct{}
}
```

The different social network methods are explained and implemented in the next section.

The NewSocialGraph method

The `NewSocialGraph` method returns a social graph consisting of nil-valued `GraphNodes` and `Links`:

```
// NewSocialGraph method
func NewSocialGraph() *SocialGraph {
  return &SocialGraph{
    GraphNodes: make(map[Name]struct{}),
    Links: make(map[Name]map[Name]struct{}),
  }
}
```

The AddEntity method

The `AddEntity` method adds the entity to the social graph. The `AddEntity` method of the `SocialGraph` class takes `name` as a parameter and returns `true` if it is added to the social graph:

```
// AddEntity method
func (socialGraph *SocialGraph) AddEntity(name Name) bool {

  var exists bool
  if _, exists = socialGraph.GraphNodes[name]; exists {
    return true
  }
  socialGraph.GraphNodes[name] = struct{}{}
  return true
}
```

The AddLink method

The AddLink method of the SocialGraph class takes name1 and name2 as parameters. This method creates the entities if the named entities do not exist and creates a link between the entities:

```
// Add Link
func (socialGraph *SocialGraph) AddLink(name1 Name, name2 Name) {
  var exists bool
  if _, exists = socialGraph.GraphNodes[name1]; !exists {
    socialGraph.AddEntity(name1)
  }
  if _, exists = socialGraph.GraphNodes[name2]; !exists {
    socialGraph.AddEntity(name2)
  }
  if _, exists = socialGraph.Links[name1]; !exists {
    socialGraph.Links[name1] = make(map[Name]struct{})
  }
  socialGraph.Links[name1][name2] = struct{}{}
}
```

The PrintLinks method

The PrintLinks method of the SocialGraph class prints the links adjacent to the root and all the links, as shown in the following code snippet:

```
func (socialGraph *SocialGraph) PrintLinks() {
  var root Name
  root = Name("Root")

  fmt.Printf("Printing all links adjacent to %d\n", root)

  var node Name
  for node = range socialGraph.Links[root] {
    // Edge exists from u to v.
    fmt.Printf("Link: %d -> %d\n", root, node)
  }

  var m map[Name]struct{}
  fmt.Println("Printing all links.")
  for root, m = range socialGraph.Links {
    var vertex Name
    for vertex = range m {
      // Edge exists from u to v.
      fmt.Printf("Link: %d -> %d\n", root, vertex)
    }
```

```
    }
}
```

The main method

The main method creates a social graph. The entities, such as john, per, and cynthia, are created and linked with the root node. The friends, such as mayo, lorrie, and ellie, are created and linked with john and per:

```
// main method
func main() {

  var socialGraph *SocialGraph

   socialGraph = NewSocialGraph()

   var root Name = Name("Root")
   var john Name = Name("John Smith")
   var per Name = Name("Per Jambeck")
   var cynthia Name = Name("Cynthia Gibas")


   socialGraph.AddEntity(root)
   socialGraph.AddEntity(john)
   socialGraph.AddEntity(per)
   socialGraph.AddEntity(cynthia)

   socialGraph.AddLink(root, john)
   socialGraph.AddLink(root, per)
   socialGraph.AddLink(root, cynthia)

   var mayo Name = Name("Mayo Smith")
   var lorrie Name = Name("Lorrie Jambeck")
   var ellie Name = Name("Ellie Vlocksen")

   socialGraph.AddLink(john, mayo)
   socialGraph.AddLink(john, lorrie)
   socialGraph.AddLink(per, ellie)

   socialGraph.PrintLinks()
}
```

Run the following command to execute the `social_graph_example.go` file:

```
go run social_graph_example.go
```

The output is as follows:

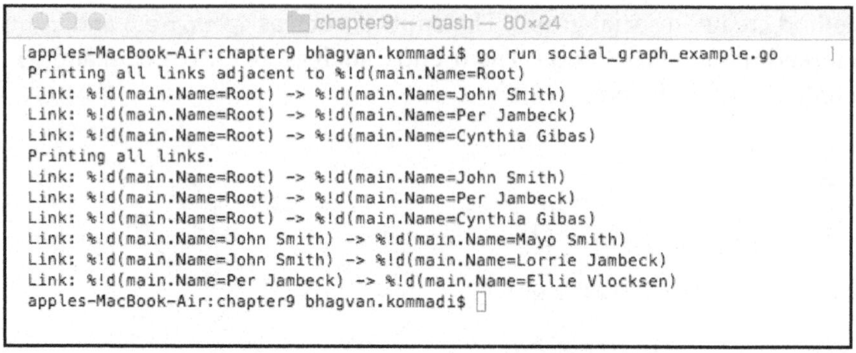

```
chapter9 — -bash — 80×24
apples-MacBook-Air:chapter9 bhagvan.kommadi$ go run social_graph_example.go
Printing all links adjacent to %!d(main.Name=Root)
Link: %!d(main.Name=Root) -> %!d(main.Name=John Smith)
Link: %!d(main.Name=Root) -> %!d(main.Name=Per Jambeck)
Link: %!d(main.Name=Root) -> %!d(main.Name=Cynthia Gibas)
Printing all links.
Link: %!d(main.Name=Root) -> %!d(main.Name=John Smith)
Link: %!d(main.Name=Root) -> %!d(main.Name=Per Jambeck)
Link: %!d(main.Name=Root) -> %!d(main.Name=Cynthia Gibas)
Link: %!d(main.Name=John Smith) -> %!d(main.Name=Mayo Smith)
Link: %!d(main.Name=John Smith) -> %!d(main.Name=Lorrie Jambeck)
Link: %!d(main.Name=Per Jambeck) -> %!d(main.Name=Ellie Vlocksen)
apples-MacBook-Air:chapter9 bhagvan.kommadi$
```

The next section talks about the **map layout** implementation.

Map layouts

A map layout is a geographical visualization of locations that are linked together. The nodes in the graph of a map consist of geo-based information. The node will have information such as the name of the location, latitude, and longitude. Maps are laid out in different scales. Cartographic design is referred to as map creation using geographic information.

A map layout is shown in the following code snippet. The `Place` class consists of `Name`, `Latitude`, and `Longitude` properties:

```
///main package has examples shown
// in Go Data Structures and algorithms book
package main

// importing fmt package
import (
  "fmt"
)

// Place class
type Place struct {

    Name string
```

```
        Latitude float64
        Longitude float64

    }
```

The next section talks about the `MapLayout` class.

The MapLayout class

The `MapLayout` class consists of `GraphNodes` and `Links`:

```
// MapLayout class
type MapLayout struct {
  GraphNodes map[Place]struct{}
  Links map[Place]map[Place]struct{}
}
```

The different `MapLayout` methods are explained and implemented in the next section.

The NewMapLayout method

The `NewMapLayout` method creates a `MapLayout`. The `MapLayout` has `GraphNodes` and links maps:

```
// NewMapLayout method
func NewMapLayout() *MapLayout {
  return &MapLayout{
    GraphNodes: make(map[Place]struct{}),
    Links: make(map[Place]map[Place]struct{}),
  }
}
```

The AddPlace method

The `AddPlace` method of the `MapLayout` class takes place as a parameter and returns `true` if the place exists. If the place does not exist, then a graph node with a new place key is created:

```
// AddPlace method
func (mapLayout *MapLayout) AddPlace(place Place) bool {

  var exists bool
  if _, exists = mapLayout.GraphNodes[place]; exists {
    return true
  }
```

```
    mapLayout.GraphNodes[place] = struct{}{}
    return true
  }
```

The AddLink method

The `AddLink` method of the `MapLayout` class takes the places as parameters and links them together:

```
// Add Link
func (mapLayout *MapLayout) AddLink(place1 Place, place2 Place) {
  var exists bool
  if _, exists = mapLayout.GraphNodes[place1]; !exists {
    mapLayout.AddPlace(place1)
  }
  if _, exists = mapLayout.GraphNodes[place2]; !exists {
    mapLayout.AddPlace(place2)
  }

  if _, exists = mapLayout.Links[place1]; !exists {
    mapLayout.Links[place1] = make(map[Place]struct{})
  }
  mapLayout.Links[place1][place2] = struct{}{}

}
```

The PrintLinks method

The `PrintLinks` method of `MapLayout` prints the places and the links:

```
// PrintLinks method
func (mapLayout *MapLayout) PrintLinks() {
  var root Place
  root = Place{"Algeria", 3, 28}

  fmt.Printf("Printing all links adjacent to %s\n", root.Name)

  var node Place
  for node = range mapLayout.Links[root] {
    fmt.Printf("Link: %s -> %s\n", root.Name, node.Name)
  }

  var m map[Place]struct{}
  fmt.Println("Printing all links.")
  for root, m = range mapLayout.Links {
    var vertex Place
    for vertex = range m {
```

```
            fmt.Printf("Link: %s -> %s\n", root.Name, vertex.Name)
        }
    }
}
```

The main method

In the main method, the map layout is created by invoking the NewMapLayout method. Places are instantiated and added to the map layout. Then, the links are added between places:

```
// main method
func main() {

  var mapLayout *MapLayout

   mapLayout = NewMapLayout()

   var root Place = Place{"Algeria", 3, 28}
   var netherlands Place = Place{"Netherlands", 5.75, 52.5}

   var korea Place = Place{"Korea", 124.1, -8.36}
   var tunisia Place = Place{"Tunisia", 9, 34}


   mapLayout.AddPlace(root)
   mapLayout.AddPlace(netherlands)
   mapLayout.AddPlace(korea)
   mapLayout.AddPlace(tunisia)

   mapLayout.AddLink(root, netherlands)
   mapLayout.AddLink(root,korea)
   mapLayout.AddLink(root,tunisia)


   var singapore Place = Place{"Singapore",103.8,1.36}
   var uae Place = Place{"UAE",54,24}
   var japan Place = Place{"Japan",139.75, 35.68}

   mapLayout.AddLink(korea, singapore)
   mapLayout.AddLink(korea,japan)
   mapLayout.AddLink(netherlands,uae)

   mapLayout.PrintLinks()
}
```

Run the following command to execute the map_layout.go file:

```
go run map_layout.go
```

The output is as follows:

```
chapter9 — -bash — 80×24
apples-MacBook-Air:chapter9 bhagvan.kommadi$ go run map_layout.go
Printing all links adjacent to Algeria
Link: Algeria -> Netherlands
Link: Algeria -> Korea
Link: Algeria -> Tunisia
Printing all links.
Link: Algeria -> Netherlands
Link: Algeria -> Korea
Link: Algeria -> Tunisia
Link: Korea -> Japan
Link: Korea -> Singapore
Link: Netherlands -> UAE
apples-MacBook-Air:chapter9 bhagvan.kommadi$
```

In the next section, we will take a look at the unit test for the NewMapLayout method.

Test

A unit test for the MapLayout class's NewMapLayout method is shown in the following code snippet:

```
///main package has examples shown
// in Go Data Structures and algorithms book
package main

// importing testing package
import (
  "testing"
)

// NewMapLayout test method
func TestNewMapLayout(test *testing.T) {

  var mapLayout *MapLayout

  mapLayout = NewMapLayout()

  test.Log(mapLayout)

  if mapLayout == nil {

    test.Errorf("error in creating a mapLayout")
  }
```

```
}
```

Run the following command to execute the preceding code snippet:

```
go test -run NewMapLayout -v
```

The output is as follows:

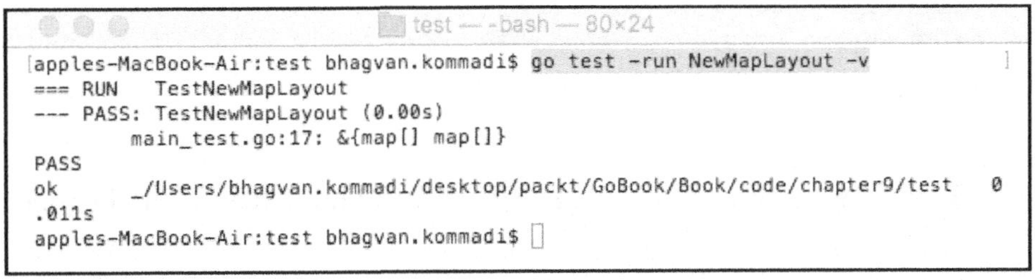

```
apples-MacBook-Air:test bhagvan.kommadi$ go test -run NewMapLayout -v
=== RUN   TestNewMapLayout
--- PASS: TestNewMapLayout (0.00s)
        main_test.go:17: &{map[] map[]}
PASS
ok      _/Users/bhagvan.kommadi/desktop/packt/GoBook/Book/code/chapter9/test    0
.011s
apples-MacBook-Air:test bhagvan.kommadi$
```

The next section talks about implementing a **knowledge graph**.

Knowledge graphs

A knowledge graph is a network representation of entities, items, and users as nodes. The nodes interact with one another via links or edges. Knowledge graphs are widely used because they are schema less. These data structures are used to represent knowledge in the form of graphs, and the nodes have textual information. Knowledge graphs are created by using item, entity, and user nodes and linking them with edges.

An **ontology** consists of a knowledge graph of information nodes. The reasoner derives knowledge from knowledge graphs. A knowledge graph consists of classes, slots, and facets, which are ontological terms. In the following code, a knowledge graph consisting of a car's bill of materials is explained. The `Class` type consists of a name, which is a string:

```
///main package has examples shown
// in Go Data Structures and algorithms book
package main

// importing fmt package
import (
  "fmt"
)

// Class Type
type Class struct {
  Name string
}
```

The next section talks about the `knowledge graph` class.

The KnowledgeGraph class

The `KnowledgeGraph` class consists of `GraphNodes` and links:

```
// Knowledge Graph type
type KnowledgeGraph struct {
  GraphNodes map[Class]struct{}
  Links map[Class]map[Class]struct{}
}
```

The different knowledge graph methods are explained and implemented in the following sections.

The NewKnowledgeGraph method

The `NewKnowledgeGraph` method creates a knowledge graph, which consists of `GraphNodes` and `Links` maps:

```
// NewKnowledgeGraph method
func NewKnowledgeGraph() *KnowledgeGraph {
  return &KnowledgeGraph{
    GraphNodes: make(map[Class]struct{}),
    Links: make(map[Class]map[Class]struct{}),
  }
}
```

The AddClass method

The `AddClass` method of the `KnowledgeGraph` class takes `class` as a parameter and returns `true` if the class exists. If the class does not exist, a `GraphNode` is created with `class` as a key:

```
// AddClass method
func (knowledgeGraph *KnowledgeGraph) AddClass(class Class) bool {

  var exists bool
  if _, exists = knowledgeGraph.GraphNodes[class]; exists {
    return true
  }
  knowledgeGraph.GraphNodes[class] = struct{}{}
  return true
}
```

The AddLink method

The `AddLink` method of the `KnowledgeGraph` class takes `class1` and `class2` as parameters, and a link is created between these classes:

```
// Add Link
func (knowledgeGraph *KnowledgeGraph) AddLink(class1 Class, class2 Class) {
  var exists bool
  if _, exists = knowledgeGraph.GraphNodes[class1]; !exists {
    knowledgeGraph.AddClass(class1)
  }
  if _, exists = knowledgeGraph.GraphNodes[class2]; !exists {
    knowledgeGraph.AddClass(class2)
  }

  if _, exists = knowledgeGraph.Links[class1]; !exists {
    knowledgeGraph.Links[class1] = make(map[Class]struct{})
  }
  knowledgeGraph.Links[class1][class2] = struct{}{}

}
```

The PrintLinks method

The `PrintLinks` method of the `KnowledgeGraph` class prints the links and nodes:

```
// Print Links method
func (knowledgeGraph *KnowledgeGraph) PrintLinks() {
  var car Class
  car = Class{"Car"}

  fmt.Printf("Printing all links adjacent to %s\n", car.Name)

  var node Class
  for node = range knowledgeGraph.Links[car] {
    fmt.Printf("Link: %s -> %s\n", car.Name, node.Name)
  }

  var m map[Class]struct{}
  fmt.Println("Printing all links.")
  for car, m = range knowledgeGraph.Links {
    var vertex Class
    for vertex = range m {
      fmt.Printf("Link: %s -> %s\n", car.Name, vertex.Name)
    }
  }
}
```

The main method

The `main` method creates the knowledge graph, and the classes are instantiated. The links between the classes are created and printed:

```
// main method
func main() {

  var knowledgeGraph *KnowledgeGraph

  knowledgeGraph = NewKnowledgeGraph()

  var car = Class{"Car"}
  var tyre = Class{"Tyre"}
  var door = Class{"Door"}
  var hood = Class{"Hood"}

  knowledgeGraph.AddClass(car)
  knowledgeGraph.AddClass(tyre)
  knowledgeGraph.AddClass(door)
  knowledgeGraph.AddClass(hood)

  knowledgeGraph.AddLink(car, tyre)
  knowledgeGraph.AddLink(car, door)
  knowledgeGraph.AddLink(car, hood)

  var tube = Class{"Tube"}
  var axle = Class{"Axle"}
  var handle = Class{"Handle"}
  var windowGlass = Class{"Window Glass"}

  knowledgeGraph.AddClass(tube)
  knowledgeGraph.AddClass(axle)
  knowledgeGraph.AddClass(handle)
  knowledgeGraph.AddClass(windowGlass)

  knowledgeGraph.AddLink(tyre, tube)
  knowledgeGraph.AddLink(tyre, axle)
  knowledgeGraph.AddLink(door, handle)
  knowledgeGraph.AddLink(door, windowGlass)

  knowledgeGraph.PrintLinks()
}
```

Run the following command to execute the `knowledge_catalog.go` file:

```
go run knowledge_catalog.go
```

The output is as follows:

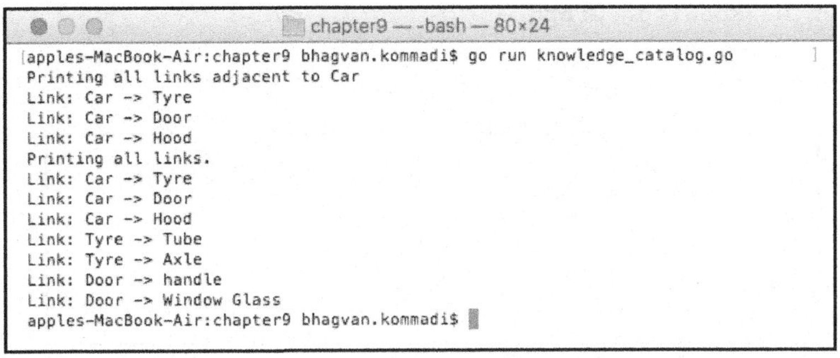

```
chapter9 — -bash — 80×24
apples-MacBook-Air:chapter9 bhagvan.kommadi$ go run knowledge_catalog.go
Printing all links adjacent to Car
Link: Car -> Tyre
Link: Car -> Door
Link: Car -> Hood
Printing all links.
Link: Car -> Tyre
Link: Car -> Door
Link: Car -> Hood
Link: Tyre -> Tube
Link: Tyre -> Axle
Link: Door -> handle
Link: Door -> Window Glass
apples-MacBook-Air:chapter9 bhagvan.kommadi$
```

In the next section, we will take a look at the unit test for the `NewKnowledgeGraph` method.

Test

The `NewKnowledgeGraph` method is unit tested in the following code snippet:

```
///main package has examples shown
// in Go Data Structures and algorithms book
package main

// importing testing package
import (
  "testing"
)

// NewKnowledgeGraph test method
func TestNewKnowledgeGraph(test *testing.T) {

  var knowledgeGraph *KnowledgeGraph

  knowledgeGraph = NewKnowledgeGraph()

  test.Log(knowledgeGraph)

  if knowledgeGraph == nil {

    test.Errorf("error in creating a knowledgeGraph")
  }

}
```

Run the following command to execute the preceding code snippet:

```
go test -run NewKnowledgeGraph -v
```

The output is as follows:

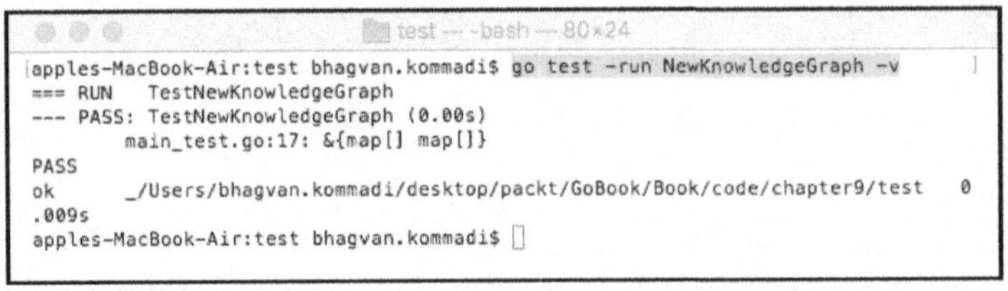

```
apples-MacBook-Air:test bhagvan.kommadi$ go test -run NewKnowledgeGraph -v
=== RUN   TestNewKnowledgeGraph
--- PASS: TestNewKnowledgeGraph (0.00s)
        main_test.go:17: &{map[] map[]}
PASS
ok      _/Users/bhagvan.kommadi/desktop/packt/GoBook/Book/code/chapter9/test    0
.009s
apples-MacBook-Air:test bhagvan.kommadi$
```

The next section talks about the representation of the **sparse matrix**.

Sparse matrix representation using a list of lists

A sparse matrix is a two-dimensional list of m rows and n columns. The shape of a matrix is $m \times n$ if it consists of m rows and n columns. Sparse matrices are used for solving large-scale problems that do not require dense matrices. For example, partial differential equations are solved by using the **finite element method** (**FEM**). Tuples of a sparse matrix are non-zero elements of the matrix.

In the following code, a sparse matrix is modeled as a list of lists. A sparse matrix consists of cells that are a list of lists. Each cell has properties such as `Row`, `Column`, and `Value`:

```
///main package has examples shown
// in Go Data Structures and algorithms book
package main

// importing fmt package
import (
  "fmt"
)

//List of List
type LOL struct {
  Row int
  Column int
  Value float64
}
```

The next section talks about the `SparseMatrix` class.

SparseMatrix class

`SparseMatrix` has a `cells` array and `shape`, which is an integer array:

```
//Sparse Matrix
type SparseMatrix struct {
  cells []LOL
  shape [2]int
}
```

In the next section, the different `Sparse` methods of the `SparseMatrix` struct are implemented.

The Shape method

The `Shape` method of the `SparseMatrix` class returns the `shape` array elements:

```
// Shape method
func (sparseMatrix *SparseMatrix) Shape() (int, int) {
  return sparseMatrix.shape[0], sparseMatrix.shape[1]
}
```

The NumNonZero method

The `NumNonZero` method finds the cells with non-zero elements. The `NumNonZero` method of the `SparseMatrix` class returns the size of the cells array in `sparseMatrix`:

```
// NumNonZero method
func (sparseMatrix *SparseMatrix) NumNonZero() int {
  return len(sparseMatrix.cells)
}
```

The LessThan method

The `LessThan` method compares the list of lists rows and columns and checks whether the row is less than `i` and that the column is less than `j`:

```
// Less Than method
func LessThan(lol LOL, i int, j int) bool {
```

```
    if lol.Row < i && lol.Column < j {

      return true
    }

    return false
}
```

The Equal method

The `Equal` method checks whether the list of lists rows and columns are equal to `i` and `j`, respectively:

```
// Equal method
func Equal(lol LOL, i int, j int) bool {
  if lol.Row == i && lol.Column == j {
    return true
  }
  return false
}
```

The GetValue method

The `GetValue` method of the `SparseMatrix` class returns the value of the cell whose row and column equal `i` and `j`, respectively:

```
// GetValue method
func (sparseMatrix *SparseMatrix) GetValue(i int, j int) float64 {
  var lol LOL
  for _, lol = range sparseMatrix.cells {
    if LessThan(lol, i, j) {
      continue
    }
    if Equal(lol, i, j) {
      return lol.Value
    }
    return 0.0
  }
  return 0.0
}
```

The SetValue method

The `SetValue` method of the `SparseMatrix` class sets the value of the cell with the row and column equal to `i` and `j`, respectively, as the parameter value:

```
//SetValue method
func (sparseMatrix *SparseMatrix) SetValue(i int, j int, value float64) {

  var lol LOL
  var index int
  for index, lol = range sparseMatrix.cells {
    if LessThan(lol, i, j) {
      continue
    }
    if Equal(lol, i, j) {
      sparseMatrix.cells[index].Value = value
      return
    }

    sparseMatrix.cells = append(sparseMatrix.cells, LOL{})
    var k int
    for k = len(sparseMatrix.cells) - 2; k >= index; k-- {
      sparseMatrix.cells[k+1] = sparseMatrix.cells[k]
    }
    sparseMatrix.cells[index] = LOL{
      Row: i,
      Column: j,
      Value: value,
    }
    return
  }
  sparseMatrix.cells = append(sparseMatrix.cells, LOL{
    Row: i,
    Column: j,
    Value: value,
  })
}
```

The NewSparseMatrix method

The `NewSparseMatrix` method takes the `m` and `n` as parameters and returns the initialized matrix:

```
// New SparseMatrix method
func NewSparseMatrix(m int, n int) *SparseMatrix {
  return &SparseMatrix{
    cells: []LOL{},
    shape: [2]int{m, n},
  }
}
```

The main method

The `main` method creates the sparse matrix by invoking the `NewSparseMatrix` method. The values are set in cells (`1`, `1`) and (`1`, `3`). The sparse matrix and the number of non-zero cells are printed:

```
// main method
func main() {

  var sparseMatrix *SparseMatrix

  sparseMatrix = NewSparseMatrix(3, 3)

  sparseMatrix.SetValue(1, 1, 2.0)
  sparseMatrix.SetValue(1, 3, 3.0)

  fmt.Println(sparseMatrix)
  fmt.Println(sparseMatrix.NumNonZero())
}
```

Run the following command to execute the sparse_matrix.go file:

```
go run sparse_matrix.go
```

The output is as follows:

```
chapter9 — -bash — 80×24
apples-MacBook-Air:chapter9 bhagvan.kommadi$ go run sparse_matrix.go
&{[{1 3 3} {1 1 2}] [3 3]}
2
apples-MacBook-Air:chapter9 bhagvan.kommadi$
```

Summary

This chapter covered how to present networks and sparse matrices using graphs and a list of lists, respectively. Social network representation, map layouts, and knowledge graphs were discussed in detail with code examples. The different sparse matrix methods were also implemented with the appropriate code.

In the next chapter, algorithms such as garbage collection, cache management, and space allocation will be presented with code examples and an efficiency analysis.

Questions

- What data structure is used to represent a set of linked objects?
- What is a two-dimensional matrix with Boolean values called?
- Give a code example for a network representation using a graph.
- Which metrics can be calculated from a social graph?
- What is a cartographic design?
- Give an example of a knowledge graph and define the class, slots, and facets.
- What are the applications of sparse matrices?
- Define a list of lists and write a code sample.
- What is a map layout?
- What different operations can be performed using graphs?

Further reading

The following books are recommended if you want to know more about graphs and list of lists:

- *Design Patterns*, by Erich Gamma, Richard Helm, Ralph Johnson, and John Vlissides
- *Introduction to Algorithms – Third Edition*, by Thomas H. Cormen, Charles E. Leiserson, Ronald L. Rivest, and Clifford Stein
- *Data structures and Algorithms: An Easy Introduction*, by Rudolph Russell

10
Memory Management

Memory management is a way to control and organize memory. Memory divisions are called **blocks**, and they are used for running different processes. The basic goal of memory management algorithms is to dynamically designate segments of memory to programs on demand. The algorithms free up memory for reuse when the objects in the memory are never required again. Garbage collection, cache management, and space allocation algorithms are good examples of memory management techniques. In software engineering, garbage collection is used to free up memory that's been allocated to those objects that won't be used again, thus helping in memory management. The cache provides in-memory storage for data. You can sort the data in the cache into locale-specific groups. The data can be stored using key and value sets.

This chapter covers the garbage collection, cache management, and space allocation algorithms. The memory management algorithms are presented with code samples and efficiency analyses. The following topics will be covered in this chapter:

- Garbage collection
- Cache management
- Space allocation
- Concepts—Go memory management

We'll look at garbage collection first, then look at the different algorithms related to garbage collection.

Technical requirements

Install Go Version 1.10 from Golang (`https://golang.org/`), choosing the right version for your OS.

The GitHub repository for the code in this chapter can be found here: `https://github.com/PacktPublishing/Learn-Data-Structures-and-Algorithms-with-Golang/tree/master/Chapter10`.

Garbage collection

Garbage collection is a type of programmed memory management in which memory, currently occupied by objects that will never be used again, is gathered. John McCarthy was the first person to come up with garbage collection for managing Lisp memory management. This technique specifies which objects need to be de-allocated, and then discharges the memory. The strategies that are utilized for garbage collection are **stack allocation** and **region interference**. Sockets, relational database handles, user window objects, and file resources are not overseen by garbage collectors.

Garbage collection algorithms help reduce dangling pointer defects, double-free defects, and memory leaks. These algorithms are computing-intensive and cause decreased or uneven performance. According to Apple, one of the reasons for iOS not having garbage collection is that garbage collection needs five times the memory to match explicit memory management. In high-transactional systems, concurrent, incremental, and real-time garbage collectors help manage memory collection and release.

Garbage collection algorithms depend on various factors:

- GC throughput
- Heap overhead
- Pause times
- Pause frequency
- Pause distribution
- Allocation performance
- Compaction
- Concurrency
- Scaling
- Tuning
- Warm-up time
- Page release
- Portability
- Compatibility

That's simple, deferred, one-bit, weighted reference counting, mark-and-sweep, and generational collection algorithms discussed in the following sections.

The ReferenceCounter class

The following code snippet shows how references to created objects are maintained in the stack. The `ReferenceCounter` class has the number of references, including the pool of references and removed references, as properties:

```
//main package has examples shown
// in Hands-On Data Structures and algorithms with Go book
package main

// importing fmt package
import (
    "fmt"
    "sync"
)

//Reference Counter
type ReferenceCounter struct {
    num *uint32
    pool *sync.Pool
    removed *uint32
}
```

Let's take a look at the method of the `ReferenceCounter` class.

The newReferenceCounter method

The `newReferenceCounter` method initializes a `ReferenceCounter` instance and returns a pointer to `ReferenceCounter`. This is shown in the following code:

```
//new Reference Counter method
func newReferenceCounter() *ReferenceCounter {
    return &ReferenceCounter{
    num: new(uint32),
    pool: &sync.Pool{},
    removed: new(uint32),
    }
}
```

The `Stack` class is described in the next section.

The Stack class

The `Stack` class consists of a `references` array and `Count` as properties. This is shown in the following code:

```
// Stack class
type Stack struct {
    references []*ReferenceCounter
    Count int
}
```

Let's take a look at the methods of the `Stack` class.

The Stack class – a new method

Now, let's look at the heap interface methods that are implemented by the `Stack` class. The new method initializes the `references` array, and the `Push` and `Pop` heap interface methods take the `reference` parameter to push and pop `reference` out of the stack. This is shown in the following code:

```
// New method of Stack Class
func (stack *Stack) New() {
    stack.references = make([]*ReferenceCounter,0)
}

// Push method
func (stack *Stack) Push(reference *ReferenceCounter) {
    stack.references = append(stack.references[:stack.Count],
    reference)
    stack.Count = stack.Count + 1
}

// Pop method
func (stack *Stack) Pop() *ReferenceCounter {
    if stack.Count == 0 {
        return nil
    }
var length int = len(stack.references)
var reference *ReferenceCounter = stack.references[length -1]
if length > 1 {
  stack.references = stack.references[:length-1]
  } else {
  stack.references = stack.references[0:]
}
    stack.Count = len(stack.references)
    return reference
```

```
}
```

The main method

In the following code snippet, let's see how `Stack` is used. A `Stack` instance is initialized, and references are added to the stack by invoking the `Push` method. The `Pop` method is invoked and the output is printed:

```
// main method
func main() {
    var stack *Stack = &Stack{}
    stack.New()
    var reference1 *ReferenceCounter = newReferenceCounter()
    var reference2 *ReferenceCounter = newReferenceCounter()
    var reference3 *ReferenceCounter = newReferenceCounter()
    var reference4 *ReferenceCounter = newReferenceCounter()
    stack.Push(reference1)
    stack.Push(reference2)
    stack.Push(reference3)
    stack.Push(reference4)
    fmt.Println(stack.Pop(), stack.Pop(), stack.Pop(), stack.Pop())
}
```

Run the following commands to execute the `stack_garbage_collection.go` file:

```
go run stack_garbage_collection.go
```

The output is as follows:

```
chapter10 — -bash — 117×29
apples-MacBook-Air:chapter10 bhagvan.kommadi$ go run stack_garbage_collection.go
&{0xc42008401c 0xc420098100 0xc420084020} &{0xc420084014 0xc4200980c0 0xc420084018} &{0xc42008400c 0xc420098080 0xc42
0084010} &{0xc420084004 0xc420098040 0xc420084008}
apples-MacBook-Air:chapter10 bhagvan.kommadi$
```

The reference counting, mark-and-sweep, and generational collection algorithms will be discussed in the following sections.

Reference counting

Reference counting is a technique that's used for keeping the count of references, pointers, and handles to resources. Memory blocks, disk space, and objects are good examples of resources. This technique tracks each object as a resource. The metrics that are tracked are the number of references held by different objects. The objects are recovered when they can never be referenced again.

The number of references is used for runtime optimizations. Deutsch-Bobrow came up with the strategy of reference counting. This strategy was related to the number of updated references that were produced by references that were put in local variables. Henry Baker came up with a method that includes references in local variables that are deferred until needed.

In the following subsections, the simple, deferred, one-bit, and weighted techniques of reference counting will be discussed.

Simple reference counting

Reference counting is related to keeping the number of references, pointers, and handles to a resource such as an object, block of memory, or disk space. This technique is related to the number of references to de-allocated objects that are never referenced again.

The collection technique tracks, for each object, a tally of the number of references to the object. The references are held by other objects. The object gets removed when the number of references to the object is zero. The removed object becomes inaccessible. The removal of a reference can prompt countless connected references to be purged.

The algorithm is time-consuming because of the size of the object graph and slow access speed.

In the following code snippets, we can see a simple reference-counting algorithm being implemented. The `ReferenceCounter` class has number (`num`), `pool`, and `removed` references as properties:

```
///main package has examples shown
// in Go Data Structures and algorithms book
package main

// importing sync, atomic and fmt packages
import (
    "sync/atomic"
    "sync"
    "fmt"
```

```
)

//Reference Counter
type ReferenceCounter struct {
    num *uint32
    pool *sync.Pool
    removed *uint32
}
```

The `newReferenceCounter`, `Add`, and `Subtract` methods of the `ReferenceCounter` class are shown in the following snippet:

```
//new Reference Counter method
func newReferenceCounter() ReferenceCounter {
    return ReferenceCounter{
        num: new(uint32),
        pool: &sync.Pool{},
        removed: new(uint32),
    }
}

// Add method
func (referenceCounter ReferenceCounter) Add() {
    atomic.AddUint32(referenceCounter.num, 1)
}

// Subtract method
func (referenceCounter ReferenceCounter) Subtract() {
    if atomic.AddUint32(referenceCounter.num, ^uint32(0)) == 0 {
        atomic.AddUint32(referenceCounter.removed, 1)
    }
}
```

Let's look at the `main` method and see an example of simple reference counting. The `newReferenceCounter` method is invoked, and a reference is added by invoking the `Add` method. The `count` reference is printed at the end. This is shown in the following code snippet

```
// main method
func main() {
    var referenceCounter ReferenceCounter
    referenceCounter = newReferenceCounter()
    referenceCounter.Add()
    fmt.Println(*referenceCounter.count)
}
```

Run the following commands to execute the `reference_counting.go` file:

```
go run reference_counting.go
```

The output is as follows:

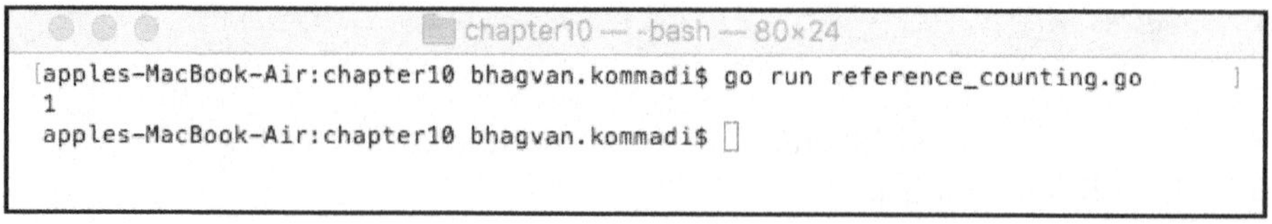

```
apples-MacBook-Air:chapter10 bhagvan.kommadi$ go run reference_counting.go
1
apples-MacBook-Air:chapter10 bhagvan.kommadi$
```

The different types of reference counting techniques are described in the following sections.

Deferred reference counting

Deferred reference counting is a procedure in which references from different objects to a given object are checked and program-variable references are overlooked. If the tally of the references is zero, that object will not be considered. This algorithm helps reduce the overhead of keeping counts up to date. Deferred reference counting is supported by many compilers.

One-bit reference counting

The **one-bit reference counting** technique utilizes a solitary bit flag to show whether an object has one or more references. The flag is stored as part of the object pointer. There is no requirement to spare any object for extra space in this technique. This technique is viable since the majority of objects have a reference count of 1.

Weighted reference counting

The weighted reference counting technique tallies the number of references to an object, and each reference is delegated a weight. This technique tracks the total weight of the references to an object. Weighted reference counting was invented by Bevan, Watson, and Watson in 1987. The following code snippet shows an implementation of the weighted reference counting technique:

```
//Reference Counter
type ReferenceCounter struct {
    num *uint32
    pool *sync.Pool
    removed *uint32
```

```
    weight int
}

//WeightedReference method
func WeightedReference() int {
    var references []ReferenceCounter
    references = GetReferences(root)
    var reference ReferenceCounter
    var sum int
    for _, reference = range references {
        sum = sum + reference.weight
    }
    return sum
}
```

The mark-and-sweep algorithm

The **mark-and-sweep algorithm** is based on an idea that was proposed by Dijkstra in 1978. In the garbage collection style, the heap consists of a graph of connected objects, which are white. This technique visits the objects and checks whether they are specifically available by the application. Globals and objects on the stack are shaded gray in this technique. Every gray object is darkened to black and filtered for pointers to other objects. Any white object found in the output is turned gray. This calculation is rehashed until there are no gray objects. White objects that are left out are inaccessible.

A mutator in this algorithm handles concurrency by changing the pointers while the collector is running. It also takes care of the condition so that no black object points to a white object. The mark algorithm has the following steps:

1. Mark the `root` object
2. Mark the `root` bit as `true` if the value of the bit is `false`
3. For every reference of `root`, mark the reference, as in the first step

The following code snippet shows the marking algorithm. Let's look at the implementation of the `Mark` method:

```
func Mark( root *object){
   var markedAlready bool
   markedAlready = IfMarked(root)
   if !markedAlready {
        map[root] = true
   }
   var references *object[]
   references = GetReferences(root)
```

```
        var reference *object
        for _, reference = range references {
            Mark(reference)
        }
    }
```

The sweep algorithm's pseudocode is presented here:

- For each object in the heap, mark the bit as `false` if the value of the bit is `true`
- If the value of the bit is `true`, release the object from the heap

The sweep algorithm releases the objects that are marked for garbage collection.

Now, let's look at the implementation of the sweep algorithm:

```
    func Sweep(){
        var objects *[]object
        objects = GetObjects()
        var object *object
        for _, object = range objects {
        var markedAlready bool
        markedAlready = IfMarked(object)
        if markedAlready {
             map[object] = true
        }
            Release(object)
        }
    }
```

The generational collection algorithm

The **generational collection algorithm** divides the heap of objects into generations. A generation of objects will be expired and collected by the algorithm based on their age. The algorithm promotes objects to older generations based on the age of the object in the garbage collection cycle.

The entire heap needs to be scavenged, even if a generation is collected. Let's say generation `3` is collected; in this case, generations `0-2` are also scavenged. The generational collection algorithm is presented in the following code snippet:

```
    func GenerationCollect(){
        var currentGeneration int
        currentGeneration = 3
        var objects *[]object
        objects = GetObjectsFromOldGeneration(3)
```

```
        var object *object
        for _, object = range objects {
            var markedAlready bool
            markedAlready = IfMarked(object)
            if markedAlready {
                map[object] = true
            }
        }
    }
```

We'll take a look at cache management in the next section.

Cache management

Cache management consists of managing static, dynamic, and variable information:

- Static information never changes
- Dynamic information changes frequently
- Variable information changes less frequently than dynamic information

The object cache is stored in various data structures, such as maps and trees. Maps have a key as an identifier and a value, which is an object.

Cache objects can be related to memory, disks, pools, and streams. Caches have attributes related to time to live, group, and region. A region consists of a collection of mapped key-values. Regions can be independent of other regions. Cache configuration consists of defaults, regions, and auxiliaries.

A typical cache manager has the following features:

- Memory management
- Thread pool controls
- Grouping of elements
- Configurable runtime parameters
- Region data separation and configuration
- Remote synchronization
- Remote store recovery
- Event handling
- Remote server chaining and failover
- Custom event logging

- Custom event queue injection
- Key pattern-matching retrieval
- Network-efficient multi-key retrieval

The `CacheObject` class and the `Cache` class are described in the following sections.

The CacheObject class

The `CacheObject` class has `Value` and `TimeToLive` properties. This is shown in the following code:

```
///main package has examples shown
// in Go Data Structures and algorithms book
package main

// importing fmt, sync and time packages
import (
	"fmt"
	"sync"
	"time"
)

// CacheObject class
type CacheObject struct {
	Value string
	TimeToLive int64
}
```

The `IfExpired` method of the `CacheObject` class is shown in the next section.

The IfExpired method

`IfExpired` checks whether the `cache` object has expired. The `IfExpired` method of `CacheObject` returns `true` if `TimeToLive` has not expired; otherwise, it returns `false`. This is shown in the following code:

```
// IfExpired method
func (cacheObject CacheObject) IfExpired() bool {
	if cacheObject.TimeToLive == 0 {
		return false
	}
	return time.Now().UnixNano() > cacheObject.TimeToLive
}
```

The Cache class

The `Cache` class consists of `objects map` with a `string` key, a `CacheObject` value, and a `sync.RWMutex` mutex. This is shown in the following code:

```
//Cache class
type Cache struct {
    objects map[string]CacheObject
    mutex *sync.RWMutex
}
```

The `NewCache`, `GetObject`, and `SetValue` methods of the `Cache` class are shown in the following sections.

The NewCache method

The `NewCache` method returns a pointer to a cache, which is initialized with the `nil` map (that is, a map without values) and `RWMutex`. This is shown in the following code:

```
//NewCache method
func NewCache() *Cache {
    return &Cache{
        objects: make(map[string]CacheObject),
        mutex: &sync.RWMutex{},
    }
}
```

The GetObject method

The `GetObject` method retrieves the object given the cache key. The `GetObject` method of the `Cache` class returns the value of `cacheKey`. The `RLock` method on the `mutex` object of the cache is invoked, and the `RUnlock` method is deferred before returning the value of `cacheKey`. If the object has expired, the key value will be an empty string. This is shown in the following code:

```
//GetObject method
func (cache Cache) GetObject(cacheKey string) string {
    cache.mutex.RLock()
    defer cache.mutex.RUnlock()
    var object CacheObject
    object = cache.objects[cacheKey]
    if object.IfExpired() {
        delete(cache.objects, cacheKey)
    return ""
```

```
    }
    return object.Value
}
```

The SetValue method

The `SetValue` method of the `Cache` class takes `cacheKey`, `cacheValue`, and `timeToLive` parameters. The `Lock` method on the `mutex` object of the cache is invoked, and the `Unlock` method is deferred. A new `CacheObject` is created with `cacheValue` and `TimeToLive` as properties. The created `cacheObject` is set as a value to map objects with the `cacheKey` key. This is shown in the following code:

```
//SetValue method
func (cache Cache) SetValue(cacheKey string, cacheValue string, timeToLive
time.Duration) {
    cache.mutex.Lock()
    defer cache.mutex.Unlock()
    cache.objects[cacheKey] = CacheObject{
        Value: cacheValue,
        TimeToLive: time.Now().Add(timeToLive).UnixNano(),
    }
}
```

We'll implement the methods we just took a look at in the `main` method in the next section.

The main method

The `main` method creates the cache by invoking the `NewCache` method. The key and value are set on the cache by invoking `setValue`. The value is accessed by calling the `GetObject` method of the `Cache` class. This is shown in the following code:

```
// main method
func main() {
    var cache *Cache
    cache = NewCache()
    cache.SetValue("name", "john smith", 200000000)
    var name string
    name = cache.GetObject("name")
    fmt.Println(name)
}
```

Run the following command to execute the cache_management.go file:

```
go run cache_management.go
```

The output is as follows:

```
apples-MacBook-Air:chapter10 bhagvan.kommadi$ go run cache_management.go
john smith
apples-MacBook-Air:chapter10 bhagvan.kommadi$
```

The next section talks about the space allocation algorithm.

Space allocation

Each function has stack frames associated with individual memory space. Functions have access to the memory inside the frame, and a frame pointer points to the memory's location. Transition between frames occurs when the function is invoked. Data is transferred by value from one frame to another during the transition.

Stack frame creation and memory allocation is demonstrated in the following code. The addOne function takes num and increments it by one. The function prints the value and address of num:

```
///main package has examples shown
// in Go Data Structures and algorithms book
package main

// importing fmt package
import (
    "fmt"
)

// increment method
func addOne(num int) {
    num++
    fmt.Println("added to num", num, "Address of num", &num)
}
```

The `main` method initializes the variable number as `17`. The number value and address are printed before and after invoking the `addOne` function. This is shown in the following code:

```
// main method
func main() {
    var number int
    number = 17
    fmt.Println("value of number", number, "Address of number",
    &number)
    addOne(number)
    fmt.Println("value of number after adding One", number, "Address
    of", &number)
}
```

Run the following command to execute the `stack_memory_allocation.go` file:

```
go run stack_memory_allocation.go
```

The output is as follows:

```
chapter10 — -bash — 80×24
apples-MacBook-Air:chapter10 bhagvan.kommadi$ go run stack_memory_allocation.go
value of number 17 Address of number 0xc420016058
added to num 18 Address of num 0xc420016068
value of number after adding One 17 Address of 0xc420016058
apples-MacBook-Air:chapter10 bhagvan.kommadi$
```

Frame pointers are explained in the next section.

Pointers

Pointers have an address that is 4 or 8 bytes long, depending on whether you have a 32-bit or 64-bit architecture. The stack's main frame consists of the number 17 with the address `0xc420016058`. After adding one, a new frame with `num` equal to `18` and an address of `0xc420016068` is created. The `main` method prints the stack's main frame after invoking the `addOne` function. The code in the following sections demonstrates memory space allocation with pointers instead of actual values passed into a function.

The `AddOne` and main methods of pointers are shown in the following sections.

The addOne method

The `addOne` function takes a pointer to `num` and increments it by 1. The function prints the value, address, and pointer of `num`. This is shown in the following code:

```
///main package has examples shown
// in Go Data Structures and algorithms book
package main

// importing fmt package
import (
    "fmt"
)

// increment method
func addOne(num *int) {
    *num++
    fmt.Println("added to num", num, "Address of num", &num, "Value
    Points To", *num )
}
```

The main method

The `main` method initializes the variable number to `17`. The pointer to the number is passed to the `addOne` function. The number value and address is printed before and after invoking the `addOne` function.

In this example, the address of the number is the same as the value of `num` in the `addOne` function. Pointers share the address of the variable for the function to access for reads and writes within the stack frame. Pointer types are specific to every type that is declared. Pointers provide indirect memory access outside the function's stack frame. This is shown in the following code:

```
// main method
func main() {
    var number int
    number = 17
    fmt.Println("value of number", number, "Address of number",
    &number)
    addOne(&number)
    fmt.Println("value of number after adding One", number, "Address
    of", &number)
}
```

Run the following command to execute the `stack_memory_pointer.go` file:

```
go run stack_memory_pointer.go
```

The output is as follows:

```
apples-MacBook-Air:chapter10 bhagvan.kommadi$ go run stack_memory_pointer.go
value of number 17 Address of number 0xc420016058
added to num 0xc420016058 Address of num 0xc42000c030 Value Points To 18
value of number after adding One 18 Address of 0xc420016058
apples-MacBook-Air:chapter10 bhagvan.kommadi$
```

The next section talks about memory management in Go.

Concepts – Go memory management

In Go, programmers don't need to worry about coding a variable's value placement in memory and space allocation. Garbage collection in Go is overseen by the memory manager. The `GOGC` variable is used to set a value for the initial garbage collection target percentage. Garbage collection is activated when the proportion of freshly allotted data to the live data that remains after the previous garbage collection reaches the target percentage. The default value of the `GOGC` variable is `100`. This setting can be turned off, which stops garbage collection. The current implementation of garbage collection in Go uses the **mark-and-sweep** algorithm.

Some of the best practices that you can follow to improve memory management are as follows:

- Small objects can be combined into larger objects
- Local variables that have escaped from their declaration scope can be promoted into heap allocations
- Slice array pre-allocation can be performed to improve memory
- Use `int8`, instead of `int`, because `int8` is a smaller data type
- Objects that do not have any pointers will not be scanned by the garbage collector
- FreeLists can be used to reuse transient objects and reduce the number of allocations

Profiling

Profiling in Go can be enabled by using the `cpuprofile` and `memprofile` flags. The Go testing package has support for benchmarking and profiling. The `cpuprofile` flag can be invoked by the following command:

```
go test -run=none -bench=ClientServerParallel4 -cpuprofile=cprofile
net/http
```

The benchmark can be written to a `cprofile` output file using the following command:

```
go tool pprof --text http.test cprof
```

Let's look at an example of how to profile the programs that you have written. The `flag.Parse` method reads the command-line flags. The CPU profiling output is written to a file. The `StopCPUProfile` method on the profiler is called to flush any pending file output that needs to be written before the program stops:

```
var profile = flag.String("cpuprofile", "", "cpu profile to output file")
func main() {
    flag.Parse()
    if *profile != "" {
        var file *os.File
        var err error
        file, err = os.Create(*profile)
        if err != nil {
            log.Fatal(err)
        }
        pprof.StartCPUProfile(file)
        defer pprof.StopCPUProfile()
    }
```

Summary

This chapter covered the garbage collection, cache management, and memory space allocation algorithms. We looked at reference counting algorithms, including simple, deferred, one-bit, and weighted. The mark-and-sweep and generational collection algorithms were also presented with code examples.

The next chapter will cover the next steps we can take after going through this book.

Questions

1. Which factors are considered when choosing a garbage collection algorithm?
2. In which reference counting algorithm are program-variable references ignored?
3. What is the type of reference counting algorithm in which a single-bit flag is used for counting?
4. In which reference counting algorithm is a weight assigned to each reference?
5. Who invented weighted reference counting?
6. Which garbage collection algorithm was proposed by Dijkstra?
7. What class handles concurrency when the mark-and-sweep collector is running?
8. What are the criteria for promoting objects to older generations?
9. Draw a flow chart for the cache management algorithm.
10. How do you get indirect memory access outside a method's stack frame?

Further reading

The following books are recommended if you want to know more about garbage collection:

- *Design Patterns*, by Erich Gamma, Richard Helm, Ralph Johnson, and John Vlissides
- *Introduction to Algorithms – Third Edition*, by Thomas H. Cormen, Charles E. Leiserson, Ronald L. Rivest, and Clifford Stein
- *Data structures and Algorithms: An Easy Introduction*, by Rudolph Russell

Next Steps

In this appendix, we share the reader's learning outcomes from this book. The code repository links and key takeaways are presented. References are included for the latest data structures and algorithms. Tips and techniques are provided to help you keep yourself up to date with the latest on data structures and algorithms.

Technical requirements

Install Go version 1.10 from `https://golang.org/doc/install`, being sure to choose the correct version for your operating system.

The GitHub repository for the code in this appendix can be found here: `https://github.com/PacktPublishing/Learn-Data-Structures-and-Algorithms-with-Golang/tree/master/Appendix`.

Learning outcomes

The learning outcomes from this book are as follows:

- Improve a web or mobile application's performance using the correct data structures and algorithms.
- Understand how an algorithm solves a problem and how the correct data structure is chosen for a problem.
- Enumerate the various solutions to a problem and identify algorithms and data structures after doing a cost/benefit analysis.
- Get a grasp of the various techniques for writing pseudocode for an algorithm, allowing you to ace white-boarding sessions and interview assignments.
- Discover the pitfalls in selecting data structures and algorithms by predicting how fast and efficient an algorithm or data structure is.

In the following section, the key takeaway points, papers, and articles to be referred to, along with tips and techniques, are discussed.

Key takeaways

The key takeaways for the reader are as follows:

- How to choose the correct algorithm and data structures for a problem.
- How to compare the complexity and data structures of different algorithms for code performance and efficiency.
- How to apply best practices to improve and increase the performance of an application.
- Real-world problems, solutions, and best practices associated with web and mobile software solutions are provided in the book as code examples.

Next steps

In this section, papers and articles are provided as further reading for each chapter.

Chapter 1 – Data Structures and Algorithms

The following articles are related to data structures and algorithms:

- *The complete guide to Go Data Structures* (`https://flaviocopes.com/golang-data-structures/`)
- *Data Structure and Algorithms* (`http://www.golangprograms.com/data-structure-and-algorithms.html`)
- *Data structures in Go: Stacks and queues* (`https://ieftimov.com/golang-datastructures-stacks-queues`)

The following papers are related to data structures and algorithms:

- *THE REPRESENTATION OF ALGORITHMS – DTIC* (`https://apps.dtic.mil/dtic/tr/fulltext/u2/697026.pdf`)
- *ON THE COMPUTATIONAL COMPLEXITY OF ALGORITHMS* (`https://fi.ort.edu.uy/innovaportal/file/20124/1/60-hartmanis_stearns_complexity_of_algorithms.pdf`)
- *Analysis and Performance of Divide and Conquer Methodology* (`http://ijarcet.org/wp-content/uploads/IJARCET-VOL-6-ISSUE-8-1295-1298.pdf`)

Chapter 2 – Getting Started with Go for Data Structures and Algorithms

The following articles are related to the content in this chapter:

- *Go – Data structures* (`https://golanglibs.com/category/data-structures`)
- *Applied – Go Algorithms and Data Structures* (`https://appliedgo.net/domains/algorithms-and-data-structures/`)
- *Effective Go* (`https://golang.org/doc/effective_go.html`)

Chapter 3 – Linear Data Structures

The following articles are related to linear data structures:

- *Data Structures for Beginners: Arrays, HashMaps, and Lists* (`https://adrianmejia.com/blog/2018/04/28/data-structures-time-complexity-for-beginners-arrays-hashmaps-linked-lists-stacks-queues-tutorial/`)
- *Stack - Array Implementation* (`https://www.cs.bu.edu/teaching/c/stack/array/`)

The following papers are related to linear data structures:

- *Linear-Space Data Structures for Range Mode Query in Arrays* (`https://cs.au.dk/~larsen/papers/linear_mode.pdf`)
- *RESEARCH PAPER ON STACK AND QUEUE* (`http://www.ijirt.org/master/publishedpaper/IJIRT101357_PAPER.pdf`)
- *Linear Data Structures for Fast Ray-Shooting amidst Convex Polyhedra* (`http://www.cs.tau.ac.il/~haimk/papers/ray.pdf`)

Chapter 4 – Non-Linear Data Structures

The following articles are related to non-linear data structures:

- *Overview of non-linear data structures* (`https://medium.com/@ankitkulhari/overview-of-non-linear-data-structures-40cb441f6d7`)
- *Non-linear Data Structures* (`http://euler.vcsu.edu:7000/9647/`)

- *What Is Forest Data Structure?* (https://magoosh.com/data-science/what-is-forest-data-structure/)
- *Tree Data Structure* (http://www.cs.cmu.edu/~clo/www/CMU/DataStructures/Lessons/lesson4_1.htm)

The following papers are related to non-linear data structures:

- *Y-Trees: An extending non-linear data structure for better organization of large-sized data* (https://ieeexplore.ieee.org/document/8234528)
- *A Shape Analysis for Non-linear Data Structures* (https://link.springer.com/chapter/10.1007/978-3-642-15769-1_13)
- *Representation of Nonlinear Data Surfaces* (https://www.semanticscholar.org/paper/Representation-of-Nonlinear-Data-Surfaces-Olsen-Fukunaga/f4f4812532ba427658ecc83d772637c076780acf)

Chapter 5 – Homogeneous Data Structures

The following articles are related to homogeneous data structures:

- *USING MATRICES IN GO(LANG)* (http://connor-johnson.com/2014/06/21/using-matrices-in-golang/)
- *Golang: Linear algebra and matrix calculation example* (https://www.socketloop.com/tutorials/golang-linear-algebra-and-matrix-calculation-example)
- *Gonum Tutorial: Linear Algebra in Go* (https://medium.com/wireless-registry-engineering/gonum-tutorial-linear-algebra-in-go-21ef136fc2d7)
- *Matrix Multiplication in Golang (3x3 matrices)* (https://repl.it/@hygull/Matrix-multiplication-in-Golang2-matrices-of-order-3x3)

Chapter 6 – Heterogeneous Data Structures

The following articles are related to heterogeneous data structures:

- Heterogeneous Arrays (`https://gist.github.com/cslarsen/5256744`)
- *OL (Ordered List)* (`https://www.w3.org/MarkUp/html3/seqlists.html`)
- *Large Ordered Lists* (`https://www.aerospike.com/docs/guide/llist.html`)
- *Implementing an Ordered List* (`https://bradfieldcs.com/algos/lists/implementing-an-ordered-list/`)

Chapter 7 – Dynamic Data Structures

The following articles are related to dynamic data structures:

- *The complete guide to Go Data Structures* (`https://flaviocopes.com/golang-data-structures/`)
- *DATA STRUCTURE AND ALGORITHMS* (`http://www.golangprograms.com/data-structure-and-algorithms.html`)
- *Data structures in Go: Stacks and queues* (`https://ieftimov.com/golang-datastructures-stacks-queues`)

The following papers are related to dynamic data structures:

- *THE REPRESENTATION OF ALGORITHMS – DTIC* (`https://apps.dtic.mil/dtic/tr/fulltext/u2/697026.pdf`)
- *ON THE COMPUTATIONAL COMPLEXITY OF ALGORITHMS* (`https://fi.ort.edu.uy/innovaportal/file/20124/1/60-hartmanis_stearns_complexity_of_algorithms.pdf`)
- *Analysis and Performance of Divide and Conquer Methodology* (`http://ijarcet.org/wp-content/uploads/IJARCET-VOL-6-ISSUE-8-1295-1298.pdf`)

Chapter 8 – Classic Algorithms

The following articles are related to classic algorithms:

- *Sorting Algorithms Primer* (`https://hackernoon.com/sorting-algorithms-primer-374b83f3ba09`)
- *Depth-First Search* (`https://medium.com/@g789872001darren/gogoalgorithm-1-depth-first-search-582eeb58f23a`)
- *Hashing in Go (Golang vs Python)* (`https://medium.com/@vworri/hashing-in-go-golang-vs-python-b7bc1194e967`)
- *Iterative vs Recursive vs Tail-Recursive in Golang* (`https://medium.com/@felipedutratine/iterative-vs-recursive-vs-tail-recursive-in-golang-c196ca5fd489`)

The following papers are related to classic algorithms:

- *A Mathematical Modeling of Pure, Recursive Algorithms* (`https://www.researchgate.net/publication/220810107_A_Mathematical_Modeling_of_Pure_Recursive_Algorithms`)
- *Recursive algorithms for estimation of hidden Markov models and autoregressive models with Markov regime* (`https://ieeexplore.ieee.org/document/979322`)
- *Recursive algorithms for approximating probabilities in graphical models* (`https://papers.nips.cc/paper/1316-recursive-algorithms-for-approximating-probabilities-in-graphical-models.pdf`)

Chapter 9 – Network and Sparse Matrix Representation

The following articles are related to network and sparse matrix representation:

- *Equations Are Graphs* (`http://gopherdata.io/post/deeplearning_in_go_part_1/`)
- *From Theory To Practice: Representing Graphs* (`https://medium.com/basecs/from-theory-to-practice-representing-graphs-cfd782c5be38`)
- *Go Data Structures: Graph* (`https://flaviocopes.com/golang-data-structure-graph/`)

The following papers are related to network and sparse matrix representation:

- *Representation Learning on Graphs: Methods and Applications* (`https://www-cs.stanford.edu/people/jure/pubs/graphrepresentation-ieee17.pdf`)
- *An overview on network diagrams: Graph-based representation* (`https://www.researchgate.net/publication/308049492_An_overview_on_network_diagrams_Graph-based_representation`)
- *Design principles for origin-destination flow maps* (`https://pdfs.semanticscholar.org/587a/730b11a4b3878142bd4995f80dc969bc5982.pdf`)

In `Chapter 9`, *Network and Sparse Matrix Representation*, use cases from real-life applications were presented. Learning how the network data structure and sparse matrices are applied in different domains, such as airlines, banking, medical, pharma, telecoms, and supply chains, is a good next step for the reader.

Chapter 10 – Memory Management

The following articles are related to memory management:

- *Getting to Go: The Journey of Go's Garbage Collector* (`https://blog.golang.org/ismmkeynote`)
- *Modern garbage collection* (`https://blog.plan99.net/modern-garbage-collection-911ef4f8bd8e`)
- *Go Lang: Memory Management and Garbage Collection* (`https://vikash1976.wordpress.com/2017/03/26/go-lang-memory-management-and-garbage-collection/`)

The following papers are related to memory management:

- *Analysis of the Go runtime scheduler* (`http://www.cs.columbia.edu/~aho/cs6998/reports/12-12-11_DeshpandeSponslerWeiss_GO.pdf`)
- *Simple Generational Garbage Collection and Fast Allocation* (`http://www.cs.ucsb.edu/~ckrintz/racelab/gc/papers/appel88simplegen.pdf`)
- *A Time- and SpaceEfficient Garbage Compaction Algorithm* (`http://www.cs.ucsb.edu/~ckrintz/racelab/gc/papers/morris-compaction.pdf`)

The different tips and tricks to be used in Go data structures and algorithm are discussed in the next section.

Tips and techniques

To keep updated on Go, you can subscribe to these forums and blogs:

- Gopherize: `https://gopherize.me/?fromhttp=true`
- Golang Weekly: `https://golangweekly.com/issues/240`
- The Gopher Conference: `https://www.gophercon.com/`
- Google Groups: `https://groups.google.com/forum/m/#!newtopic/golang-dev`
- Slack Groups: `https://techbeacon.com/46-slack-groups-developers`
- Stack Overflow: `http://stackoverflow.com/questions/tagged/go`
- Dave Cheney's Resources for New Go Programmers: `https://dave.cheney.net/resources-for-new-go-programmers`

The following section contains tips for writing good code in Go.

Using channel with a timeout interval

The software program that connects to resources can be set with timeouts. Channels are used for implementing timeouts. You can configure a channel with a timeout interval as follows:

```
//main package has examples shown
// in Go Data Structures and algorithms book
package main

// importing errors, log and time packages
import (
    "errors"
    "log"
    "time"
)

// delayTimeOut method
func delayTimeOut(channel chan interface{}, timeOut time.Duration)
(interface{}, error) {
    log.Printf("delayTimeOut enter")
    defer log.Printf("delayTimeOut exit")
    var data interface{}
```

```
    select {
        case <-time.After(timeOut):
        return nil, errors.New("delayTimeOut time out")
        case data = <-channel:
        return data, nil
    }
}

//main method
func main() {
    channel := make(chan interface{})
    go func() {
        var err error
        var data interface{}
        data, err = delayTimeOut(channel, time.Second)
        if err != nil {
            log.Printf("error %v", err)
            return
        }
        log.Printf("data %v", data)
    }()
    channel <- struct{}{}
    time.Sleep(time.Second * 2)
    go func() {
        var err error
        var data interface{}
        data, err = delayTimeOut(channel, time.Second)
        if err != nil {
            log.Printf("error %v", err)
            return
        }
        log.Printf("data %v", data)
    }()
    time.Sleep(time.Second * 2)
}
```

Run the following command to execute the preceding code snippet:

```
go run chan_timeout.go
```

The output is as follows:

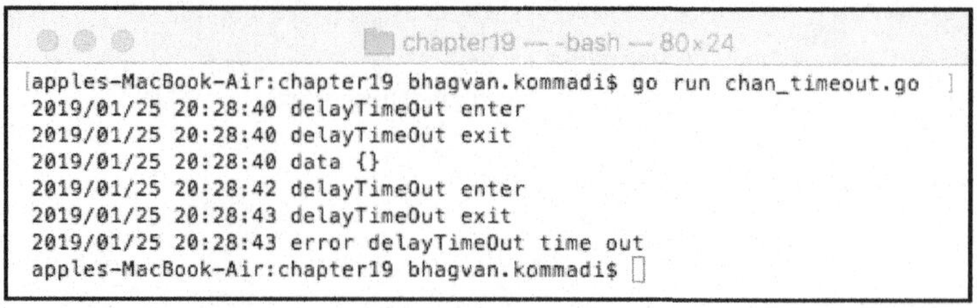

```
chapter19 — -bash — 80×24
apples-MacBook-Air:chapter19 bhagvan.kommadi$ go run chan_timeout.go
2019/01/25 20:28:40 delayTimeOut enter
2019/01/25 20:28:40 delayTimeOut exit
2019/01/25 20:28:40 data {}
2019/01/25 20:28:42 delayTimeOut enter
2019/01/25 20:28:43 delayTimeOut exit
2019/01/25 20:28:43 error delayTimeOut time out
apples-MacBook-Air:chapter19 bhagvan.kommadi$
```

Using context instead of channel

Contexts can be implemented in functions executed in Go routines. Contexts are used instead of channel in the code for passing information between processes. The following code snippet shows the usage of context:

```
//main package has examples shown
// in Go Data Structures and algorithms book
package main

// importing errors,context,log and time packages

import (
  "errors"
  "golang.org/x/net/context"
  "log"
  "time"
)

// main method
func main() {

  var delay time.Duration

  delay = time.Millisecond

  var cancel context.CancelFunc

  var contex context.Context

  contex, cancel = context.WithTimeout(context.Background(), delay)

  go func(context.Context) {
    <-contex.Done()
    log.Printf("contex done")
  }(contex)

  _ = cancel
```

```
    time.Sleep(delay * 2)

    log.Printf("contex end %v", contex.Err())

    channel := make(chan struct{})

    var err error
    go func(chan struct{}) {
      select {
      case <-time.After(delay):
        err = errors.New("ch delay")
      case <-channel:
      }
      log.Printf("channel done")
    }(channel)


    time.Sleep(delay * 2)

    log.Printf("channel end %v", err)
}
```

Run the following command to execute the preceding code snippet:

```
go run context.go
```

The output is as follows:

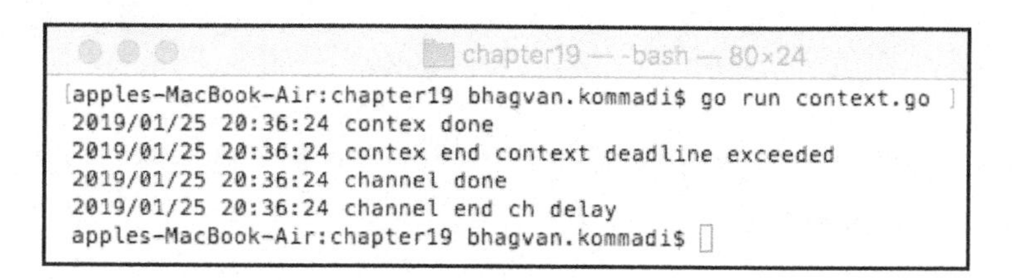

Logging with the line number

While logging, you can log with the line number and the method name. The following code snippet shows how logging can be executed with the line number and the method name:

```
//main package has examples shown
//in Go Data Structures and algorithms book
package main

//importing path, runtime, fmt, log and time packages
```

```
import (
  "path"
  "runtime"
  "fmt"
  "log"
  "time"
)

//checkPoint method
func checkPoint() string {
    pc, file, line, _ := runtime.Caller(1)
    return fmt.Sprintf("\033[31m%v %s %s %d\x1b[0m", time.Now(),
      runtime.FuncForPC(pc).Name(), path.Base(file), line)
}

//method1
func method1(){
  fmt.Println(checkPoint())
}

//main method
func main() {

  log.SetFlags(log.LstdFlags | log.Lshortfile)

  log.Println("logging the time and flags")

  method1()

}
```

Run the following command to execute the preceding code snippet:

```
go run log_linenumber.go
```

The output is as follows:

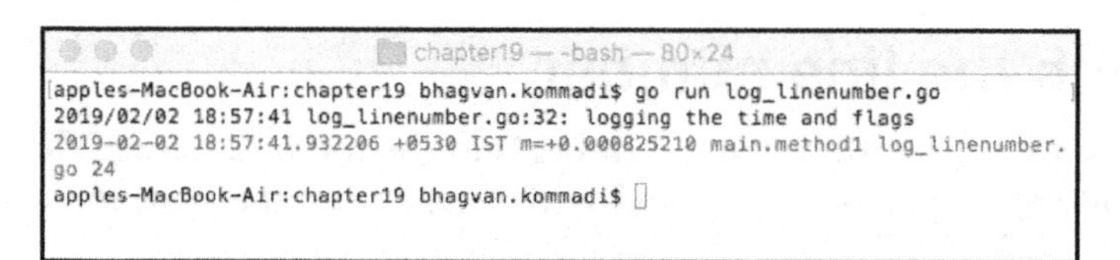

Go tool usage

The Go tool compiler can be invoked with the following command:

```
go build -gcflags="-S -N"
```

The list options command syntax is as follows:

```
go build -x
```

To test the race conditions, you can use the following command:

```
go test -race
```

Running a test method by name can be done using the following syntax:

```
go test -run=method1
```

To update your version of Go, you can use the following command:

```
go get -u
```

Copying can be done with the following command:

```
go get -d
```

To get depths, you can use the following command:

```
go get -t
```

To get a list of software, you can use the following command:

```
go list -f
```

Go environment variables

The `GOROOT` variable can be configured as an environment variable with this command:

```
export GOROOT=/opt/go1.7.1
```

The `PATH` variable can be configured as an environment variable with this command:

```
export PATH=$GOROOT/bin:$PATH
```

The `GOPATH` variable can be configured as an environment variable with this command:

```
export GOPATH=$HOME/go
```

The GOPATH variable can be configured in the PATH variable with this command:

```
export PATH=$GOPATH/bin:$PATH
```

Test table

Tests are driven by a test table. The following code snippet shows how a test table can be used:

```
//main package has examples shown
// in Go Data Structures and algorithms book
package main

// importing testing packages

import (
  "testing"
)

func TestAddition(test *testing.T) {


  cases := []struct{ integer1 , integer2 , resultSum int }{
    {1, 1, 2},
    {1, -1, 0},
    {1, 0, 1},
    {0, 0, 0},
    {3, 2, 1},
  }

  for _, cas := range cases {
    var sum int
    var expected int
    sum = cas.integer1 + cas.integer2
    expected = cas.resultSum
    if sum != expected {
      test.Errorf("%d + %d = %d, expected %d", cas.integer1, cas.integer2,
sum, expected)
    }
  }

}
```

Run the following command to execute the preceding code snippet:

```
go test -run TestAddition -v
```

The output is as follows:

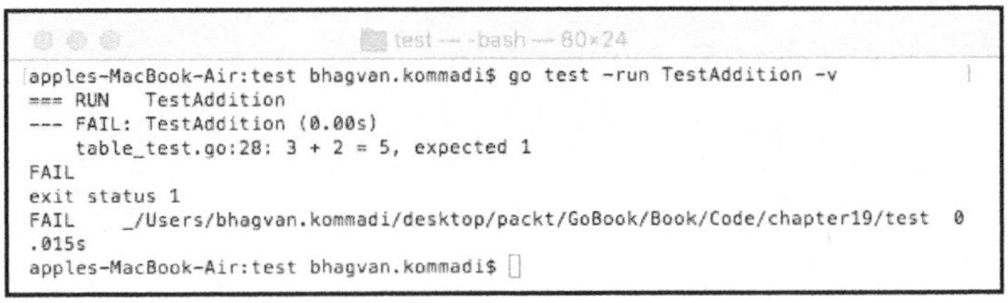

```
apples-MacBook-Air:test bhagvan.kommadi$ go test -run TestAddition -v
=== RUN   TestAddition
--- FAIL: TestAddition (0.00s)
    table_test.go:28: 3 + 2 = 5, expected 1
FAIL
exit status 1
FAIL    _/Users/bhagvan.kommadi/desktop/packt/GoBook/Book/Code/chapter19/test  0
.015s
apples-MacBook-Air:test bhagvan.kommadi$
```

Importing packages

You can import packages with the following statements. Here, we show three different syntactical options:

```
import "fmt"
import ft "fmt"
import . "fmt"
```

Panic, defer, and recover

Panic, defer, and recover are used to handle complex errors. The last returned variable in a function is used as an error. The following code snippet is an example of this:

```
//main package has examples shown
// in Go Data Structures and algorithms book
package main

// importing fmt and errors packages

import(
  "fmt"
  "errors"

)

//First Func method
func FirstFunc(v interface{}) (interface{}, error) {
  var ok bool

  if !ok {
    return nil, errors.New("false error")
  }
  return v, nil
}
```

```
//SecondFunc method
func SecondFunc() {
  defer func() {
    var err interface{}
    if err = recover(); err != nil {
      fmt.Println("recovering error ", err)
    }
  }()
  var v interface{}
  v = struct{}{}
  var err error
  if _, err = FirstFunc(v); err != nil {
    panic(err)
  }

  fmt.Println("The error never happen")
}

//main method
func main() {
  SecondFunc()
  fmt.Println("The execution ended")
}
```

Run the following command to execute the preceding code snippet:

```
go run handling_error.go
```

The output is as follows:

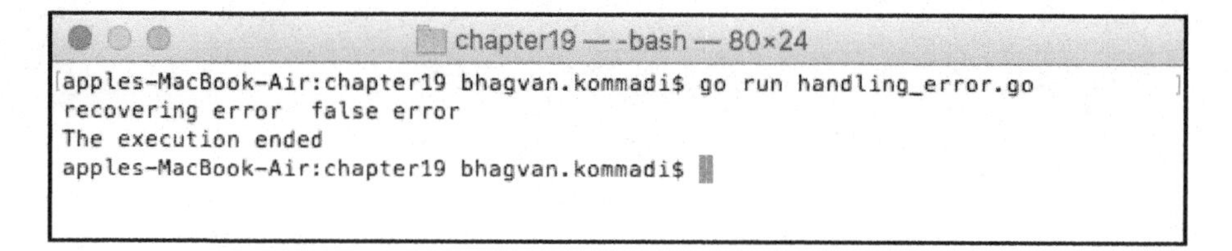

The following link contain some useful tips and techniques for writing Go code: `https://golang.org/doc/effective_go.html`.

Other Books You May Enjoy

If you enjoyed this book, you may be interested in these other books by Packt:

Hands-On Software Architecture with Golang
Jyotiswarup Raiturkar

ISBN: 978-1-78862-259-2

- Understand architectural paradigms and deep dive into Microservices
- Design parallelism/concurrency patterns and learn object-oriented design patterns in Go
- Explore API-driven systems architecture with introduction to REST and GraphQL standards
- Build event-driven architectures and make your architectures anti-fragile
- Engineer scalability and learn how to migrate to Go from other languages
- Get to grips with deployment considerations with CICD pipeline, cloud deployments, and so on
- Build an end-to-end e-commerce (travel) application backend in Go

Hands-On Dependency Injection in Go
Corey Scott

ISBN: 978-1-78913-276-2

- Understand the benefits of DI
- Explore SOLID design principles and how they relate to Go
- Analyze various dependency injection patterns available in Go
- Leverage DI to produce high-quality, loosely coupled Go code
- Refactor existing Go code to adopt DI
- Discover tools to improve your code's testability and test coverage
- Generate and interpret Go dependency graphs

Leave a review - let other readers know what you think

Please share your thoughts on this book with others by leaving a review on the site that you bought it from. If you purchased the book from Amazon, please leave us an honest review on this book's Amazon page. This is vital so that other potential readers can see and use your unbiased opinion to make purchasing decisions, we can understand what our customers think about our products, and our authors can see your feedback on the title that they have worked with Packt to create. It will only take a few minutes of your time, but is valuable to other potential customers, our authors, and Packt. Thank you!

Index

D

F

G

H

I

K

L

M

N

T

U

V

W

Z

Made in the USA
Las Vegas, NV
27 June 2022